MARTIN LUTHER : CREATIVE TRANSLATOR

Luther portrayed as St. Jerome in his study. After Albrecht Dürer's copper engraving [of St. Jerome] by Wolfgang Stuber

Luther's translation of Psalm 23 in his own handwriting

Reproduced from Robert Koenig, *Deutsche Litteraturgeschichte*, 29th ed. (Bielefeld and Leipzig: Velhagen & Klasing, 1895)

Martin Luther

CREATIVE TRANSLATOR

BY HEINZ BLUHM

CONCORDIA PUBLISHING HOUSE

ST. LOUIS, MISSOURI

Concordia Publishing House, St. Louis, Missouri
Concordia Publishing House Ltd., London, E. C. 1
© 1965 Concordia Publishing House

Library of Congress Catalog Card No. 65-28162

CONTENTS

Introduction   vii

Part I. *The Making of a Translator*

Chapter 1.	On the Evolution of Luther's Bible: Matthew (1517-1521)	3
Chapter 2.	The First Translation of a Pericope	37
Chapter 3.	Translation in Transition: The Christmas Postil	49
Chapter 4.	Translating the Twenty-third Psalm	
	a. The Predecessors	78
	(1) The Printed High German Bibles	78
	(2) The Printed Low German Bibles	97
	b. The Evolution of Luther's Masterpiece	104

Part II. *Interpreting the Translator's Task*

Chapter 5.	Responsible Freedom: The New German Psalter	117
Chapter 6.	The Original's Intent and the Modern Idiom	125
	a. "Allein durch den Glauben"	125
	b. "Wes das Herz voll ist"	138
	c. "Gegrüsset seist du, Holdselige"	151

Part III. *Shaping the English Bible*

Chapter 7.	William Tyndale: Ephesians	169
Chapter 8.	Miles Coverdale	181
	a. The Twenty-third Psalm	181
	b. Galatians	194
Chapter 9.	The Authorized Version	223
	a. Psalm 26 : 8	223
	b. Psalm 45 : 13	225

Indexes   233

INTRODUCTION

THE TRANSLATION of the Bible into German is Martin Luther's greatest single work. It is both a literary and a religious achievement of the first order.

Nietzsche once remarked that Richard Wagner thought of himself as a synthesis of Shakespeare and Beethoven. He accused the music dramatist of megalomania. If Nietzsche had cared enough about theology and if he had known Martin Luther better than he did, he might very well have called the German Reformer a synthesis of Jerome and Augustine, of the great literary shaper of the Vulgate and the profoundest of the church fathers. Had Nietzsche actually made such a statement, he would have come close to the truth. Luther is indeed one of the supreme literary geniuses of the entire Christian tradition at the same time that he is one of the keenest and boldest Christian thinkers of all time.

It is not the purpose of the following essays to examine Luther's stature as a theologian. Theodosius Harnack[1] and Paul Althaus,[2] not to mention Karl Holl,[3] have admirably and convincingly presented and analyzed Luther's theological thought. This book attempts to contribute to a better understanding and deeper appreciation of Luther's achievement as a writer. However, it does not deal with Luther's immense literary output as a whole but only with his translation of the Bible.

Luther's German Bible is a famous book, a classic not only of German but of world literature. Its eminence is universally recognized. Beyond being the first as well as the foremost of the major Protestant versions of the Bible, it is one of the two greatest translations the Christian church of the West has produced. It was the earliest and most successful rival of the Vulgate. Catholic as well as Protestant scholars fully recognize the high artistic level of Luther's German Bible. It is superior to the Vulgate both in accuracy and in literary quality.

---

[1] Theodosius Harnack, *Luthers Theologie* (Erlangen, 1862–86), 2 vols.
[2] Paul Althaus, *Die Theologie Martin Luthers* (Gütersloh, 1962).
[3] Karl Holl, *Gesammelte Aufsätze zur Kirchengeschichte,* vols. I and III, 6th ed. (Tübingen, 1928–32).

Three translations of the Bible have thus far become preeminent in Western culture: the Vulgate, Luther's, and the Authorized Version. Of these three, Luther's is in some respects the most remarkable. In evaluating Jerome's work on the Vulgate, one should remember that only parts of the Bible were translated by him from the Hebrew and Greek; for large sections he merely revised already existing Latin versions. Luther, on the other hand, is practically independent of the available German translations; though of course indebted to what has been called the language of the German Bible tradition, his rendering is essentially the product of his own genius. There is a profound meaning in the accepted designations of the Latin Bible as the *Vulgate* and of the German Bible as *Luther's Bible:* the Vulgate is incomparably less Jerome's personal achievement than the German Bible is Luther's. As to the great King James Bible, it is common knowledge that it is not the work of a single individual, William Tyndale's lasting contributions notwithstanding. Thus of the three most significant and influential Bible translations used in the West, only Luther's is definitely the work of a single man. This fact alone puts his translation in a category of its own.

Though the German Bible enjoys worldwide renown, its essence is not really known. Millions have read it, listened to it, memorized greater or lesser parts of it, but only a handful of scholars have actually examined its nature in the full meaning of the word examine. Since it is sure to be used indefinitely, however, its distinctive character should be better known.

The bald fact is that the nature, the real nature, of Luther's German Bible is still largely unexplored and uncomprehended. Our ignorance of the true essence of this masterpiece is as profound as it should be disturbing to scholar and layman alike. A major reason for this regrettable state of affairs is that Luther's Bible is a very complex organism. The apparent simplicity of its utterance is misleading. It could be argued that one should just expose oneself to its power and tenderness, its overall majesty, and not even try to analyze the secret of its manifest success during almost four centuries and a half. Why should we endeavor to examine its texture closely, more closely than has been done up to now? A straightforward answer is that the unexamined Luther Bible is fundamentally and ultimately an unappreciated Luther Bible. The countless readers of this amazing document have been the poorer for not fully, or not better, grasping what the master translator placed before them. We still have no real idea what Martin Luther actually accomplished and what an extraordinary achievement his Bible is. Its incomparable depth and beauty have not yet been fathomed. It is high time that this peerless rendering should begin to be understood.

A start has of course been made. Wilhelm Walther,[4] Emanuel Hirsch,[5] and Michael Reu[6] among more recent scholars have led the way toward making us aware of the treasure the world possesses in the German Bible. A number of essays in learned periodicals have been similarly helpful. But all these put together have merely scratched the surface of Luther's *magnum opus*. The most advanced students in this field have been only too painfully conscious that even their most careful work is inadequate. They all realize we are only on the threshold of the immense task that is still before us. Yet it is perhaps not so much a task as it is a high privilege to move ever closer to a fuller realization of the amazing work done by Martin Luther. Exciting and rewarding though the road before us is, we should not underestimate the philological *Kleinarbeit* required to approach the goal of a more responsible and informed appreciation of one of the main results of the Reformation. Not until we have examined every single verse of Luther's Bible from its earliest formulation to its final shape shall we be in a position to comprehend the man's incredible achievement and to do justice to his genius. What I have just said is a sober statement of fact and a tremendous program for the future.

This, then, is where we stand. A few New Testament passages, one or two Psalms, a verse here and there have been investigated with the philological acumen they need and deserve. The little that has been done has definitely sharpened our awareness of the magnitude and sheer brilliance of Luther's achievement.

The essays collected in this volume should be seen against the background of our present inadequate knowledge of the Luther Bible. Written on different occasions over a period of years, they endeavor to subject to close scrutiny a number of significant passages from the Scriptures. No one can be more painfully conscious of their fragmentariness than the author. But we must never forget that the real study of the nature of Luther's German Bible has hardly begun. We simply are in no way ready to make sweeping statements and meaningful generalizations. Instead, we must labor with painstaking care, examining small parts of Luther's Bible one by one, in the hope that at some distant date our knowledge of the whole may be more adequate than

---

[4] Wilhelm Walther, *Luthers deutsche Bibel* (Berlin, 1917), 218 pp.
[5] Emanuel Hirsch, *Luthers deutsche Bibel* (Munich, 1928), 109 pp.
[6] Michael Reu, *Luther's German Bible* (Columbus, Ohio, 1934), 226 pp.

it is today. In the meantime each contribution, however minute, serves an important, albeit preliminary, function.

The essays in this volume touch on a variety of aspects of Luther's translation. The first deals with the ever intriguing problem of the Biblical quotations in Luther's German writings. These constitute alternative renderings of significance and wide appeal. When Luther wanted to quote a passage from the Bible, he apparently never took the trouble to look it up in his own official translation, not even after the translation was available. Instead he almost invariably made a new translation *ad hoc*. His quick mind produced new variants in great abundance. Hardly ever did he repeat himself. Such was the wealth of potential variants at his disposal that he could pour them forth at will—surely another indication of the astonishing mastery of language that allowed him to move with sovereign ease through the length and breadth of the Bible and render into superb German whatever was needed at the moment. Luther's German works are filled to overflowing with exciting new formulations of familiar verses, many of them superior to those of the excellent official German Bible. It would be very much worth while to assemble Luther's Biblical quotations into a book. They would actually yield a new Bible as it were, differing significantly from the rendering to which we are accustomed.

As a first step into this uncharted region, a comprehensive index of the Biblical quotations in Luther's German writings was compiled at Yale by my assistants and myself. One of the first uses I made of the index was to investigate the quotations from the Gospel according to St. Matthew. However, I soon found that there were altogether too many to be treated in their entirety from 1517 to 1546. Therefore I selected those in Luther's German works from the beginning of his literary activity in 1517 (a short piece Luther wrote in 1516 contains no Matthew quotation) to the end of the year 1521, when Luther began the formal translation of the New Testament. The main questions to which answers were sought concern the source (Greek or Latin) and the literary quality of the quotations.

It would be very valuable if some scholar would examine in the same way the Matthew quotations from 1522 to 1546. Similar investigations of the other books of the Bible should also be undertaken.

The second essay is a close examination of Luther's earliest translation of a pericope, Matt. 16 : 13-19, which is prefixed to an important sermon Luther delivered in Leipzig at the time of his famous debate with Johann Eck in 1519. The question of the sources is uppermost in the mind of the reader. One would like to know whether Luther, an

Introduction

enthusiastic user of Erasmus' edition of the Greek New Testament from the day it reached Wittenberg in 1516, is still using the Vulgate or has already turned to the Greek original for the purpose of this *ad hoc* translation.

The third essay shows us Luther at work in 1521. In this epoch-making year of Luther's stand at the Diet of Worms he worked, among other things, on his Christmas Postil, a series of sermons each one of which is introduced by a new translation into German of an important text from the New Testament. It is exciting to compare the special translation of Matt. 2 : 1-12, presumably made in the late fall of 1521, with his formal translation of the same text made, probably in December of the same year, as part of the official translation of the New Testament published in the following year. In the course of this investigation I come to conclusions different from those of Walter Köhler, Albert Freitag (who edited the New Testament volumes in the Weimar edition), and Gerhard Bruchmann,[7] the most recent worker in this field. Again it is fascinating to see how the excellent translator of a number of New Testament texts of 1521 (and before) turns into the outstanding translator of the *Septembertestament,* as Luther's first edition of his German New Testament is usually called because it left the Wittenberg presses on September 21, 1522. One's respect and admiration for the great translator grow by leaps and bounds as one watches him at work. Naturally it is necessary to direct one's attention to the minutest details. If one is willing to do that, the reward is great. Luther's moving from one realm of translation to an entirely different one is exciting to watch.

The fourth essay is really a series of three closely related pieces. They all deal with the Twenty-third Psalm. The first two discuss how the printed pre-Lutheran High and Low German Bibles rendered this most popular of all psalms. The third analyzes the evolution and nature of Luther's own incomparable translation. The genius of Luther the translator nowhere shines more brightly than in the psalms. His translation of every single psalm deserves a detailed examination of its own. Unless this slow and painstaking work is undertaken, we can never hope to come to a full appreciation of the Reformer's extraordinary achievement.

We rightly speak of *Luther's* Bible. It *is* his, in a special way. It *is* the most personal of all the great renderings of the Scriptures. And of all the books of the Bible, of the Old Testament at any rate, the

[7]Gerhard Bruchmann, "Luther als Bibelverdeutscher in seinen Wartburgpostillen." In *Luther–Jahrbuch,* 1935, pp. 111–131.

Psalter was closest to his heart. There one poet speaks to another poet, Martin Luther, who had the genius to make the original author express himself more than adequately in the new language. Since Luther himself was a poet at heart, he outdid himself in giving Hebrew poetry a truly German form. On no other part of the Bible did he lavish so much time, energy, and sheer love. While it is perfectly true that he kept revising the Bible as a whole to the end of his all-too-short life, the Psalter was singled out for special attention and received two major revisions after the first edition of 1524. The 1528 revision moves on the same high level as the notable 1530 revision of the New Testament. But the third revision of the Psalter of 1531 is unique, utterly unique. Here the Hebrew Psalter was put into the most idiomatic German of which the greatest master of the German language was capable. The consummate skill here demonstrated by Luther is without parallel in the long and distinguished history of the translation of the Bible into other tongues. The evolution of the final version of the Twenty-third Psalm shows what heights Luther could reach.

The fifth essay discusses how Luther felt about his own translation of the Psalms, especially the German Psalter of 1531. Luther did not hide his light under a bushel. He knew full well what he had accomplished. He was very much aware of the unusualness, even singularity, of the Psalter of 1531. Since he was not sure the rest of the world quite realized what he had done, he decided to announce publicly the principles that had guided him. Luther, fortunately, was one of the most articulate of men, able to give a theoretical account of his performance. It is not often that a great artist can explain as adequately as Luther did what he had endeavored to do and what he actually carried out with so much success. Luther could be, and in fact was, both creator and critic, as the occasion demanded. The span of his abilities and activities is breathtaking.

The subject of the following essay—again a series of three pieces—is one of Luther's greatest writings in the vernacular, his world-famous Treatise on Translation. He had been bitterly attacked by Hieronymus Emser, secretary to Duke George of Saxony, for his translation of the New Testament. Luther took the occasion to explain and justify in detail and with great vigor, verve, and irony his translation of a number of key passages. I have selected for detailed analysis three passages, each full of great interest to all Christians. They are, as rendered in the Authorized Version,[8]

[8]Unless they are otherwise identified, all English quotations from the Bible are from the Authorized Version.

Romans 3 : 28: "Therefore we conclude that a man is justified by faith without the deeds of the law."

Matthew 12 : 34b: "For out of the abundance of the heart the mouth speaketh."

Luke 1 : 28: "Hail, *thou that art* highly favoured, the Lord *is* with Thee."

These three passages I have discussed against a fuller background than Luther himself saw fit to provide. The Reformer was such a prolific author and such a busy man that it is not surprising if he could not always remember everything he had previously written on a particular subject. Neither could he foretell of course what changes he would make in the future. It is part of the literary historian's function to see and set things in perspective so that what is said in the understandable heat and excitement of the moment is toned down and viewed as part of the larger whole. Luther's creative performance can be appreciated even more when the historian has put all available data together and has related all parts of the argument and achievement to each other.

In the final cluster of essays the influence of Luther's German Bible on the English Bible is traced in a few representative passages. This is a complicated matter, about which our information is still, after these many centuries, at best rudimentary. I have merely scratched the surface here.

Three stages of the English Bible are considered in this connection. There is first of all William Tyndale, the preeminent genius in the history of the Bible in English. L. Franklin Gruber[9] and Albert H. Gerberich[10] have written ably on his debt to Luther. I have added to their studies a detailed analysis of Luther's influence on Tyndale's translation of Paul's Epistle to the Ephesians. Through this close examination of a single book of the New Testament things are perhaps brought into sharper focus.

My main work in this section is contained in the two essays on the Coverdale Bible of 1535. This, the first printed Bible in English, is more heavily indebted to Luther than any other in the great succession of Bibles from Tyndale to the Authorized Version. Although the original title page of the Coverdale Bible speaks of "Douche and Latyn" sources, the name of Luther is not specifically mentioned. My two

---

[9] L. Franklin Gruber, *The First English New Testament and Luther* (Burlington, Iowa, 1928), 128 pp.

[10] Albert H. Gerberich, *Luther and the English Bible* (Lancaster, Pa., 1933), 58 pp.

essays establish Luther as the primary source of one Old and one New Testament passage which I subjected to detailed analysis, inasmuch as the Zurich Bible, so far held to be Coverdale's "Douche" source, is itself based on Luther. For the Old Testament, the Twenty-third Psalm was once more chosen; for the New, the Epistle to the Galatians. In both instances the sustained influence of Luther is evident.

Even though we must and shall again refrain from generalizing too soon, one cannot easily escape the impression that the Coverdale Bible is the most "Lutheran" of all major English Bibles. Its high literary qualities are all but proved by its continuing role in the Anglican communion. Perhaps it is not too widely known that the Psalter in the Book of Common Prayer is not the Psalter of the King James Bible but the Psalter of the Coverdale Bible. This means that a number of the most beautiful English phrases in this great Psalter are ultimately Luther's. Miles Coverdale was a master of the English language, quite able to put much of Luther's magnificent German into superb English. It has occurred to me more than once that the Lutheran Church in English-speaking countries might well consider introducing the Prayer-book Psalter into its own service to replace the far less Lutheran Psalter of the King James Bible. I do not really see why Lutherans, much closer to Luther by tradition and preference, should allow the Anglican communion—unwittingly to be sure—to be in more intimate touch with their greatest religious and literary genius. The days when Johann Sebastian Bach was heard more often in Anglican than in Lutheran churches of this country are happily past. Why not reclaim also the "Lutheran" Coverdale Psalter for English-speaking Lutherans? I even wonder whether the Coverdale Bible as a whole, or at least the New and Old Testament lessons, could not be reexamined for possible use in the Lutheran liturgy. If the Coverdale Psalter is so outstanding that the Anglican world clearly prefers it to the King James Psalter, other parts of the Coverdale Bible might deserve further study at least from this practical point of view. The Coverdale Bible is as close as English-speaking Lutheranism can come to Luther's Bible short of translating the German Bible itself into English. Whoever has really seen something of the glory of Luther's Bible will perhaps not be taken aback too much by this somewhat diffident suggestion.

The Authorized Version of 1611 is itself not without Lutheran traces, as I show in the last two essays. I am sure there are many more examples than the two I have presented. There is work for a multitude of laborers in this field too.

To summarize, what is presented in this book is a collection of essays toward a better understanding of one of the greatest translations of the Bible ever made in the West, perhaps anywhere. If they should induce others to explore the riches of Luther's Bible in an ever increasing measure, I should be the first to welcome such results. These essays are a beginning, with the end not even in sight. We are but on the threshold of an immense *terra incognita*: Luther's German Bible. May many cross it and stand amazed.

I cannot say too often that the time for generalization has not yet arrived. All we can do at present and in the foreseeable future is to keep on analyzing individual passages of the Bible. This is admittedly a slow process. But no one who has ever really tried his hand at it can ever weary of it. There are too many breathtaking discoveries to be made in this *corpus mirabile*. I for one have found every step exciting, and I am convinced others, too, will find their own ventures into this rich field equally rewarding. More than one lifetime and many investigators are needed to bring a project of such magnitude to completion. The task is well worth all the tremendous effort it will require.

PART I. THE MAKING OF A TRANSLATOR

Chapter 1

On the Evolution of Luther's Bible:
Matthew (1517–1521)

FOR A LONG TIME one of the most important desiderata in the study of Luther's German Bible has been an investigation of the nature of the Biblical quotations in the German writings of the Reformer. The late Walther Köhler, a leading student of the Reformation, insisted years ago on the need to examine closely the numerous scriptural citations found throughout Luther's works in the vernacular.

The literary ability of Martin Luther, so clearly revealed on practically every page he ever wrote, usually left its mark even on an isolated Biblical verse quoted more or less casually in the course of an essay. Whatever this past master of the German tongue threw off in the white heat of creative writing necessarily partook of the general excellence of his literary utterance. It requires no more than an ordinary acquaintance with Luther to realize that Köhler was right in urging a detailed analysis of the quotations from the Bible.

Luther's German Bible is a strikingly distinctive and individual work. Like Goethe's *Faust*, Part II, it is *sui generis*. The matter was put very well by the able author of the quadricentennial article on Luther in the February 18, 1946, issue of the *Times Literary Supplement*. He pointed particularly to the extraordinary singularity, even uniqueness, of Luther's Bible. Its assured place of honor and distinction in the history of the translation of the Bible into the various languages of the world is due not only to its scholarly and undisputed aesthetic qualities but also to the highly individual and personal characteristics that set it apart from other famous renderings.

In the light of the literary eminence and marked individuality of Luther's Bible it is only natural that special interest should attach to the Biblical quotations in his German writings. How did the man who, all by himself, gave the world one of the greatest of all translations of the Bible proceed when he saw fit to quote verses or significant parts of verses in his many German writings? Are they based on the original

Greek and Hebrew or on the Vulgate or on both? Are there several, even many, renderings of the same verse or phrase? Could some of the more or less informal renderings possibly excel his "official" translation of the Bible? In general, how did this thoroughgoing individualist of unquestioned genius acquit himself in the workaday world of the unpretentious Biblical quotation?

Quotations from the Bible, in the original or in translation, have often been examined from various points of view. What makes the investigation of Martin Luther's quotations of such absorbing interest is primarily that, in this case, we are dealing with one of the foremost translators and at the same time with a writer whose work fairly bristles with Biblical quotations, allusions, and references.

It stands to reason that an investigation of this magnitude cannot be undertaken all at once. In this essay only one gospel and only one period of Luther's literary activity will be examined, the Gospel According to St. Matthew in Luther's vernacular writings from 1517 to 1521, the important quinquennium prior to the launching of the formal translation of the New Testament.

These five years before the so-called *Septembertestament* of 1522 form a natural first division of the entire period to be investigated. The quotations from 1517 to 1521 were made by a man who as yet entertained no serious thought, if any thought at all, of translating the Bible into the vernacular. They antedate the days when Luther, pushed by his friends, especially by Melanchthon, almost abruptly resolved to provide a readable German Bible for the benefit of the people. The chief question we are concerned with is this: What are the salient characteristics of these early, pre-*Septembertestament* quotations from the Gospel of St. Matthew?

Before embarking on the main problem, a few preliminary observations are in order. First, we must ignore the popular Protestant notion that the Vulgate is either a somewhat inferior piece of work or full of mistakes. Let it be stated emphatically that, with reference to the quotations from Matthew at any rate, this important rendering is a generally correct and excellent translation of the Greek original. There are, to be sure, a few divergences between the Greek and Latin texts; these are for the most part due to the manifest endeavor of the men responsible for the Vulgate to produce a smooth and idiomatic rendering. We should realize that Luther's splendid attempt to employ only idiomatic language was anticipated, pretty successfully on the whole, by the creators of the Vulgate.

The second preliminary point is the relation of Luther's Bible to the German pre-Lutheran translations. There is now a fair measure of agreement that no discernible influence of the printed High German versions from the Mentel Bible of about 1466 to the Silvanus Otmar edition of 1518 has been established. This sweeping statement is not intended to deny unmistakable similarities of a number of phrases or words. It is only fair to assume that Martin Luther, particularly in the early years under review in this essay, stands in the stream of a tradition beginning with the earliest efforts to put the Christian message into German.

Rather more important than the printed pre-Lutheran Bibles are the Plenaria, renderings of selected Biblical passages, chiefly the liturgical lessons appointed to be read in the vernacular, the so-called pericopes. Since these precious documents are only partially available in printed editions, definite conclusions cannot be drawn as yet. Inasmuch as Luther's German Bible appears to be more indebted to the Plenaria (so far as they go) than to the printed complete Bibles, one might easily suppose that the relation between these Plenaria and Luther's Biblical quotations is decidedly closer than that between the quotations and the pre-Lutheran Bibles. Until the full array of Plenaria becomes accessible, very little can be said on this interesting point.

Besides the printed Bibles and the Plenaria there remains the rich store of Biblical quotations in the relevant German writings of pre-Lutheran authors. This is another related subject which has been investigated only fractionally thus far. The several German dissertations on this topic do not begin to exhaust it. Moreover, they do not contain sufficient data to be of more than casual value.

The third major preliminary observation refers to the important matter of the "completeness" of Luther's individual quotations from the Bible. It has been pointed out that Luther frequently—in fact more frequently than not—quotes less than a whole verse at one time. This is a correct statement so far as it goes. Its actual relevance, however, is considerably diminished when we remember that the division of the Bible into verses is a post-Lutheran phenomenon of the second half of the sixteenth century. Luther's quotations cannot very well be expected to conform to a verse pattern established after his death. The only fair yardstick of completeness that can or should be applied is whether a quotation is what might be called a "unit of meaning." This unit can, and upon occasion does, exceed in length our conventional "verse"; usually, however, it is shorter than this often fairly arbitrary division. In general Luther is fond of quoting the most important part of a verse, or, if the verse has several important phrases, that portion which he needs in the connection in which he is using it. There is nothing static or cut and dried about Luther's technique; on the contrary, it is dynamic and spontaneous. In fact, the extent of a quotation of Luther's is often quite unpredictable. Luther takes *what* he needs *when* he needs it. It follows from this comparatively free manner of handling citations that Luther, almost invariably quoting from memory as he is, pays very little attention to verbal accuracy. What seems important to him is to catch the gist of a verse and to couch it in as idiomatic German as he can, thus putting it across to the general reader. Needless to say, he almost always succeeds, sometimes admirably. Even the briefest Biblical quotation often becomes all aglow when touched by Luther's magic wand. The German master's quotations at their best are as alive, imaginative, and artistically creative as his official translation of the Bible as a whole. From time to time there is a rendering, informal, even casual, which even surpasses the magnificent German of the formal Luther Bible.

After these introductory remarks we are ready to turn to a close analysis of Luther's quotations from the Gospel According to St. Matthew as found in his German writings from 1517 to 1521. Doubtless the question uppermost in the minds of all scholars interested in this problem has been the matter of the source that Luther followed. Did he use the Vulgate or are there evidences that he is turning to the Greek original? If the latter is the case, when does the Greek text tend to replace the Vulgate?

It will be recalled from our preliminary discussion that this question is perhaps more difficult to answer than has usually been assumed. Since the Vulgate is, by and large, a faithful rendering of the Greek, in Matthew at any rate, we cannot make a general statement. We shall be compelled to concentrate on the comparatively small number of divergences between the Vulgate and the original. Only in these few passages can we arrive at a more or less definite decision. Our procedure will be chronological in order that we may become aware of any change or development in Luther's practice.

1517

Of the six relevant quotations in Luther's German writings of 1517 only one lends itself to the problem at hand: Matt. 7:6. This is the only passage in which the Vulgate differs sufficiently from the Greek to enable us to try to determine Luther's source. The important phrase is "neither cast ye your pearls before swine." The Vulgate uses the verb *mittatis*, while the Greek has βάλητε. Luther put down *furwerffen*.¹ Although this would seem to point in the direction of the Greek verb, it is nevertheless practically impossible to come to a decision. Since the great majority of Luther's quotations are couched in excellent, idiomatic German, it is quite conceivable that Luther, without reference to the Greek original, simply wished to express himself idiomatically and came upon the very satisfactory word *furwerffen*. If we remember further that Luther seldom quoted literally but generally quite freely, there appears to be no particular need to call in the original to explain his natural German rendering. Still, the possibility of Greek entering into the picture as early as 1517 cannot be ruled out altogether, however remote it may be.

1518

The 19 quotations from Matthew of 1518 yield but three that are pertinent to our quest: Matt. 4:17; 9:13; 16:23. Two (4:17; 16:23) point toward the Vulgate, one (9:13) toward the Greek original.

Matt. 4:17

The famous word "repent" (Greek μετανοεῖτε), is rendered by *poenitentiam agite* in the Vulgate. Luther's translation *Thut pusz*² is probably based on the Vulgate, though one cannot be absolutely certain, because in his New Testament revision of 1526 Luther chose this rendering, replacing the preceding versions' *Bessert euch*.

Matt. 16:23

The words "Get thee behind me, Satan," are rendered by Luther: *Gehe hinter mich*.³ Greek: ὕπαγε ὀπίσω μου. Vulgate: *vade post me*. The simple word *gehe* in lieu of a less common one (cf. September-testament: *heb dich Satan von myr*) suggests the Vulgate as its source.

Matt. 9:13

"For I am not come to call the righteous, but sinners to repentance." The important phrase in our connection is "to repentance." It is not found in the Vulgate: *Non enim veni vocare iustos, sed peccatores*. The editions of Erasmus and Gerbel add the words: εἰς μετάνοιαν, to re-

---

[1] Martin Luther, *Werke*, Kritische Gesamtausgabe (Weimar: Hermann Böhlaus Nachfolger, 1883 ff.). Hereafter cited as WA (Weimarer Ausgabe). WA 1, 181.
[2] Ibid., 383.   [3] Ibid., 276.

pentance. Of these, only the first edition of Erasmus' New Testament of 1516 was available to Luther in 1518. Erasmus was quick to point out in the *Adnotationes* the discrepancy between the Vulgate and the Greek text with which he was working: "graeci addunt ad poenitentiam, εἰς μετάνοιαν, etiamsi non addit Hieronymus, apud Chrysostomum tamen reperio." Indisputable proof that Erasmus himself considered his Greek text, not the Vulgate, to be correct is found in Erasmus' own new translation into Latin, printed in a parallel column of his edition of the New Testament. Here we read: *Non enim veni ad vocandum iustos, sed peccatores ad poenitentiam.* The words *zu der busse*[4] in Luther's early quotation of 1518 are in all likelihood due to Erasmus' edition. The question of course remains whether they are based on the Greek text or on Erasmus' own Latin translation accompanying the Greek. It is also possible, even probable, that Luther looked at both. But even if Luther's translation should rest, in this particular case and in other instances, primarily on the Latin text provided by Erasmus, it would still go beyond the Vulgate and would definitely be related to the new humanistic scholarship of the early 16th century. It should not be forgotten, however, that Luther's addition to the Vulgate, occurring as it does in a relatively free quotation, may have been inserted more or less unconsciously as an expression of his own religious depth. Still, there is a much greater probability that Luther's clearly established early acquaintance with, and active use of, Erasmus' New Testament suggested the phrase.

The Vulgate predominates as the source of the relevant quotations of the year 1518. There is, however, rather strong evidence that Luther consulted Erasmus' famous edition of the original Greek text. This does not mean that Luther looked up Matt. 9:13 just prior to quoting it; it simply means that he must have done so sometime between 1516 and 1518. We are probably dealing with the reminiscence of a passage that impressed itself on his mind when he first came across it and noticed its divergence from the then accepted text. The further fact that the expanded text speaks of *repentance*, a word and an idea absolutely central in the theology of the author of the Ninety-five Theses, surely tended to embed it in his memory.

1519

Among the more than 60 quotations from Matthew in 1519, only six reveal differences between the Greek and Vulgate versions sufficient to give us a clue as to Luther's preferred source.

[4]Ibid., 274.

Matt. 6:7

"But when ye pray, use not vain repetitions." The Greek μὴ βατταλογήσητε is expressed in the Vulgate, somewhat flatly, by *nolite multum loqui*. Luther's translation, *solt nit vil redenn*,[5] is clearly based on the Vulgate. This conclusion becomes all the more likely if one considers that the *Septembertestament*, done out of the Greek text, has *plappern*. In further corroboration one might add that all printed High German pre-Lutheran Bibles, which are based on the Vulgate, have essentially the same German phrase that Luther has in 1519: *nichten wölt vil reden*.

Matt. 6:11

"Give us this day our daily bread." The interesting word is of course "daily." The Greek ἐπιούσιον is rendered in the Vulgate by *supersubstantialem*. Luther translates it twice in 1519 by *teglich*.[6] In the careful exposition of this verse Luther gives unmistakable evidence of his knowledge of Greek in general and of his awareness of the peculiar philological problem connected with this verse in particular. "Das wortlein 'Teglich,'" he writes, "heyst yn Krichischer tzungen Epiusion, das hat man mancherley auszgelegt. Etlich sagen, es heyssz ein uberwesenlich broth, Etlich, ein auszerwelet und besonders brot, Etlich, der Hebreischen tzungen nach ein morgen broth, nit wie wir deutschen ein morgen und abenth broth heyssen, sundern das auff den andern tag bereyt sey, auff Lateynisch crastinum."[7] Luther sees some value in all these interpretations. For translation into German he decides in favor of *teglich*, undergirding his rendering with the following significant explanation: ". . . auff deutsch heyst teglich das, das man teglich tzur handt hat und yn bereytschafft, ab man des selben schon nit an underlas braucht."[8] Thus Martin Luther, quite familiar with the Greek word and the difficulties it contains, reverts to its traditional German rendering, hallowed by long usage, giving it, however, a meaning enriched by his knowledge of the history of the learned interpretation of the word.

Matt. 7:18

". . . neither can a corrupt tree bring forth good fruit." Greek: δένδρον σαπρόν. Vulgate: *mala autem arbor*. Luther's translation of this phrase by *eyn böszer baum*[9] appears to be based on the Vulgate's *mala* rather

[5] WA 2, 81. [6] Ibid., 86 and 105. [7] Ibid., 109.
[8] Ibid., 110. [9] Ibid., 71.

than the Greek original's σαπρὸν meaning "rotten." The *September-testament* has, as one would expect, *eyn fawler bawm*, unmistakably translated from the Greek.

Matt. 8 : 26

"O ye of little faith." Greek: ὀλιγόπιστοι. Vulgate: (*quid timidi estis,*) *modicae fidei*? In a quotation of 1519 Luther's rendering is: *Eins geringen glauben seyt yr*.[10] This genitival construction coupled with the use of an adjective and a noun stems rather clearly from the Vulgate. In the *Septembertestament* we find, in full agreement with the Greek original, *yr kleynglewbigen*. The printed pre-Lutheran Bibles[11] are very interesting in their treatment of this phrase. Mentel has *Lutzeler trew waz seit ir vorchtsam*? Pflanzmann changes *lutzeler* to *weniger*. From the Zainer redaction of about 1475 to the last of these High German Bibles, that of Silvanus Otmar of 1518, a considerably revised version occurs: *ir eins wenigen glauben*. If any further proof were needed that Luther's early incidental quotation of this verse is based on the Vulgate, the pre-Lutheran Bibles, especially from Zainer on, furnish it readily.

Matt. 9 : 2

"Son, be of good cheer." Greek: θάρσει, τέκνον. Vulgate: *Confide fili*. Luther in a quotation of 1519: *Meyn sun, glaub*.[12] The word *glaub* appears to be based on the Vulgate's *confide* rather than on the stronger Greek θάρσει meaning "to be of good courage, to be bold." The *Septembertestament* has: *sey getrost*, a rendering quite clearly coming from the Greek original.

Matt. 9 : 22

"Daughter, be of good comfort; thy faith hath made thee whole." Greek: θάρσει, θύγατερ· ἡ πίστις σου σέσωκέν σε. Vulgate: *Confide filia, fides tua te salvam fecit*. Luther's quotation of 1519: *Glaub, meyn tochter, deyn glaub hatt dich gesund macht*.[12] As in the second verse of the same chapter, discussed in the preceding passage, the word *glaub* appears quite definitely to stem from the Vulgate's *confide* rather than from the Greek θάρσει. The phrase *gesund macht* also seems to be based on the Vulgate's *salvam fecit*, which would suggest

---

[10] Ibid., 129.

[11] Most easily accessible in W. Kurrelmeyer, *Die erste deutsche Bibel* (Tübingen: Litterarischer Verein in Stuttgart, 1904 ff.).

[12] WA 2, 720.

itself as the source in preference to the original Greek σέσωκεν. In contrast, the translation contained in the *Septembertestament* is manifestly from the Greek: *sey getrost meyn tochter, dein glawb hatt dir geholffen.*

The interesting examples from the year 1519 again indicate the strong preponderance of the Vulgate influence. Luther, in quoting casually from the Gospel According to Matthew in 1519, followed the Vulgate rather than the original Greek wherever these deviate sufficiently from each other to allow us to determine the probable source. This is not to say that Luther is altogether unfamiliar with the Greek version. As a matter of fact, he does quote the Greek word *Epiusion*. But, although he is quite aware of the original and does, in an especially important case such as Matt. 6 : 11 (our *daily* bread) refer to it for exegetical purposes, he makes his quotations in 1519 from the Vulgate, with which he had grown up and which he knew practically by heart.

1520

Among the almost 100 quotations from Matthew in the year 1520, only four phrases show enough differences between the Greek and Vulgate versions to be useful for determining the source on which they are based.

Matt. 6 : 31

"Therefore take no thought, saying, What shall we eat?" Greek: μὴ οὖν μεριμνήσητε. Vulgate: *Nolite ergo soliciti esse*. Luther's phrase of 1520, *nit sorgfeltig sein*,[13] appears to stem from the Latin *soliciti esse*. In the *Septembertestament* he uses the simple verb form as it occurs in the Greek: *Darumb sollt yhr nitt sorgen*. It should be added that, in the nature of the case, this is a very difficult question to settle; one could argue that the difference between *sorgfeltig sein* and *sorgen* is minor and quite inconclusive as to the source followed. However, the fact that the pre-Lutheran printed versions all have predicate adjectives rather than a single verb tends to point in the direction of the Vulgate for Luther's early quotation too—from Mentel to the second edition of Anton Sorg of 1480: *sein sorgsam;* from Koberger (1483) to Silvanus Otmar (1518): *sein sorgfeltig*.

Matt. 7 : 18

"... a corrupt tree...." Cf. the same passage in 1519.[14] Luther repeats, in 1520, *ein böszer bawm*,[15] thus showing that he is still guided by the Vulgate's *mala arbor* and not by the Greek version's δένδρον σαπρὸν.

[13] WA 6, 271. [14] Cf. p. 9 of this essay. [15] WA 7, 32.

Matt. 10:9

"(Provide neither gold, nor silver,) nor brass (in your purses)." Greek: μηδὲ χαλκὸν. Vulgate: *neque pecuniam*. Luther's phrase *nit gelt*[16] appears rather strongly to be based on the Vulgate's *neque pecuniam*. The *Septembertestament* has *ertz*, as the Greek original obviously requires.

Matt. 18:16

"... that in the mouth of two or three witnesses every word may be established." Greek: ἵνα ἐπὶ στόματος ... σταθῇ πᾶν ῥῆμα. Vulgate: *ut in ore ... stet omne verbum*. This phrase occurs twice in Luther's German writings of 1520. In *Ein Sermon von dem Bann* it is worded as follows: *auff das do bestee eyn iglich wort odder geschefft*.[17] It is very difficult to say whether *wort* is based on the Vulgate's *verbum* or not. The word *geschefft*, which Luther uses as an alternative rendering, would seem to suggest an awareness at least of the Greek original, meaning both "word" and "thing." We may conclude that *wort* could very easily still be due to the Vulgate, but *geschefft* cannot readily be accounted for except by linking it up with the Greek original. The second occurrence of this phrase in 1520 is in *Von dem Papstthum zu Rom*, where it is found in the form *ein igliche sache sol bestehn*,[18] The word *sache* can come only from the Greek original, it would seem, for there is no bridge from the Vulgate's *verbum* to Luther's *sache*. In the *Septembertestament* Luther uses *sach*, whereas, characteristically enough, all printed pre-Lutheran Bibles have *wort*.

The four relevant quotations of 1520 again show indubitable predominance of the Vulgate over the Greek text. Three of the four citations are based on the Vulgate, while only one (occurring twice, however) appears to go back to the original. It is clear that Luther is making some use of the Greek version, but it is equally clear that he follows the Vulgate as a rule.

1521

Of more than 175 quotations in 1521 (up to the Diet of Worms) only six are of interest to us in this connection.

Matt. 5:15

"(Neither do men light a candle, and put it under a bushel, but on a candlestick;) and it giveth light. ..." Greek: καὶ λάμπει. Vulgate: *ut*

---

[16] WA 6, 434.   [17] Ibid., 65.   [18] Ibid., 311.

luceat. Luther, in a quotation of 1521, has this phrase: *auff das es . . . leuchte.*[19] This translation is definitely based on the Vulgate, retaining as it does the clause of purpose *ut luceat,* a construction found only in the Vulgate. In the *Septembertestament* Luther, as may be expected, follows the Greek original, using a main clause with the verb in the indicative: *so leuchtet es.*

Matt. 9:12

". . . They that be whole (need not a physician, but they that are sick)." Greek: οἱ ἰσχύοντες. Vulgate: *Non est opus valentibus medicus.* . . . Luther in 1521: *Die gesunden durffen keynsz artzt.*[20] The word *gesunden* seems to be a rendering of the Vulgate's *valentibus* rather than of the original's ἰσχύοντες, meaning primarily the "strong." The *Septembertestament,* definitely translating the Greek, reads: *Die starcken.*

Matt. 11:17

". . . We have piped unto you, (and ye have not danced;). . . ." Greek: ηὐλήσαμεν ὑμῖν. Vulgate: *Cecinimus vobis.* Quoting this verse in 1521, rather freely to be sure and with a change of person, Luther renders it as follows: *Singt man yhn, szo tantzen sie nit.*[21] The important thing is the use of the word *singen,* which suggests very strongly that Luther had the familiar Vulgate passage in mind when he set it down casually in the vernacular: *canere—singen.* It happens that in this particular instance the Greek original is so markedly different from the Vulgate that one can tell quite easily whether the word is done out of one or the other. The *Septembertestament* leaves no room for doubt that our passage is based on the Greek text: *wyr haben euch gepfyffen.*

Matt. 24:24

". . . if it were possible . . ." Greek: εἰ δυνατόν. Vulgate: *si fieri potest.* Luther quotes this phrase of v. 24 as many as three times in 1521: *wenn es geschehen künt,*[22] *wenn es muglich were,*[23] and, identically with the preceding except for spelling, *wens müglich were.*[24] This little phrase appears to be rendered from the Vulgate the first time (*wenn es geschehen künt*), and from the Greek the second and third times (*wenn es muglich were,* etc.). However, it is also quite conceivable that the words *wenn es muglich were* are just another idiomatic rendering into German of *si fieri potest.* Anyone acquainted with Luther's pronounced preference for idiomatic German and with the wealth of

[19] WA 7, 315.   [20] Ibid., 697.   [21] Ibid., 637.
[22] WA 8, 530, 1. 26.   [23] WA 7, 663.   [24] WA 8, 530, 1. 15.

14   *Martin Luther: Creative Translator*

synonyms at his disposal could easily argue that it may not be necessary to resort to the Greek original to account for the phrase under review. It is very difficult to decide the issue unequivocally.

Matt. 15 : 8

"This people draweth nigh unto me with their mouth." Greek: In the Nestle edition this passage does not occur. Vulgate: This passage is also omitted. Luther quotes it as follows in 1521:[25] *da mit kummen sie mir nah mit dem mund.*[26] This is in all likelihood based on Erasmus' edition of the Greek New Testament: Ἐγγίζει μοι ὁ λαὸς οὗτος τῷ στόματι αὐτῶν. The new Latin translation which Erasmus provided with his Greek text reads like this: *Appropinquat mihi populus hic ore suo.* In the course of a long note on this passage Erasmus makes this remark: "Apud grecos plusculum est verborum." It would seem that the extra phrase is due to Luther's consulting the Greek text of Erasmus or at least the latter's new translation of the Greek into Latin, but the additional words can also be fully explained on the basis of the Vulgate. Matt. 15 : 8 happens to be a somewhat condensed quotation from Is. 29 : 13; it is therefore not inconceivable that Luther, who had an almost uncanny knowledge of the Bible, may have remembered the full text of Isaiah and substituted it, quite unconsciously perhaps, for the abbreviated version contained in Matthew. The relevant phrase from Is. 29 : 13 reads as follows in the Vulgate: *Eo quod appropinquavit populus iste ore suo.*

Matt. 15 : 9

"But in vain they do worship me." Greek: μάτην δὲ σέβονταί με. Vulgate: *Sine causa autem colunt me.* Luther in 1521: *Es ist umbsonst, das sie.* ... It would seem that Luther's *umbsonst* was suggested by the Greek μάτην rather than by the Vulgate's *sine causa*. One might also consider Erasmus' own translation furnished along with his edition of the original text: the word he uses for μάτην is *frustra*. Erasmus' annotation on the Vulgate's *sine causa* is as follows: "sine causa, graece est μάτην . . . frustra . . . sine fructu potius quam sine causa."

Of the six suitable examples of the year 1521, four are rather definitely based on the Vulgate, and two, or perhaps only one, on the Greek original. It is pretty safe to say that the Vulgate is the predominant source as late as 1521, less than one year before the translation of the *Septembertestament* was undertaken.

[25]There is also in the same year another quotation of the same verse without the additional phrase. This quotation (WA 8, 145) is apparently based on the Vulgate.
[26]WA 7, 661.

If we take the five pre-*Septembertestament* years (1517–1521) as a unit, the Vulgate is the preponderant and preferred source in those relatively few verses in which it differs substantially from the Greek original. We have also found some pretty good evidence that Luther was quite aware of the Greek text published by Erasmus and that in two or three instances he chose to follow the Greek original rather than the accepted Latin version of the church. It is extremely difficult to assess the influence of the new Latin translation Erasmus made available in his edition of the Greek New Testament; there can be little doubt, however, that Luther made extensive use of it.

Another important question is whether Luther was influenced by the pre-Lutheran German Bibles. As we have noted, so far as Luther's actual translation of the Bible is concerned, there is now practical agreement among scholars that it is essentially uninfluenced by earlier German versions. What little influence there is is held to come from the Plenaria and from what has been called the general tradition of Biblical material in German rather than from the printed full pre-Lutheran Bibles. As regards the quotations from Matthew, I have observed no definite links to any of the printed German Bibles beyond certain fundamental similarities in simple phrases that are hardly translatable in any other way. But it should be pointed out again that Luther stands, in the individual quotations as well as in the Bible as a whole, in a general German tradition: even Luther did not create in a vacuum. Unfortunately the rich body of the Biblical quotations in pre-Lutheran German writings has not been sufficiently investigated as yet, or at least has not been made available in such a way as to permit comparison. Hence we are unable at this time to determine the relation of Luther's Biblical quotations to those in the German works of preceding German writers. Without a full array of these abundant materials we are rather helpless in this important aspect of the problem. I once examined the Biblical quotations in the *Theologia deutsch* and found no recognizable relation to Luther's quotations from 1517 to 1521. If this is true of a book Luther loved so well that he edited it twice early in his career, it is possible that Luther is as independent of previous translations in his quotations of individual verses as he appears to be in his official German Bible. This tentative and provisional statement is not intended to deny, of course, Luther's general debt to the broad stream of the German Bible tradition which was part of his medieval heritage.

At least as important for our purposes as the matter of sources is the idiomatic nature of Luther's Biblical quotations in German, irrespective of questions of origin and influence. An effort will now be made to characterize these from this point of view. The worst and the best that can be said about them will be set forth. Let us begin with the least successful.

I. Inferior Variants

1518

Matt. 11 : 28

Komet zu mir alle die ir arbeitet und beschweret seid....[27]

This is by no means a bad rendering. Cf. the Authorized Version: "Come unto me, all ye that labour and are heavy laden." It is of course necessary to make due allowance for the older use of *arbeiten* if we wish to be fair to Luther's early rendering. In fact, the quotation of 1518 is inferior only if one measures it by the standard set by Luther's *Septembertestament: Kompt her zu mir, alle die yhr muheselig vnnd beladen seytt....*

1519

Matt. 11 : 28

Kommet zu myr all die yhr beladen seyt und arbeytet....[28]

Here we have *beladen* (retained in the *Septembertestament*) instead of *beschweret*, with the order of the two synonyms reversed. It is the obsolescent word *arbeytet* that grates on the modern ear. Compared with the matchless rendering of the *Septembertestament*, the quotation of 1519 is not much better than that of 1518; it does however contain the word *beladen*, anticipating thereby the later version so familiar to readers of the German Bible.

1520

Matt. 18 : 20

... da bin ich in yhrem mittel.[29]

The mediocrity of this rendering strikes one hardest if one holds it up against the *Septembertestament: da byn ich mitten vnter yhn.* The superiority of the *Septembertestament* version is not due to the Greek original at all! (*sum in medio eorum* corresponds exactly to εἰμι ἐν μέσῳ αὐτῶν.) It is solely a matter of expressing the thought in more idiomatic German. Luther's quotation of 1520 moves on the level of the printed

[27]WA 1, 255.
[28]WA 2, 689.
[29]WA 6, 457. Cf. Ibid., 368: "... da sey er yn yhrem mittel."

pre-Lutheran Bibles. Mentel has: *do bin ich in mitzt ir;* Pflanzmann: *do bin ich in mitten ir;* Zainer: *do bin ich in mit ir.* Koberger in 1483 creates the translation that was to remain to the last of the High German pre-Lutheran Bibles of 1518: *do bin ich in irem mittel.*

1521
Matt. 6:13

Und nicht uns eynleyt ynn versuchen.[30]

This is a disturbingly literal rendering of the Latin *et ne nos inducas in tentationem.* It is interesting that as late as 1521 such an inferior German phrase still occurs in so important a work as *Vom Missbrauch der Messe.*

Characteristically enough, the number of such second-rate phrases is very small. One should bear in mind, however, that they do occur from time to time. We may conclude then that there are weak passages, however few and far between, throughout the period from 1517 to 1521, prior to the undertaking of the translation of the New Testament as a whole.

II. Good Variants
1518
Matt. 16:23

Gehe hinter mich, Sathan....[31]

Considerably simpler but less idiomatic than the *Septembertestament's heb dich Satan von myr,* this rendering, probably based on the Vulgate,[32] is nevertheless couched in good German and is an interesting variant of the *Septembertestament.*

1519
Matt. 5:25

Du salt mit deynem widdersacher eins sein....[33]

This is a delightful variant of *Sey willfertig deynem widersacher* as found in the *Septembertestament.* It is idiomatic and worth noting as a direct statement of the idea of the passage. The essential meaning of the verse is rendered freely, as the "man in the street" might choose to express it himself.

[30] WA 8, 530. [31] WA 1, 276.
[32] Cf. p. 7 of this essay. [33] WA 2, 101.

Matt. 9:38

... *das er werck leuth sende in seine erne.*[34]

Werck leuth is a good variant of the plain *erbeyter* of the *Septembertestament*.

Matt. 11:28

Komment tzu mir alle, die yr beengstiget seyt und beschweret seyd.[35] Also: *Kumet zu mir, die yhr beschweret seyd und muhesam.*[36]

It will be readily granted that words like *beengstiget* and *muhesam* are important variants, worth pointing out. They are typical of Luther's incessant attempts, long before he entertained the idea of rendering the whole Bible, to find good German phrases to convey what he held to be the basic meaning of the text. Perhaps one should also take note of some interesting synonyms for the second part of the verse, *ich will euch erquicken: helffen*[37] and *trosten.*[38] Although both are very free renderings of *reficiam* or ἀναπαύσω, they do express the underlying idea with imagination and insight.

Matt. 18:15

So dein bruder etwas sundiget, das dir wyddert....[39]

This is an interesting expository variant of what was to be translated much more literally in the *Septembertestament* as follows: *Sundigt aber deyn bruder an dyr....* The expansiveness of the early quotation is due neither to the Vulgate (*in te*) nor to the available Greek text (εἰς σε).

Matt. 27:43

Er vortrawt gott, lasz sehen, ob ehr yhn erlosze....[40]

One is struck by this engaging variant of the more staid *Septembertestament: Er hatt gott vertrawet, der erlose yhn nu, lusts yhn.* The variant of 1519, which, incidentally, recurs in 1521,[41] is refreshingly idiomatic. We hear as it were Christ's enemies mocking Him in words such as they might very well have used if their native tongue had been German. The informality and realism of this variant are scarcely to be outdone. Compared with this, the rendering of the passage in the *Septembertestament* seems considerably more formal and reserved, though it is of course excellent and is a close translation of *si vult* and εἰ θέλει. The jeering of the crowd is caught more realistically in *lasz*

---

[34] Ibid., 114.   [35] Ibid., 94. Cf. 107.   [36] Ibid., 720.
[37] Ibid., 689.   [38] Ibid., 720.   [39] Ibid., 120.
[40] Ibid., 692.   [41] WA 8, 375.

sehen, ob er yhn erlosze than in the more detached *der erlose yhn nu, lusts yhn.* Whichever one may prefer, it is good to have both versions.

1520

Matt. 7 : 15

Huttet euch vor den falschen propheten.[42]

The phrase *huttet euch* is a good variant of *sehet euch fur* in the Septembertestament. There is another fine variant in 1520: *wir sollen mit fleysz acht haben.*[43] These variants are not caused by a divergence between the Greek text and the Vulgate. προσέχετε and *attendite* correspond to each other very closely.

Matt. 16 : 18

... *die pfortenn der helle solten nit vormugen widder sein gebew auff den fels.*[44]

Vormugen is a good variant of the Septembertestament's *Vbirweldigen*. There is no denying, however, that the latter is superior. It is conceivable, though not necessary, that *vormugen* was inspired by the Vulgate's *praevalebunt* rather than by the Greek κατισχύσουσιν. But the difference between the Latin and the Greek is so minor that this verse was not included in the first section of this paper, on the sources of Luther's early quotations.

Matt. 18 : 6

Es were yhm besser gewest ... Man hett yhm ein mölsteyn an seynen halsz gepunden. ...[45]

Septembertestament: ... *dem were besser, das eyn mulsteyn an seynen hals gehenckt wurd.* ... Aside from the construction of the sentence, which is better than in the Septembertestament, the word *gepunden* of the quotation is perhaps just as good as the later *gehenckt*. At any rate it is another acceptable expression.

Matt. 18 : 18

... *furwar sag ich euch.*[46]

The Septembertestament has it this way: *Warlich ich sage euch.*

Matt. 24 : 24

Vil falscher Christen und Prophetenn werdenn in meinem namenn kommenn.[47]

[42]WA 6, 210. [43]Ibid., 202. [44]Ibid., 315.
[45]WA 7, 657. [46]WA 6, 309. [47]Ibid., 293. Cf. also 414.

Kommenn is a pleasant, informal variant of the formal *es werden . . . auff stehen* of the *Septembertestament*.

Matt. 24 : 26

. . . sihe da, in den heymlichen heusern ist er.[48]

This is an interesting variant of the *Septembertestament: Sihe, er ist ynn der kamer.* The Vulgate rendering *in penetralibus* is a literal translation of the Greek original ἐν τοῖς ταμιείοις. Luther's variant was not suggested by any difference between the Greek and the Vulgate, for there is none.

Matt. 25 : 43

Ich byn blosz geweszen.[49]

A good variant of *ich bynn nacket gewesen* in the *Septembertestament*.

1521

Matt. 5 : 24

. . . so lass das opffer ligen. . . .[50]

The addition of *ligen* gives a delightful informality to the more restrained version of the *Septembertestament: so las alda fur dem altar, deyn gabe.*

Matt. 5 : 39

Wer dich schlecht an den rechten backen. . . .[51]

This again is a highly idiomatic, informal rendering of the formal *Septembertestament: so dyr yemant eyn streych gibt auff deyn rechten backen. . . .*

Matt. 7 : 6

. . . unnd die hund sich umb keren.[52]

A variant of *vnnd sich wenden* in the *Septembertestament*.

Matt. 8 : 11

Viel werden kummen vom auffgang und nydergang.[53]

An interesting variant of *vom morgen vnd vom abent* in the *Septembertestament*.

Matt. 10 : 24

Der junger sol nit besser denn der meister sein.[54]

This is a fine, free variant of the *Septembertestament: der iunger ist nit vbir den meyster.*

[48]Ibid., 265. [49]Ibid., 45. [50]WA 7, 250. [51]WA 8, 284.
[52]Ibid., 685. [53]Ibid., 32. [54]WA 7, 274.

Matt. 10 : 25

... sie werden das gesind auch szo heyssen.[55]
A good variant of *hauszgenossen* in the *Septembertestament*.

Matt. 11 : 7

... eyn rohr, das da hyn ynd her wancket vom wind.[56]
This is a good but also more literal translation of what is rendered freely in the *Septembertestament*: ... *das der wind hyn unnd her webt*.

Matt. 11 : 28

... ich wil euch erlaben. ...[57]
A very good variant of *ich will euch erquicken* in the *Septembertestament*.

Matt. 11 : 30

Meyn purde ist leycht ynd meyn ioch ist suesse.[58]
This is an important variant of the *Septembertestament*'s familiar and beloved phrase, *denn meyn ioch ist senfft, vnnd meyne last ist leycht*.

Matt. 13 : 29

... *das hedderich auszrotten*.[59]
A very interesting variant of *so yhr das vnkraut aus gettet* in the *Septembertestament*. Paul Pietsch has an important note on this passage: "Das hedderich (meist der H.) ist ein über Nieder- und Mitteldeutschland bis ins Elsass verbreiteter Pflanzenname. ... Luther hat hier das Wort offenbar der grösseren Anschaulichkeit wegen statt des nachher in der Bibelübersetzung gebrauchten 'Unkraut' ... angewendet."[60]

Matt. 15 : 8

... *kummen sie mir nah*.[61]
A good variant of the *Septembertestament*: *dis volck nehit sich zu mir*.

Matt. 15 : 9

Es ist umbsonst, das sie mir dienen. ...[62]
This is a fine variant, especially noteworthy for its sentence structure, of the version of the *Septembertestament*: *Aber vergeblich dienen sie myr*.

[55]Loc. cit. [56]WA 8, 30. [57]WA 7, 258. [58]WA 8, 21.
[59]WA 7, 583. [60]Ibid., 583, 584, n.2. [61]Ibid., 661. [62]Loc. cit.

Matt. 16 : 18

Die hellische pfortten sollen nichts vormugen.[63]

A good variant of the *Septembertestament:* . . . *die pfortten der hellen sollen sie nicht vbirweldigen.*

Matt. 18 : 17

. . . *szo sey er dyr wie eyn heyd.* . . .[64]

This is a good literal variant of the free *Septembertestament* rendering: *So halt yhn als eynen heyden.*

Matt. 18 : 19

There are as many as three good variants of an important part of this verse in 1521:
1. *waruber sie bitten wollen, das wirt yhn geben werden.*[65]
2. *es sey waryn es woll, das sie begeren, das soll yhn geschehen.*[66]
3. *waruber es sey, das sie bitten, das soll yhn geschehen.*[67]

This passage reads as follows in the *Septembertestament: warumb es ist, das sie bitten wollen, das soll yhn widderfaren.* The variants of 1521 have considerable merit.

Matt. 21 : 5

Sich an, dein konigk kompt dir demütigk. . . .[68]

This is a very acceptable variant of the *Septembertestament's* excellent rendering *sanfftmutig.*

Matt. 26 : 50

Freund, wo tzu bistu komen?[69]

The *Septembertestament* has *warumb* for the *wo tzu* of the quotation.

III. Excellent Variants

1518

Matt. 21 : 3

. . . *sie seyn dem herren not.*[70]

This is a superbly idiomatic variant of what the *Septembertestament* was to render in this way: . . . *der herr bedarff yhr.* One could easily

---

[63]WA 7, 686. For *vormugen* cf. p. 19 of this essay.
[64]WA 8, 270.   [65]Ibid., 173.   [66]Ibid., 178.   [67]Ibid., 184.
[68]WA 9, 709.   [69]WA 8, 361.   [70]WA 1, 388.

On the Evolution of Luther's Bible 23

hold that the early variant of 1518, probably jotted down quite casually, is somehow superior to the good translation of Luther's official German Bible.

1519

Matt. 6 : 33

Sucht vor allen dingen das reich gottis.[71]

The well-known rendering of the *Septembertestament* reads as follows: *tracht am ersten nach dem reych gottis*. While the word *sucht* is a good but not superior variant of *tracht*, the phrase *vor allen dingen* is in its delightful idiomatic informality almost an improvement upon the literal *am ersten* ($\pi\rho\hat{\omega}\tau o\nu$; *primum*). Some may even prefer it to the official rendering. At any rate, it is a quotation quite worth noting.

Matt. 6 : 34

Dan der morgen wirt sein eygen sorge mit bringen.[72]

This variant is probably at least as good as the excellent translation found in the *Septembertestament*: *denn der morgene tag, wirt fur das seyn sorgenn*. Both the official version and the quotation are free and highly idiomatic renderings. The ability to produce, more than two years before undertaking the translation of the New Testament, a variant which is a serious rival of the justly famous *Septembertestament* surely testifies to Luther's early mastery of the German language and to the relative ease with which he could throw off an alternate rendering of distinction.

Matt. 15 : 28

O weib, wye gros ist dein glaub....[73]

There can be little doubt that this is a superb variant, more vibrant than the literal *Septembertestament*: *o weyb, deyn glawbe ist gros*. By audaciously and felicitously turning the declaratory sentence into an exclamation, Luther, without changing the underlying spirit of the passage, has underlined and reinforced it by the emphasis expressed in the *wye gros*.

Matt. 18 : 15

Du solt es nit sagen, dan ym allein.[74]

Again a very free and idiomatic variant of the literal rendering of the *Septembertestament*: *so gang hyn vnnd straff yhn zwisschen dyr vnd yhm alleyn*. Luther's most informal phrase of 1519 catches fully

[71] WA 2, 97. [72] Ibid., 115.
[73] Ibid., 126. [74] Ibid., 121.

the language of everyday life: This is the way one German is apt to speak to another; this is indeed the language of the home and the marketplace.

1520

Matt. 10 : 8

Gebt umbsonst, den yhr habts auch umbsonst.[75]

An abbreviated, informal variant of the *Septembertestament* version: *Vmbsunst habt yhrs empfangen, vmbsonst gebet es auch.* The variant of 1520 again is couched in the language of the common man. This is probably the way he spoke with his family and his neighbors.

Matt. 16 : 15

Was haltet yhr von mir?[76]

This thoroughly idiomatic variant is a very informal rendering in lieu of the fairly formal phrase of the *Septembertestament: Wer, sagt denn yhr, das ich sey?* It is most simple and direct. Either translation is a far cry from the awkward way the first printed German Bible put it: *Wann wen sagt ir mich zesein?*

Matt. 17 : 27

There are two splendid variants of an important phrase of this verse in 1520:
1. *Der erste fisch der do kumpt den nym.*[77]
2. *Den ersten fisch du fehist, den nym.*[78]

The *Septembertestament* reads as follows: *den ersten fisch der auffer fert, den nym.* The first variant puts the matter as simply as possible, much more so than the fairly elaborate *Septembertestament* version. The second variant is really superb! A very free rendering of the original, it expresses the situation in the most natural German imaginable: *der erste Fisch, den du fängst.* That is the way the man in the marketplace and the mother in the home are likely to talk about it. Luther has again caught the speech habits of the common folk, of all Germans for that matter.

Matt. 23 : 13

Weh euch schrifftgelereten, yhr . . . schlisset zu das hymelreich fur den menschen, yhr geht nit hynein, und weret den, die hynein gehen.[79]

The last phrase is an excellent variant of the formal and literal

[75] WA 6, 288. [76] Ibid., 310. [77] Ibid., 214.
[78] WA 7, 36. [79] WA 6, 445.

translation contained in the *Septembertestament*: . . . *vnd die hyneyn wollen, last yhr nit hyneyn gehen*. The variant of 1520 is a simple and direct statement compared with the more cumbersome official rendering.

Matt. 23:14

Sie werden nur mehr peyn damit vordienen.

A very free and interesting variant of the *Septembertestament* phrase: . . . *deste mehr verdamnis empfahen.*

1521

Matt. 5:13

Das saltz, szo es den schmack verlorn hat, ists keyn nutz, denn das die leutt drober lauffen.[80]

This is one of the most noteworthy variants, completely different from the famous rendering of the *Septembertestament*: . . . *wo nu das saltz thum wirtt, ... vnd lasz die leutt zur trettenn*. It is of interest to the English-speaking world that the King James Bible is very much like Luther's variant of 1521: ". . . if the salt have lost his savour . . . ." In other words, Luther's casual quotation of 1521 is as good as the superb Authorized Version. The variant is probably more readily intelligible to the modern reader than the somewhat quaint rendering of the *Septembertestament, wo nu das saltz thum wirtt*. The second important phrase, *denn das die leutt drober lauffen*, is a free but engagingly idiomatic variant of the more literal *vnd lasz die leutt zur trettenn*. The variant as a whole shows the remarkable ability of Luther at his best to produce, on the spur of the moment as it were, alternative renderings which not only can stand on their own feet but even compare most favorably with the admittedly excellent work done and the high level achieved in the *Septembertestament.*

Matt. 8:4

. . . *gib dein opffer, wie Moses . . . gepotten hatt.*[81]

The *Septembertestament* has this rendering: *opffere die gabe, die Moses befohlen hat*. The variant is free but is couched in excellent German.

Matt. 10:10

. . . *eyn wanderstab . . .*[82]

This is a fine variant of the word *stecken* used in the *Septembertestament*.

[80] WA 8, 199.　　[81] Ibid., 152.　　[82] WA 9, 710.

Matt. 24 : 13

Wer da bestendig bleibt bisz ansz ende, der wirt selig.[83]

This variant is in all likelihood as good as the version of the *Septembertestament*: *Wer aber beharret bis ans ende, der wirt selig.*

Matt. 24 : 15

Wer das lieset der vorstehe es wol[84]

Another variant of 1521 has *vorstehe es* but omits *wol*. These are excellent variants of the *Septembertestament*: *wer das lieset, der merck drauff.*

Matt. 24 : 24

. . . das . . . die auszerwelten schier verfurt werden.[85]

The *Septembertestament* reads as follows: *. . . das verfuret werden . . . (wo es muglich were) auch die auserweleten.* The single word *schier* is a superb variant of the whole phrase *wo es muglich were*. It can easily be maintained that the variant is superior to the official rendering, which is of course good in its own right.

IV. Wholly Idiomatic Variants

1519

Matt. 5 : 45

. . . unser vater . . . lest regnen uber die im dancken und die im nit dancken.[86]

This would seem to be a thoroughly vernacularized variant of the literal *Septembertestament* version: *. . . lest regnen vbir gerechten vnd vngerechten.* One might hold that the non-theologian can probably grasp the idea of gratefulness more easily than that of righteousness.

Matt. 6 : 34

Last die sorge eins tags gnug sein . . .[87]

This is a more direct, simple, and idiomatic way of putting the *Septembertestament*'s more literal version: *Es ist gnug das eyn iglich tag seyn eygen vbell habe.*

Matt. 7 : 12

Was du willt, das man dir thu, das thu du auch dem andern.[88]

The official rendering is much more literal and heavy-footed: *Alles*

[83] WA 8, 368.   [84] WA 7, 423, 424   [85] WA 8, 490.
[86] WA 6, 16.   [87] WA 2, 115.   [88] Ibid., 120.

nu, das yhr wollet, das euch die leutte thun sollenn, das thutt yhn auch yhr.

1520
Matt. 23 : 24

... *die mucken fahen und Elephanten lassen faren.*[89]

This is a very free, rather amusing and humorous rendering of what the *Septembertestament* expresses literally as follows: ... *die yhr mucken seyget, vnd kameel verschluckt.* The (involuntary?) substitution of *Elephanten* for *kameel* is too good to be missed!

1521
Matt. 7 : 27

... *ungestümme der wasser unnd wind.*[90]

An unusually free but excellent variant of the more literal *Septembertestament* version: ... *kam eyn gewesser, vnd webeten die winde.*

Matt. 11 : 17

Singt man yhn, szo tantzen sie nit, klaget man sie, szo weynen sie nit, wie mansz mit yhn macht, szo hilfft widder ernst noch schimpff.[91]

In the present connection we are not interested in the first half of this verse; it will be recalled that this was discussed when we dealt with the question of sources. We are at this time concerned with the second half of the passage, which expresses the basic idea of the verse very freely, to be sure, but in really excellent, idiomatic German. The translation, if indeed it can still be called a translation at all, is so extraordinarily free that it is almost an addition to, or summary of, the actual text. It is a superb example of how Luther can give the fundamental thought of a passage in such a manner that the meaning must have become absolutely clear to the humblest German reader.

Matt. 18 : 9

... *das aug muss ausgestochen seynn.*[92]

This is a splendid variant of the literal *Septembertestament* rendering: *vnd so dich deyn auge ergert, reys es aus.*

Matt. 21 : 5

... *uff einem iungen esel.*[93]

A straightforward, most simple rendering of the formal, literal *Septembertestament* version: ... *auff eynem fullen der lastbaren esellynn.*

[89]WA 6, 289. [90]WA 8, 482. [91]WA 7, 637.
[92]Ibid., 563. [93]WA 9, 709.

Matt. 21 : 31

Hurn und buben werden fur ewch gahn ynsz himelreich.[94]

The word *buben* as part of the well-known phrase *hurn und buben* would seem to be a stronger, more "domestic" rendering than the word *tzolner* occurring in the literal translation of the *Septembertestament:* ... *die tzolner vnnd hurnn werden ehe yns hymelreych komen denn yhr.*

V. Intensifying Variants

As one may fairly be led to expect from so intensely personal a writer as Martin Luther, some of his "quotations" are characterized by interesting augmentations and reinforcements of the text. These accretions generally intensify the meaning of a passage as Luther understood it. They often underscore heavily what Luther felt to be the heart of the verse. The following are the chief examples of this peculiarity of Luther's manner of "quoting."

1518

Matt. 7 : 12

Was ir wollet, das euch die menschen thun sollen, dasselb thut yr yn auch, das ist das gantz gesetze unnd alle propheten.[95]

Neither the Greek original nor the Vulgate has anything corresponding to *gantz* and *alle*. The comparatively literal *Septembertestament* version also omits these additional words. In the casual quotation, however, in which the stamp of Luther's individuality is much more evident than in the official German Bible, an intensification of meaning such as that produced by adding *gantz* and *alle* is occasionally found. Luther's full heart and head overflowed into phrases of this sort.

Matt. 11 : 28

Komet zu mir alle die ir arbeitet und beschweret seid mit sünden, ich wil euch erquicken.[96]

The exciting interpolation *mit sünden* is of course not found in Luther's sources; it is pretty definitely Luther's personal addition. Yet it readily affords us a glimpse into Luther's heart and mind. He is not so much concerned with relief from general discomfort as with deliverance from sin. The core of the theology of Luther finds linguistic expression—probably quite involuntarily—in a casual Biblical quotation.

[94]WA 7, 359.   [95]WA 1, 251.
[96]Ibid., 255.

1519
Matt. 21 : 22

Wan yr bettet, so gleubt fest, das yrs werdeth erlangenn, szo geschicht es gewisz.[97]

Luther has again intensified the intrinsic meaning of the verse by adding *fest* to the idea of faith and *gewisz* to the idea of its realization. The reader feels the full weight of the man Luther and his religion behind these significant additions to the text.

1520
Matt. 18 : 17

Höret er sie nit, szo sag es der gantzen gemeyn der kirchen.[98]

Aside from the addition of the intensifying adjective *gantzen*, this verse is highly interesting in that it uses, in one and the same passage, both *gemeyn* and *kirchen*. It is widely known that Luther preferred to say *gemeyn* rather than *kirche;* the latter word in his view was too often applied to the building or the hierarchy to serve as a translation of the Biblical *ecclesia*. Here we have then the curious phenomenon of the employment of both designations, one piled upon the other as it were!

Matt. 24 : 15

Wen yhr werdett sehen den stinckenden grewell, der alle dinge wüst macht . . . .[99]

This is a very strongly worded variant of the more literal phrases *den wusten grewel* of the *Septembertestament* and *grewel der verwüstunge* of the revised edition of the New Testament of 1527. The vehemence and vigor of which Luther was at all times capable surely come to the fore in this early alternative rendering.

VI. Simplifying Variants

There are a few splendid examples of quotations simplifying the sometimes heavy and involved Biblical text. What Luther did not quite dare to do in his formal translation of the Bible, he occasionally permitted himself in an informal citation.

1519
Matt. 26 : 29

Ich werd disz weynsz nit mehr dringken . . . .[100]

This is a considerable simplification when compared with the *Sep-*

[97] WA 2, 126.   [98] WA 6, 65.   [99] WA 7, 177.   [100] WA 2, 754.

tembertestament: . . . *ich werde von nu an nit trincken von dem gewechs des weynstocks* . . . .

1520
Matt. 17 : 25

. . . *ob nit künigs kynder frey weren zynsz su geben.*[101]

An unusually abbreviated form of what reads as follows in the *Septembertestament:* . . . *von wem nemen die konige auff erden den zoll oder tzinsze? von yhren kyndern odder von frembden?*

1521
Matt. 13 : 33

. . . *sawr teyg, den das weyb menget ynn drey scheffel meel.*[102]

The *Septembertestament* is rather long and more formal: . . . *sawer teyg, den eyn weyb nam vnnd vermengt yhn vnter drey scheffel mehls* . . . .

VII. Expanded Variants

One of the interesting characteristics of the early quotations from Matthew is what might be termed Luther's fondness for using synonyms where the source has only a single word. He is not satisfied sometimes to express the matter once: he likes to repeat the idea in a slightly different form, almost suggesting Hebrew parallelism.

1518
Matt. 5 : 29

. . . *das auge, das uns scandalizirt und ergert.*[103]
The *Septembertestament* has merely *ergert.*

Matt. 16 : 23

Gehe hinter mich, Sathan, du Teufel.[104]
Only the word *Satan* occurs in the *Septembertestament.*

Matt. 21 : 3

Sie seyn dem herren not, das ist, er darf yhrer.[105]
Der Herr bedarff yhr is all the *Septembertestament* has.

[101] WA 7, 36. [102] Ibid., 337.
[103] WA 1, 269 f. [104] Ibid., 276.
[105] Ibid., 388.

1519

Matt. 5 : 42

Und wer von dyr borgen odder entleyhen will, von dem kere dich nit, das ist, vorsags yhm nicht.[106]
Septembertestament: ... wende dich nit von dem, der von dyr borgen will.

Matt. 7 : 3

... aber den cleynen steckel ader ruthen in ires nehesten auge.[107]
Septembertestament: spreyssen. Dezembertestament: splitter.

Matt. 15 : 28

... dir geschee, wie du wilt, und gebeten hast.[108]
Septembertestament: dyr geschehe wie du wilt.

1520

Matt. 16 : 18

Du bist oder heissest Petrus.[109]
Septembertestament: du bist Petrus.

Matt. 18 : 4

Eyn yglicher sol sich den vntirsten und geringsten halten.[110]
Septembertestament: wer nu sich selbs nydriget. ...

1521

Matt. 7 : 27

Szo yhr aber auff dem sandt stehet, wirtt euch eyn schwinder grosser fall begegen.[111]
Septembertestament: ... vnd sein fall war grossz.
Revision of 1530: ... thet einen grossen fall.

Matt. 10 : 22

Ir werdet veracht werden vnnd verworffen von den menschen.[112]
Septembertestament: ... musset gehasset werden.

Matt. 10 : 34, 35

... bynn nit kummen frid, sondernn schwerd und hadder zu sendenn.[113]

---

[106]WA 6, 3, line 18. [107]WA 2, 118. [108]Ibid., 126. [109]WA 6, 309.
[110]Ibid., 410. [111]WA 8, 482. [112]WA 7, 244. [113]Ibid., 281.

Septembertestament: ... das schwerd. ...
Denn ich bynn kummen, uneynisz zu machen und scheyden den sun wider den vatter.
Septembertestament: ... den menschen tzu erregen widder seynen vater.

Matt. 11 : 28

... ich wil euch erlaben und erfristen.[114]
... ich wil euch erquicken und helffen.[115]
Septembertestament: ... ich wil euch erquicken.

Matt. 15 : 3

... haben ... schadet und vortunckelt gottliche gesetz.[116]
Septembertestament: ... vbirtrettet. ...

Matt. 24 : 24

... das die auszerwelten sollen verfurtt und betrogen werden.[117]
Septembertestament: ... das verfurt werden ... auch die auserweleten.

VIII. Alliterative Variants

Contrary to the frequent occurrence of alliteration in the *Septembertestament*, there is but one clear-cut example of it in the early quotations from Matthew. It is, however, an excellent one that should be more widely known.

1520

Matt. 6 : 24

Yhr mugt nit zu gleych dem gutt und gott dienen.[118]
The official version lacks alliteration in this instance altogether: *Yhr kunt nitt gott dienen vnnd dem Mammon.* It is probably not safe to say that Luther consciously abandoned the alliterative structure of the early quotation. He apparently did not even remember it when he undertook the translation of the New Testament as a whole! But this extraordinary citation of 1520 should not be entirely forgotten. It has real value as an important alternative rendering.

IX. Variants with Foreign Words

As is the case in the earlier German writings of the Reformer in general, the Biblical quotations from 1517 to 1521 contain rather more

---

[114]Ibid., 258. [115]Ibid., 697. [116]Ibid., 633.
[117]WA 8, 532. [118]WA 7, 173.

foreign words than the corresponding verses of the *Septembertestament*.

1518

Matt. 5 : 26

... *bis sie bezalen den minsten quadranten.*[119]
Septembertestament: ... *den letzten heller.* ...

Matt. 5 : 29

... *das auge, das uns scandalizirt* ....[120]
Septembertestament: ... *ergert* ...

1520

Matt. 18 : 17

... *szo hallt yhn alsz eynen heyden und publican.*[121]
Septembertestament: ... *so halt yhn als eynen heyden vnd zolner.*

Matt. 21 : 9

... *gebenedeyt sey, der do* ... *kompt* .... [122]
An indication of how late some foreign words were replaced by German words is the fact that the *Septembertestament* and the various revised editions between 1522 and 1527 still retain the foreign word: ... *gebenedeyet sey.* ... It is not till the famous revision of 1530 that the foreign word dropped out: its place was then taken by *gelobet*.

1521

Matt. 8 : 8

... *Centurion.* ...[123]
Septembertestament: ... *der hawbtman.* ...

X. Quotations Anticipating the Septembertestament

It is interesting to note that there are a number of cases in which the rendering of the *Septembertestament* is anticipated in the quotations from 1517 to 1521. This list includes several striking passages that are characteristically Lutheran, i.e., they do not anticipate the *Septembertestament* merely because there is no other way of rendering the phrase: they rather bear the unmistakable stamp of Luther's individuality. To bring this out more clearly, the corresponding renderings of the printed German Bibles before Luther will be appended.

[119] WA 1, 277.   [120] Ibid., 269.   [121] WA 6, 65.
[122] Ibid., 359.   [123] WA 7, 377.

1517
Matt. 5 : 4

... *dann sie sollen getrostet werden.*[124]

All pre-Lutheran Bibles read as follows: ... *wann sy werdent getröst.*

Matt. 7 : 23

... *ubeltheter.* ...[125]
Mentel Bible: *ir do werckt die vnganckheit.*
Pflanzmann Bible: *ir do werckt die bossheit.*
Zainer Bible to Silvanus Otmar Bible: *die ir wurckent die bossheit.*

Matt. 12 : 36

... *rechenschafft geben am jungsten tag.*[126]
Mentel: *sy gebend rede ... an dem tag des vrteils.*
Zainer to Silvanus Otmar: *sy gebend rechnung an dem tag des vrteils.*

1518
Matt. 15 : 14

... *laszt si faren.* ...[127]
Mentel to Silvanus Otmar: ... *lasst sy.* ...

1519
Matt. 11 : 29

Lernet von mir, dan ich bin sanfftmutigk und von hertzen demutig.[128]
Mentel to Schönsperger (1490): ... *wan ich bin senfft vnd demutigs hertzen.*
Hans Otmar to Silvanus Otmar: ... *diemütig im hertzen.*

1520
Matt. 18 : 24

... *der seynem herrn schuldig war zehen tausent pfundt.*[129]
All pre-Lutheran Bibles: ... *er solt im X M pfunt.*

Matt. 24 : 9

Ihr werdet umb meynes namens willen von allen menschen gehasset werdenn.[130]
All pre-Lutheran German Bibles: *ir werdet in hasse allen leuten vmb meinen namen.*

[124]WA 1, 214.   [125]Ibid., 164.   [126]Ibid., 220.   [127]Ibid., 393.
[128]WA 2, 88.   [129]WA 6, 66.   [130]Ibid., 274.

1521

Matt. 7 : 15

Sehet euch fur fur den falschen lerern,[131] *die zu euch komen yn schaffs kleyder und ynnewendig sein sie reyssende wolff.*[132]

All pre-Lutheran German Bibles: *Mit fleiss hutet euch vor den valschen weyssagen die zu euch kument in scheffin gewande: wann inwendig seint sy grimig wolff.*[133]

Matt. 12 : 34

... das maul ubir gehen lassen, des das hertz voll ist.[134]

While this is not yet fully the famous *Septembertestament* phrasing of *Wes das hertz voll ist, des geht der mund vbir*, it is certainly not far from this superb rendering.

Mentel: *Wann vor der begnugsam des hertzen redt der mund.*
Zainer to Silvanus Otmar: *uberflussigkeit* is used in place of *begnugsam*.

Matt. 22 : 21

Gebt dem keyszer was des keysers ist.[135]
All pre-Lutheran German Bibles: *gebt dem keyser die ding die do seint des keysers.*

In addition to these rather significant examples there are a number of less important ones which also show an early anticipation of the *Septembertestament*:

1520

Matt. 6 : 19; 18 : 15; 24 : 23.

1521

Matt. 13 : 58; 15 : 7; 15 : 8; 16 : 11; 16 : 24; 18 : 15; 18 : 18; 21 : 12; 21 : 13; 21 : 43; 23 : 3; 23 : 10; 23 : 32; 23 : 33; 24 : 5; 24 : 15; 24 : 24; 26 : 26; 26 : 27; 26 : 28; 27 : 42; 28 : 19; 28 : 20.

XI. Quotations Anticipating the New Testament Revision of 1530

1520

Matt. 7 : 27

... zuletzt einenn grausammen fal thun.[136]
Septembertestament: *... vnnd seyn fall war grossz.*
Revision of 1530: *... thet einen grossen fall.*

---

[131]The *Septembertestament* has: *propheten*. [132]WA 7, 662. Cf. 8, 140.
[133]Zainer to S. Otmar: *zuckend* for *grimig*.
[134]WA 8, 682. [135]WA 7, 626. [136]WA 6, 209.

This famous passage, which is all Luther's own phrasing, was thus anticipated, roughly of course, as early as 1520, in a casual quotation.

In conclusion it may be said that Luther's quotations from Matthew prior to the beginning of his work on the *Septembertestament* are of more than passing interest. Generally speaking, they reveal an expert and an artist in the handling of highly idiomatic German. Their variety and more than occasional excellence provide an important clue to what was to be offered to the world in the *Septembertestament*. When Luther was persuaded to undertake this formidable task, he was in a position to draw, unconsciously of course, on a large and ready storehouse of previously, and sometimes frequently, rendered passages. Boundless as this vast supply of variants would seem to be, in some verses Luther appears to have exhausted the very possibilities of expressing the idea in the vernacular. The scholar patient enough to peruse these early quotations is impressed by the apparent ease with which one of the greatest masters of the German language can render in various superb ways a veritable deluge of Biblical verses.

The early quotations then give us a good idea of the well-stocked and well-equipped workshop of the master craftsman who was to present the Western world with one of the most distinguished translations of the Bible. If emperor or pope had put an untimely end to Luther at Worms or soon thereafter, the wealth and excellence of the Biblical quotations prior to 1522 would make us forever long for a complete German Bible from this literary genius. Fortunately, Frederick the Wise intervened and preserved the life of his most famous professor, who was, among many other things, also an incomparable translator, Martin Luther.

Chapter 2

The First Translation of a Pericope

LUTHER's first translation of a New Testament pericope was made as early as the summer of 1519, when, during the early days of the Leipzig Disputation, Luther was asked by Duke Barnim of Pomerania to deliver a sermon for the feast of St. Peter's and St. Paul's, on June 29.[1] Luther chose for his text the Gospel of the day, Matt. 16 : 13–19. The vernacular version of this text, prefixed to the actual sermon, constitutes Luther's earliest translation of a New Testament pericope.[2]

Was Luther in this early translation, which antedates *Das Newe Testament Deutzsch* by several years, still basing himself on the Vulgate, or was he already using Erasmus' Greek text? This is not an idle question, since it is well known that Luther made almost instantaneous use of Erasmus' *Novum Instrumentum Omne* when that epoch-making book first appeared in 1516. Luther consulted it for his famous lectures on the Epistle to the Romans as soon as he could lay his hands on it. While a popular sermon is naturally different from a formal university lecture, it is not wholly inconceivable that he should have used the Greek text when he made what appears to be his first extant German version of a highly significant pericope, to serve as the text for an important sermon given before important people on an unusually important occasion. Whatever one's preconceived opinion in this matter, it stands to reason that only a careful investigation of the problem can hope to answer the question of Luther's source.

It will be necessary to compare Luther's vernacular version with the Vulgate,[3] Erasmus' Greek text, and the new Latin version which Erasmus supplied alongside the Greek original. As regards the Erasmus

[1] WA 2, 241.
[2] Aside from numerous isolated New Testament quotations scattered throughout the early German works of Luther, there is also a translation of the Lord's Prayer of 1519, which deserves an investigation of its own.
[3] The Basel edition of 1509 is used because a copy of this was presumably in Luther's hands.

text, both the first edition of 1516 and the second edition of 1519 will have to be considered, since both were, so far as the publication date is concerned, available to Luther, Erasmus' second edition having appeared in March of 1519. In order to proceed as cautiously as possible, only one verse at a time will be compared and discussed.

MATT. 16 : 13 Luther, 1519.[4] *Es ist Jesus kummen in dy gegent der stad Cesarea, die Philippus erbawet hat, und aldo fragt er seine jünger: was sagen die leut von dem sun des menschen.*

Vulgate: *Venit autem iesus in partes cesaree philippi: et interrogabat discipulos suos dicens: Quem dicunt homines esse filium hominis?*

Erasmus' Greek, 1516: Ἐλθὼν δὲ ὁ Ἰησοῦς εἰς τὰ μέρη καισαρείας τῆς φιλίππου, ἠρώτα τοὺς μαθητὰς αὐτοῦ λέγων· τίνα με λέγουσιν οἱ ἄνθρωποι εἶναι τὸν υἱὸν τοῦ ἀνθρώπου;

Erasmus' Latin, 1516: *Cum venisset autem Jesus in partes Cesareae eius, quae cognominatur Philippi, interrogavit discipulos suos dicens. Quem me dicunt homines esse filium illum hominis?*

Erasmus' Greek, 1519: Identical with the text of 1516.

Erasmus' Latin, 1519: Identical with the text of 1516.

It is quite clear that Luther's German version of v. 13 is not a literal translation at all. Let us first take its relation to the Vulgate. From a strictly philological point of view Luther both omits from and adds to the Latin text. On the one hand, he omits the words *autem* and *dicens* and he condenses the question *Quem dicunt homines esse filium hominis*. On the other hand, he expands the brief phrase *in partes cesaree philippi* to *in dy gegent der stad Cesarea, die Philippus erbawet hat,* and he adds the word *aldo*, which is not in the Vulgate, to the next phrase.

The same remarks apply to the Erasmian Greek text. Both δὲ and λέγων are omitted by Luther, and the question τίνα με λέγουσιν οἱ ἄνθρωποι εἶναι τὸν υἱὸν τοῦ ἀνθρώπου is condensed. The short phrase εἰς τὰ μέρη καισαρείας τῆς φιλίππου is expanded, and the word *aldo*, lacking in the Greek text, is added.

There can be no doubt that Luther's German version is not dependent on Erasmus' Latin translation. It is of considerable interest, however, that Erasmus also "expands" the phrase εἰς τὰ μέρη καισαρείας τῆς φιλίππου. But the important thing to remember is that Luther's expansion is quite different from that of Erasmus. It seems that both men felt it necessary to enlarge on the compact original text (whether this

[4] WA 2, 246.

was Greek or Latin for Luther does not matter in this instance). Of major significance for our purpose, however, is the fact that there is an important difference between what Erasmus and Luther chose to add. Erasmus' supplementary clause *quae cognominatur Philippi* is more clearly implied in the text than Luther's *die Philippus erbawet hat.* Luther added an idea not necessarily contained in the text while Erasmus' version adds nothing extraneous to it. As regards the origin of Luther's phrase *die Philippus erbawet hat,* it may very well stem from a work such as the *Postilla . . . Hugonis cardinalis,* which in the 1504 edition (accessible to me) comments as follows on this passage: "quā in honorē tyberii cesaris philippus frater herodis extruxit." Or the suggestion may have come to him from the following passage in Erasmus' *Adnotationes: "quam extruxit Herodes filius in honorem Tyberii Caesaris."* But Luther was bold enough to incorporate in the text itself what Erasmus put merely into the notes.

Luther's translation of v. 13 does not permit us to draw any conclusion as to whether it was based on the Vulgate or the Greek text. Aside from the fact that Luther's rendering is far from literal, the Vulgate version of this verse adheres so closely to the Greek original that no decision regarding the text used is possible.

MATT. 16:14 Luther, 1519: *Do haben sie gesagt: Etlich sagen, du seyest Johannes der teuffer: etlich, du seyest Helias: Etlich, Hieremias adder sunst einer aus den propheten.*

Vulgate: *At illi dixerunt: Alii iohanem baptistam: alii autem heliam: alii vero hieremiam: aut unum ex prophetis.*

Erasmus' Greek, 1516: οἱ δὲ εἶπον· οἱ μὲν Ἰωάννην τὸν βαπτιστήν, ἄλλοι δὲ Ἠλίαν, ἕτεροι δὲ Ἱερεμίαν, ἢ ἕνα τῶν προφητῶν.

Erasmus' Latin, 1516: *illi vero dicebant. Alii quidem Ioannem baptistam, alii vero Eliam, alii vero Hieremiam, aut unum de numero prophetarum.*

Erasmus' Greek, 1519: Identical with the text of 1516.

Erasmus' Latin, 1519: Identical with the translation of 1516 except in orthography: 1516—*baptistam, Eliam;* 1519—*Baptistam, Heliam.*

This verse is somewhat more literally translated by Luther than the preceding one. So far as its relation to the Vulgate is concerned, *autem* and *vero* are omitted and the initial *at* is rendered by *do,* surely not as close a rendering as possible. Additions are: *sagen, seyest* (twice), and *sunst.* With reference to the Greek text, Luther omits μὲν and, twice, δὲ. For the δὲ in οἱ δὲ εἶπον he substitutes *do.* The additions are the same as those to the Latin text. One look at Erasmus' Latin translation suffices to convince the reader that Luther did not use it. Erasmus' attempt to restore classical Latin was not the basis of Luther's version.

Inasmuch as the Vulgate and the Greek text are again very close to each other, it is again impossible to arrive at any conclusion regarding the source of Luther's vernacular rendering.

MATT. 16 : 15 Luther, 1519: *Da sprach Jesus zu yn: was sagt dann yhr von mir?*

The Vulgate: *Dicit illis iesus: Vos autem quem me esse dicitis?*
Erasmus' Greek, 1516: λέγει αὐτοῖς· ὑμεῖς δὲ τίνα με λέγετε εἶναι;
Erasmus' Latin, 1516: *Dicit illis. At vos, quem me dicitis esse?*
Erasmus' Greek, 1519: Identical with the text of 1516.
Erasmus' Latin, 1519: Identical with the Latin translation of 1516.

Luther's translation again is not strictly literal. With reference to the Vulgate, Luther adds the initial *da* and substitutes *dann* for *autem*. The entire phrase, *was sagt dann yhr von mir*, is a free rendering of the Latin *vos autem quem me esse dicitis*. The artistic merits of the translation[5] are not our primary concern in this connection. It will be recalled that the same kind of splendid idiomatic German was also found in v. 13: *was sagen die leut von dem sun des menschen?*

Looking now at the Greek text, we note first that the second half of v. 15 has the δὲ corresponding to the Latin *autem*, which Luther "rendered" by *dann*. Of far greater importance for our investigation, however, is the first half of the verse. Here we are provided with a reasonably good indication that Luther's translation is not based on the Greek text. The passage reads: *da sprach Jesus zu yn* and *dicit illis iesus* in the German and Latin versions respectively. The Greek text of both editions of 1516 and 1519 does not have *Jesus* for the subject but simply the implied *He:* λέγει αὐτοῖς. While this fact seems to suggest quite strongly that Luther used the Vulgate rather than the Greek text, it still cannot be considered as an absolute proof. Nestle in a footnote to v. 15 indicates that the Latin text occurs also without the subject *Jesus*. However, it should be pointed out that the Basel edition of the Vulgate of 1509, which Luther is now believed to have used, has the word *Jesus*. Moreover, the twenty-odd Vulgates published between 1509 and 1520 which are available in the great collection of Bibles at the General Theological Seminary in New York all contain the word *Jesus*. About the same number of samples taken from the Vulgates published between 1455(?) and 1509 also have the subject *Jesus*. Thus

---

[5] An isolated quotation of this verse in 1520 has another excellent German wording: *was haltet yr von mir?* (WA 6, 310).

the roughly 45 Vulgates examined by me have without exception the word in question. On the basis of these facts it would seem that the probability that Luther used an edition containing *Jesus* is distinctly greater than that he should have used one without this word in the verse under consideration. If this hypothesis is correct, the presence of the subject *Jesus* in this verse may be taken as evidence that Luther's translation is based on the Vulgate.

So far as Erasmus' Latin version is concerned, the first half of the verse, *dicit illis*, with its omission of *Jesus* in accordance with the Greek text, makes it quite unlikely that Luther used it. In the second half, Luther's *dann*, as contrasted with Erasmus' *at*, only strengthens this conviction.

In summary, the first half of this brief verse is of paramount importance for the main problem of this investigation. Luther's use of the word *Jesus* is a fairly good indication that his translation is based on the Vulgate. Although a Vulgate reading without *Jesus* does occur, none of the more than 40 editions I have consulted has this variant. While it cannot be said with complete certainty that the omission of the word *Jesus* would mean that Luther used the Greek text, the fact that Luther does employ the word allows us to conclude that his translation is not based on the Greek text. Paradoxical as it may sound, we cannot prove that Luther used the Vulgate, but we can all but prove that he did not use the Greek text.

MATT. 16:16 Luther, 1519: *Da antwortet Simon Petrus und sprach: Du bist Christus, ein sun des lebendigen gottis.*

Vulgate: *Respondens simon petrus/dixit: Tu es Christus filius dei vivi.*

Erasmus' Greek, 1516: ἀποκριθεὶς δὲ σίμων πέτρος εἶπεν· σὺ εἶ ὁ χριστὸς ὁ υἱὸς τοῦ θεοῦ τοῦ ζῶντος.

Erasmus' Latin, 1516: *Respondens autem Simon Petrus, dixit. Tu es Christus ille filius dei viventis.*

Erasmus' Greek, 1519: Identical with the text of 1516.

Erasmus' Latin, 1519: Identical with the translation of 1516.

As regards the relation of the verse to the Vulgate, there is one minor addition in Luther's translation: the introductory *da*. This *da* does not prove any use of the Greek text, however, since it can hardly be said to be a translation of the second word, δὲ.

While the first part of this verse is of little significance for our purposes, the second part presents a highly interesting problem. On the face of it, this second half seems to rule out the possibility that

Luther used the Greek original. The indefinite article *ein* before *sun* would appear to argue eloquently against its being based on the Greek phrase ὁ χριστὸς ὁ υἱὸς. However, the case is not so simple as all that. Otto Behaghel points out that in an appositional phrase like *Christus, ein sun...gottis* the indefinite article was formerly employed: "bei einer bereits bekannten Vorstellung... steht der unbestimmte Artikel ... in der älteren Sprache."[6] In addition to pertinent Middle High German illustrations such as "Christ,...ein freunt der sundaere" Behaghel gives also examples from the age of the Reformation, e.g., "wie Lucifer, ain künig der hellen, ain fürst der finsternus."[7] Against the background of this linguistic usage, Luther's phrase *ein sun* loses much of its evidential power. The further fact that Luther in a quotation of this isolated verse in 1518[8] also used *ein* but in another quotation of the same verse in 1520[9] used *der* is probably an indication of changing German usage. It is suggestive that the article *der* is found in all printed High German Bibles from 1466 to 1518 as well as in the Teplitz and Freiberg manuscripts. Tempting as it may seem to deduce from this fact that Luther's employment of *ein* proves his rendering is not based on the Greek text, it cannot really be done in the light of Behaghel's observations. Luther's use of *ein* is primarily a phenomenon of German grammar.

Erasmus' Latin translation of the second half of this verse is of more than passing interest in its relation to the problem just discussed. He takes great pains to translate the Greek definite article into Latin: *Tu es Christus ille filius dei viventis.* Even this excellent way of suggesting the Greek article in the Latin language, which has to get along without articles, is not yet satisfactory to Erasmus, who apparently set his heart on reproducing the Greek definite article at all cost. In the *Adnotationes* he goes so far as to suggest *ille Christus,...ille filius dei*[10] as the real equivalent of the original Greek ὁ χριστὸς ὁ υἱὸς. Erasmus must have been very much impressed by the Greek use of the definite article in this instance. He somehow must have felt that the Vulgate phrase *Christus, filius Dei* was an inadequate rendering of the original. Even the modern reader of the *Adnotationes* senses the keen delight Erasmus must have experienced upon the discovery of the Greek text, which caused him to be quite dissatisfied with the existing Vulgate version. In the light of Erasmus' new Latin translation and elaborate annotation it seems rather unlikely that Luther could have consulted

---

[6] O. Behaghel, *Deutsche Syntax* (1923), I, 99, 100.
[7] Ibid., 100.   [8] WA 1, 276.   [9] WA 6, 310.
[10] The second edition of 1519 has the more elaborate note on this passage.

it when making his early vernacular version. Erasmus' tenacious insistence on expressing the Greek definite article in his Latin translation does not seem to be reflected in Luther's rendering unless we interpret the *ein* as intensifying.

MATT. 16 : 17 Luther, 1519: *Do antwortet ym Jesus und sagt: wol dir, o Simon Barjona, dann fleisch and blut hat dir das nit offenbaret, sundernn mein vatter, der ym hymel ist,*

Vulgate: *Respondens autem iesus/dixit ei: Beatus es simon bariona: quia caro et sanguis non revelavit tibi: sed pater meus qui in celis est.*

Erasmus' Greek, 1516: καὶ ἀποκριθεὶς ὁ Ἰησοῦς εἶπεν αὐτῷ· μακάριος εἶ σίμων βαριωνά, ὅτι σὰρξ καὶ αἷμα οὐκ ἀπεκάλυψέν ἀλλ' ὁ πατήρ μου ὁ ἐν τοῖς οὐρανοῖς.

Erasmus' Latin, 1516: *Et respondens Jesus dixit illi. Beatus es Simon Bar Iona, quia caro et sanguis non revelavit tibi, sed pater meus qui est in celis.*

Erasmus' Greek, 1519: Identical with the text of 1516.

Erasmus' Latin, 1519: Identical with the translation of 1516 except that *celis* is now spelled *coelis*.

So far as the relation of Luther's translation of this verse to the Vulgate is concerned, its first half is again scarcely literal. The important fact that it is delightfully idiomatic is not our first concern in this connection. Luther's introductory *do* apparently takes the place of *autem* as it had taken the place of *at* in v. 14. The drawing of *ym (ei)* away from *dixit* to *antwortet* is another case of Luther's free (though idiomatic) rendering of this passage. Similarly, the following words *wol dir, o Simon Barjona* are surely not a literal (albeit highly idiomatic) translation of *beatus es simon bariona*. It should be noted that an isolated quotation of this phrase *beatus es*, going back to 1518,[11] has the literal translation *selig bistu*, a rendering to which the *Septembertestament* returns and which persists through the 1546 revision. The remainder of this verse is a close translation of the Vulgate.

As regards the relation of Luther's 1519 version to Erasmus' Greek text, two important points are to be noted. First, there is the fact that Erasmus' introductory καὶ is not translated by Luther. As has been pointed out above, the *do* in Luther's version probably takes the place of *autem*. It seems unlikely that it replaces καὶ. If this argument is correct, the omission of Erasmus' καὶ would be an indication that Luther did not base his translation on the Greek text, particularly since

[11] WA 1, 276.

the *Septembertestament,* which was made from the Greek original, faithfully reproduces the καί. The second point, to which particular attention should be paid, is the concluding phrase ὁ πατήρ μου ὁ ἐν τοῖς οὐρανοῖς. Luther's 1519 rendering *der ym hymel ist* appears to be based on the Vulgate line *qui in celis est* rather than on the Greek text. Luther, it would seem, translated the relative clause of the Vulgate and not the appositional phrase of the Greek original. By way of comparison, one should remember Luther's translation of these words in the *Septembertestament,* which was definitely based on the Greek original: *meyn vatter ym hymel.* However, the hypothesis that the use of the relative clause points clearly to the Vulgate is somewhat impaired by the consideration that Luther in his catechisms retained throughout his life the relative clause in the similar phrase *der du bist im Himmel.*

With reference to Erasmus' Latin translation, there is no indication that Luther consulted it in any way. If Luther's rendering were based on it, he would have had to begin this verse with *und,* which he did not.

MATT. 16 : 18 Luther, 1519: *Und ich sag dir auch: Du bist Petrus (das ist ein fels), und auff diszen fels will ich bawen meine kirche, und die gewalt der hellen sollen nit sie uber mügen.*

Vulgate: *Et ego dico tibi: quia tu es petrus: et super hanc petram edificabo ecclesiam meam: et porte inferi non prevalebunt adversus eam.*

Erasmus' Greek, 1516: κἀγὼ δὲ σοι λέγω, ὅτι σὺ εἶ πέτρος, καὶ ἐπὶ ταύτῃ τῇ πέτρᾳ οἰκοδομήσω μου τὴν ἐκκλησίαν. καὶ πύλαι ᾅδου οὐ κατισχύσουσιν αὐτῆς.

Erasmus' Latin, 1516: *At ego quoque tibi dico, quod tu es Petrus, et super hanc petram aedificabo meam ecclesiam, et portae inferorum non valebunt adversus illam.*

Erasmus' Greek, 1519: Identical with text of 1516.

Erasmus' Latin, 1519: Identical with the translation of 1516 with one important exception: 1516—*At ego quoque tibi dico;* 1519—*At ego vicissim tibi dico.*

This verse offers unusually interesting material for discussion. As regards its relation to the Vulgate, the translation is reasonably faithful on the whole if we disregard the fact that Luther adds the parenthetical explanatory words *(das ist ein fels).* There are, however, two departures from a literal rendering. The first occurs at the beginning of the verse. The equivalent of the word *auch* is not in the Vulgate text. Here the question naturally arises whether Luther's *auch* is merely one of his not infrequent additions to the text or whether it might be due to Erasmus' Greek text or his Latin translation. This matter will be discussed fully below. The other departure from the Vulgate is the translation of *porte* by *die gewalt*. On first sight, this seems a strange rendering. But apparently there must have been a tradition of the figurative use of *gewalt* for *portae*. Harper's Latin Dictionary uses this word as a legitimate translation, quoting our very verse, Matt. 16 : 18: "portae inferi, the power of hell." Luther's translation *gewalt* is thus merely a metaphorical rendering of *portae*. Of the five isolated quotations of this verse occurring from 1520 to 1522 four translate *portae* by *pfortenn*[12] and one by *gewalt*.[13] Thus it appears that Luther freely alternated between the literal and metaphorical renderings, with the accent on the literal, however. Both are of course correct. Neither indicates that Luther went beyond the Vulgate for the translation of this passage.

So far as the relation of Luther's translation of this verse to the Greek text is concerned, the important question is the one referred to above, whether Luther's *auch* could possibly be explained on the basis of the Greek δέ. If we take the Greek text by itself, it hardly seems likely that *auch* should result from δέ. Looking, however, at Erasmus' Latin translation of this passage by *at ego quoque* in the 1516 edition, it does not appear impossible that Luther's *auch* might have been inspired by the combined Greek and Latin Erasmian texts. The 1519 edition of the New Testament, which changed the *quoque* to *vicissim*, seems to be more remote from Luther than the first edition of 1516. While this general explanation of Luther's *auch* is quite within the realm of the possible, the *auch* may be no more than a mere expletive with no relation whatsoever to the Greek text or Erasmus' Latin version of it. Since the general evidence up to the use of *auch* in this passage has been rather against Luther's dependence upon the Greek and Latin of Erasmus' edition, it may very well be that the *auch* is only an accidental addition unrelated to the Greek δέ and Erasmus' Latin *at . . . quoque*. It might also easily be due to Luther's unconscious striving for a smooth German text. Whatever its origin, it cannot be said to be unequivocally related to δέ or even *quoque*.

MATT. 16 : 19 Luther, 1519: *und dir will ich geben die schlussel des hymelreichs: was du wirst binden auff erden, das soll gebunden sein ym hymel, und was du wirst auflösen auf erden, das soll aufgelost sein ym hymel.*

[12]WA 6, 315 (1520); 7, 411 (1521); 7, 686 (1521); 8, 714 (1522).
[13]WA 6, 310 (1520).

Vulgate: *Et tibi dabo claues regni celorum. Et quodcunque ligaveris super terram: erit ligatum et in celis; et quodcunque solveris super terram: erit solutum et in celis.*

Erasmus' Greek, 1516: καὶ δώσω σοι τὰς κλεῖς τῆς βασιλείας τῶν οὐρανῶν. καὶ ὅσα ἂν δήσῃς, ἐπὶ τῆς γῆς, ἔσαι δεδεμένα ἐν τοῖς οὐρανοῖς. καὶ ὅσα ἂν λύσῃς ἐπὶ τῆς γῆς, ἔσαι λελυμένα ἐν τοῖς οὐρανοῖς.

Erasmus' Latin, 1516: *Et dabo tibi claves regni coelorum, et quicquid solveris in terra, erit solutum in coelis, et quodcumque alligaveris in terra, erit alligatum in coelis.*

Erasmus' Greek, 1519: καὶ δώσω σοι τὰς κλεῖς τῆς βασιλείας τῶν οὐρανῶν, καὶ ὃ ἐὰν δήσῃς, ἐπὶ τῆς γῆς ἔσαι δεδεμένον ἐν τοῖς οὐρανοῖς, καὶ ὃ ἐὰν λύσῃς ἐπὶ τῆς γῆς ἔσαι λελυμένον ἐν τοῖς οὐρανοῖς.

Erasmus' Latin, 1519: *Et dabo tibi claves regni coelorum, et quicquid solveris in terra, erit solutum in coelis, et quicquid alligaveris in terra, erit alligatum in coelis.*

Regarding the relation of Luther's translation to the Vulgate, it must be said that it is as literal as any that we have had thus far. Additions are *das*, twice. *Et* is omitted three times. So far as the Greek text is concerned, Luther's differs from that only in the omission of the second καὶ and in the addition of *das*, twice.

Taking first the addition of *das*, it is clear that this is without significance for determining which text Luther used, since it is not found either in the Vulgate or in the Greek text. Luther's omission of the second *et* from the Vulgate and the second καὶ from the Greek text does not help us either in our main question. If the copula were lacking from either the Greek text or the Vulgate, it could conceivably be used as an argument for Luther's dependence upon that text in which it was lacking. But since it is lacking in both texts it is of no value to us whatever. There remains the fact that Luther's translation agrees with Erasmus' Greek text and Latin translation in the omission of the copula in the phrase *ym hymel*. While the Vulgate has *et in celis*, the Greek text and Erasmus' Latin translation have ἐν τοῖς οὐρανοῖς and *in coelis*, thus agreeing with Luther's *ym hymel*. The extent to which this fact may be used as evidence in our question is most difficult to establish.

The 22 isolated quotations of this verse from 1518 to 1522 do not throw any additional light on the text Luther used. Once, in 1520, Luther quotes in a German work a portion of Matt. 16:19 in the Vulgate's version: *Quodcunque ligaveris.*[14] While this points of course

---

[14] WA 7, 171.

toward the Vulgate, it is partially offset by the omission of *et* referred to above. Still, the evidence tends to be more in favor of Luther's use of the Vulgate than of the Greek text at this early period.

The time has come for summing up the results of this detailed inquiry into Luther's probable source for his earliest translation of a longer passage from the New Testament. Before hazarding any conclusion it must be stated emphatically that Luther's first vernacular rendering of Matt. 16 : 13-19 is to a certain extent not a meticulously literal translation. It is partially characterized by both expansion and condensation of the text he used. The chief reason for this phenomenon, aside from the fact that it was a not uncommon feature of the Middle Ages, may have been Luther's striving, conscious or unconscious or both, to present his hearers and readers with as clear and idiomatic a German version as possible. It may prove helpful to visualize Luther in the role of a popular preacher who, on coming to the words *in partes cesaree philippi*, felt compelled to explain this compact phrase by enlarging upon it: *in die gegent der stad Cesarea, die Philippus erbawet hat*. Similarly, when he reaches the name *Petrus*, he adds *das ist ein fels* by way of explanation as it were for the untutored in the assemblage. Again it may be enlightening to think of the audience in the case of such superb renderings as *was sagen die leut von dem sun des menschen* and *was sagt dann yhr von mir* instead of more literal translations.

Suggestive and important as these expansions and condensations of the text are, they fail to throw light on the main question of this essay: Did Luther use the Vulgate or did he go back to the Greek original for his first translation of a New Testament pericope that has come down to us? Fortunately, despite the freely rendered passages just discussed, the main body of this New Testament passage can be considered a literal translation on the whole, so that an attempt could be made to examine it for its source. It must be admitted that this was not an easy task, because the Vulgate version of this particular passage is a pretty accurate translation of the Greek original.

These are the difficulties besetting the path of the scholar who would like to try to determine Luther's source for this important early document. Nevertheless, the results are not wholly negative. There is one passage which, on minute inspection, yields a clue that, although not entirely incontestable, still tends to 'solve' this delicate question in a fairly definite manner. This evidence supports the view that Luther used the Vulgate rather than the Greek text. The passage is the *da sprach Jesus* of v. 15. All the Vulgates examined, including the Basel edition of 1509, have the phrase *dicit . . . Jesus* while the Greek text has merely λέγει, omitting the subject *Jesus*.

This passage constitutes in my opinion the only acceptable evidence that this early translation of 1519 is based on the Vulgate. No important evidence to the contrary could be found in this entire pericope. While there is, in the nature of the subject matter, no *absolute proof* either way, there is *relatively* more evidence for Luther's having used the Vulgate than for his having used the Greek text.

Chapter 3

Translation in Transition : The Christmas Postil

ONE OF THE MOST regrettable events in German literary history is the loss of Luther's manuscript of the first edition of the translation of the New Testament of 1522, the so-called *Septembertestament*. Perhaps only those who have worked with the manuscript of Luther's rendering of the Psalms or other parts of the Old Testament can fully appreciate the tragedy of the disappearance of the New Testament manuscript. It was this *Septembertestament*—no matter how often and how thoroughly Luther revised it in the following quarter of a century—which created a literary sensation in the early 16th century, far beyond the borders of the Holy Roman Empire of the German Nation, among Luther's sympathizers and opponents alike. It was the publication of the *Septembertestament* which first really testified, even more than the rich and provocative early German essays, to the breathtaking literary eminence of the religious genius of the age of the Reformation. The loss of the manuscript of this crucial publication will always be a source of regret.

The difference between the pre-Lutheran German Bibles, whether printed or unprinted, whether High German or Low German, on the one hand, and Luther's achievement on the other, is so vast that one would give anything to be able to trace the evolution of the Luther version from its earliest jottings to the published text. The student of the New Testament in the pre-Lutheran Bibles and in Luther's initial venture is so completely overwhelmed by the abyss that separates the two efforts at translation that he cannot easily bring himself to believe that Luther's creation sprang, Athena-like, from the master's head, a finished product. The scholar, awed but incredulous that it emerged full-formed, desperately wants to know what the manuscript pages looked like. He wants to know which of the now world-famous phrases were the gift of the inspiration of the moment and which had to undergo long and arduous birth pangs as evidenced by words crossed out, written above or below the line, and jotted in the margin—the same sight presented in the happily preserved manuscript of sections of the Old Testament. The student of the subject would like somehow to bridge the gap from the obscurity of the pre-Lutheran Bibles to the brilliance of the Lutheran achievement. The manuscript of the *Septembertestament*, if preserved and rediscovered, would probably close this gap somewhat.

Small wonder then that Reformation scholars, greatly impressed by Luther's extraordinary, practically unique accomplishment, have racked their brains in efforts to look behind the scenes, to gain admittance to the workshop of the master craftsman, even by the back door. Needless to say, these attempts have so far proved in vain. Nobody has rediscovered the lost manuscript. Neither has there been, to the best of my knowledge, any forgery. Yet hope springs eternal in the breast of students of Luther, as dedicated a group as ever tried to understand genius. When the darkness was deepest and the gloom heaviest, a ray of light suddenly seemed to penetrate the scholar's night. No, the missing manuscript was not found. But an ingenious theory was advanced by one of the learned editors of the great Weimar edition of Luther's works.

Albert Freitag called attention to the long-known fact that Martin Luther, just prior to undertaking the monumental task of translating the Bible, had been engaged, while on the Wartburg, in composing his Christmas Postil. This postil, begun in June and finished in November 1521, included a number of new translations of New Testament selections prefixed to the sermons based on them. These translations of 1521, it was suggested, came as close as possible to constituting a kind of manuscript version of the relevant portions of the New Testament. At the very least they could be considered a substitute for the lost manuscript of the *Septembertestament* itself.

This theory was made more plausible by the indisputable fact that these postil translations are not identical with the rendering found in the *Septembertestament*. In fact, they are clearly inferior to it, despite the comparatively high level on which they move. It is not surprising that these facts conspired to formulate the thesis that in these translations of the *Weihnachtspostille* we have something approximating the lost manuscript, a virtual substitute for it under the circumstances. The claim was thus made, or strongly implied, that the unfortunately vanished manuscript of the *Septembertestament* must have looked something like the renderings contained in the Christmas Postil. Here at last was the long sought missing link in a manner of speaking. Albert Freitag put it this way: "Jedenfalls wird der Grundstock dieser

Perikopen durchaus ins NT übergeführt. Sie bilden für dessen Übersetzung gleichsam die 'ersten Niederschriften', wie solche für das AT noch vorhanden sind...."[1]

A close examination of all the translations occurring in the Christmas Postil is quite beyond the limits of an essay. Instead, a single pericope was selected, to be treated exhaustively. It seemed to me that a good choice would be the passage presumably translated last, the text prefixed to the final sermon of this postil, Matt. 2 : 1–12. It is highly probable that less than a month separates the translation of this text in the Christmas Postil and in the *Septembertestament*. The Christmas Postil was finished in the second half of November 1521. Work on the *Septembertestament* was in all likelihood started before the middle of December. It seems reasonable to assume that Luther reached the second chapter of Matthew within a day or so after undertaking the project, especially if one bears in mind that a major portion of the first chapter is filled with the very simple material of the genealogy of Jesus.

What we have in the Matthew passage, then, is an almost ideal situation: the final translation in the *Weihnachtspostille* (henceforth abbreviated WP) and one of the very first translations (discounting Matt. 1 : 1–25) of the *Septembertestament* (henceforth abbreviated ST). If there is any similarity to be found anywhere between WP and ST, it should be in the last, and presumably most advanced, phase of WP and the first, or practically first, and presumably least advanced, phase of ST.

In order to do justice to the problem and to show its complexity it will be necessary to present the picture as fully as we may. We shall, however, not discuss at this time the much simpler question of the possible influence of the pre-Lutheran German Bibles and Plenaria upon Luther. This requires a special examination. What we are primarily concerned with here is the intriguing question whether WP can in any way be regarded as a kind of substitute for the lost manuscript of ST. It is this really exciting matter that I wish to deal with in this essay.

For an adequate discussion of the issue at stake, it will be necessary to present the following data for the entire passage under review:

1. The Vulgate. In view of the many variants found in the various early editions of the Vulgate, one must use the edition presumably at Luther's disposal: Basel, 1509.

2. The Greek text as made available to Luther in the second (then

[1] WA, *Deutsche Bibel* 6, 611.

the most recent) edition of Erasmus of 1519. One should also refer to the first edition of 1516 and to Gerbel's reprint of Erasmus' second edition in 1521.

3. Erasmus' new Latin translation printed in a second column alongside the Greek text in the second edition of 1519, with constant reference to the first edition. (Gerbel reproduced only the Greek text of Erasmus.)

4. Erasmus' *Adnotationes* appended to his editions of 1519 and 1516. Gerbel did not reproduce these either.

5. *Lexicon graecolatinum* of Hieronymus Aleander of 1512.

6. *Weihnachtspostille* (WA 10, *erste Abteilung, erste Hälfte*).

7. *Septembertestament* (WA, *Deutsche Bibel* 6).

With this indispensable information before us, each verse of our text will be analyzed by itself before we summarize our findings at the end of the investigation.

MATT. 2 : 1 Vulgate, 1509: *Cum ergo natus esset iesus in bethleem iude in diebus herodis regis: ecce magi ab oriente venerunt hierosolymam dicentes:*

Erasmus, 1519: (Erasmus' second edition will be copied out because it was presumably Luther's *editio princeps* for his translation; divergences, if any, of the first edition and of Gerbel will be noted.)

Greek

τοῦ δὲ Ἰησοῦ γεννηθέντος ἐν βηθλεὲμ τῆς Ιουδαίας ἐν ἡμέραις Ἡρώδου τοῦ βασιλέως. ἰδοὺ μάγοι ἀπὸ ἀνατολῶν παρεγένοντο εἰς ἱεροσόλυμα λέγοντες.

Latin

Cum autem natus esset Jesus in Bethleem vico Judaeae temporibus Herodis regis, Ecce magi ab oriente accesserunt Hierosolyma, dicentes

Erasmus' first edition of 1516 has the following variants:
... *in Bethleem Judaeae in diebus* ...
... *ecce* ... *Hierosolymam,* ...

WP: *Da Jhesus gepornn war zu Bethlehem Jude, ynn den tagen Herodis des kunigis, nempt war, da sind kommen die weyssager vom auffgang gen Hierusalem und haben gesagt:*

ST: *Do Jhesus geporn war zu Bethlehem, yhm Judischen land, tzur tzeyt des konigs Herodis, sihe, da kamen die weysen vom morgenland gen Hierusalem, vnnd sprachen.*

In each verse we shall discuss two questions: first, the *source* or sources, whether Greek or Latin; secondly, the *nature* of Luther's renderings.

SOURCE

The Vulgate and Greek texts are practically identical, with the exception of one minor divergence: the Greek δὲ is rendered somewhat loosely by *ergo*. Erasmus' Latin version is more accurate in this point. It replaced the Vulgate's *ergo* by *autem*.

This small difference between the Greek text and the Vulgate is of no help to us in our effort to determine the source of WP and ST. It so happens that Luther saw fit to omit this little word altogether, in both the WP and ST versions. Matt. 2:1 therefore does not allow us to determine the source followed by Luther. The only word which might give us ever so slight a clue does not occur in the Lutheran renderings!

NATURE OF TRANSLATION

It is obvious that there are important differences between WP and ST. Let us first consider the translation found in WP.

With the exception of the omission of δὲ/*ergo*, WP contains a correct literal translation. The literalness is carried so far that the Greek and Latin word order is reproduced in the phrase *Herodis des kunigis*. The translation of ἰδοὺ/*ecce* by *nempt war* is somewhat awkward. It also occurs, incidentally, in Luther's early German tracts. The phrase *Bethlehem Jude* is the closest translation imaginable.

Luther's translation of Matt. 2:1 is correct but definitely undistinguished. It is indifferent at best. Luther himself seems to have been aware that his translation left something to be desired so far as using the best German was concerned. He was particularly eager to put across the meaning of the words *magi ab oriente venerunt*. Thus he tried again in the body of the sermon proper and produced yet another version in "real German." He prefaced this by saying: "Wenn wyr nu ... eygentlich vordeutschen wolten, musten wyr alszo sagen: Es sind kommen die naturlichen meyster vom auffgang, oder: die naturkündigen ausz reych Arabien."[2] This is how he would put it were he to use living German. But the conservative translator of November 1521 did not incorporate this bold rendering in the translation he prefixed to the sermon; he mentioned it merely in passing when he elaborated on the meaning of *magi* and *ab oriente*.

It seems rather clear that Luther, before undertaking the major task

[2] WA 10¹, 1. *Hälfte*, 563.

of the formal rendering of the New Testament as a whole, had no theory of translation. Translating and what he calls "eygentlich vordeutschen" were still two different procedures. He had not yet decided to merge the two, so far as possible, in a higher synthesis such as became his goal, never wholly realized of course, from December of the year 1521 on.

The version of this verse in the official *Septembertestament,* probably made less than a month later, is a noteworthy improvement on its shape in the Christmas Postil. Let us consider specific points. Instead of the former awkward phrase *zu Bethlehem Jude* we now find *zu Bethlehem, yhm Judischen land.* This is clear, intelligible German, leaving no doubt as to the meaning of the passage: Bethlehem is the town and Judea the country. How did Luther arrive at this new rendering?

Without wishing to detract from his ability as a master of the German language, I suggest it was perhaps Erasmus who helped him considerably in this matter. It will be remembered that Erasmus added to the Greek text a new Latin translation of his own, differing markedly from the Vulgate, and that he appended extensive annotations at the end of the Greek and Latin texts.

In view of the Vulgate's unsatisfactory performance Erasmus furnished this clarifying note: *Judaea regionis nomen est . . . Solemus . . . regionis nomen addere.* So far as his actual translation of this phrase is concerned, Erasmus provided a literal rendering in the first edition of 1516: *in Bethleem Judaeae.* But in the second edition of 1519 he struck out on his own and explained the meaning of the Greek phrase in an expanded translation: *in Bethleem vico Judaeae,* that is, in Bethlehem, a town or hamlet of Judea.

It seems to me that Luther's new explanatory phrase, *yhm Judischen land,* employed by him to render the brief Greek genitive τῆς 'Ιουδαίας, may stem more or less directly from Erasmus' translation and annotation of 1519. Luther of course did not translate Erasmus verbatim, but he probably formulated his own excellent rendering after consulting what the great humanist and Greek scholar had to say. As a matter of fact, Luther was less adventurous than Erasmus. He did not go so far as to take over Erasmus' delightful *vico.* He did not write, as well he might have done if he had followed Erasmus all the way, *in Bethlehem, einem Flecken im jüdischen Land* or something similar to that. Luther remained independent. He was willing to take suggestions, even eager to take them, but he went ahead on his own. He was great enough for that.

Whatever the origin of Luther's *yhm Judischen land* in ST, whether wholly original or, as I believe, at least in part suggested by Erasmus, it is a phrase which the man in the street—Luther's *gemein man auff dem marckt*—had no trouble at all in understanding. It is safe to assume that the same reader experienced considerable difficulty in grasping the import of the Christmas Postil's *zu Bethlehem Jude*. In the *Septembertestament* Luther had clearly eliminated the trouble spot. The reader's path, obstructed in WP, was now—to use one of Luther's own inimitable expressions—*ein gehoffelt bret*.

The next phrase differing from the Christmas Postil is *tzur tzeyt*. This takes the place of the earlier *ynn den tagen*, which corresponded exactly to the Vulgate's *in diebus* and the Greek original's ἐν ἡμέραις. Luther, in his official version, no longer looked with favor upon the literal *ynn den tagen*, with which he had been satisfied only a month or so before in WP. He must have thought the free rendering *tzur tzeyt* was more idiomatic German. Impartial readers are likely to agree with him. A last trace of "foreignness" still attaching to *tagen* in this sense is absent from *tzeyt*, which is completely and thoroughly German.

Yet one should perhaps be careful in calling the replacement of *ynn den tagen* by *tzur tzeyt* exclusively a move toward more idiomatic German. Erasmus, probably as great a master of Latin style as Luther was of German, appears to have felt similarly about the proper Latin idiom. He changed his own early (1516) version of *in diebus* to *temporibus* in the second edition of 1519. It is not altogether improbable that Luther owes his *tzeyt* to Erasmus' *temporibus*, even though he used the singular instead of Erasmus' plural. This substitution is just another indication of the sureness with which Luther moved in his native tongue.

Closely connected with this phrase, actually a part of it, is the genitive that follows it, the whole passage reading in ST: *tzur tzeyt des konigs Herodis*. The Christmas Postil had read: *Ynn den tagen Herodis des kunigis*. The word order of *Herodis des kunigis* was exactly like that of the Latin *Herodis regis* and of the Greek Ἡρώδου τοῦ βασιλέως. When Luther reached this phrase in ST, he found it wanting. A German would put the name after the title. Luther's *tzur tzeyt des konigs Herodis* reads as though it were written in German to begin with. He translated as if he were writing an original piece of German, and this is how he wanted his rendering judged by fair-minded critics. Of course no violence was to be done to the text in the process of such germanizing. All that took place in this instance was a successful transplanting of a Greek phrase to a German milieu. A German reader would feel thoroughly at home with Luther's rendering. The Bible was becoming, in the hands of the master translator, a German book.

We can more fully realize the significance of Luther's method and achievement by considering the treatment of the same phrase in the King James Bible. This justly famous translation, in general much more literal than Luther's Bible, was apparently perfectly content to accept "in the days of Herod the king," a phrase employed by Luther as we have seen in the informal Christmas Postil but rejected soon after when he was shaping the idiomatic German of his unique official Bible.

The next word in ST to catch our eye (and ear, for one should always read Luther aloud) is *sihe*. This single word takes the place of the rather heavy *nempt war* of WP. It is a manifest improvement. *Sihe*, which in 1521 and earlier was used interchangeably with *nempt war* in the many informal, occasional translations of scriptural verses occurring throughout Luther's German writings, henceforth replaces the less felicitous longer phrase.

Little need be said about ST's *weysen* in lieu of WP's *weyssager* except that the former would seem to be the more dignified word. Could it be that *weyssager* was also rejected because of its implied suggestion of magic, taken by Luther in its non-Renaissance meaning of black magic? The preferred word *weysen* would do away with any such possible misunderstanding on the part of the readers envisaged by Luther. Interestingly enough Luther, in the formal translation which the *Septembertestament* is, did not go as far as he had done in the body of the sermon of the Christmas Postil, where he had translated *magi* by *die naturlichen meyster* and, still more daringly, by *die naturkündigen*. It is clear that Luther differentiated between translating, even idiomatic translating, on the one hand and *eygentlich vordeutschen*[3] on the other. That is to say, ST is not total *Verdeutschung* but still *Übersetzung*. It is true that the word *Naturkundiger* does occur in ST, but only in a marginal note, not in the text itself.

MATT. 2 : 2 Vulgate, 1509: *Ubi est qui natus est rex iudeorum: Vidimus enim stellam eius in oriente: et venimus adorare eum.*

Erasmus' Greek, 1519: Ποῦ ἐστιν ὁ τεχθεὶς βασιλεὺς τῶν ἰουδαίων; Εἴδομεν γὰρ αὐτοῦ τὸν ἀστέρα ἐν τῇ ἀνατολῇ, καὶ ἤλθομεν προσκυνῆσαι αὐτῷ.

Erasmus' Latin, 1519: *Ubi est ille, qui natus fuit rex Judaeorum? vidimus enim illius stellam in oriente, et accessimus, ut adoremus eum.*

[3]Loc. cit.

WP: *Wo ist der new geporne kunig der Juden? wyr haben seynen sternn gesehen ym auffgang unnd sind kommen, das wyr yhn anbeten.*

ST: *Wo ist der newgeborne konig der Juden? wyr haben seynen stern gesehen ym morgen land, vnd sind komen, yhn antzubeten.*

SOURCE

The Vulgate is a correct rendering of the Greek text. It is therefore impossible, on the basis of the evidence presented by the second verse, to indicate the source of Luther's rendering.

The changes made by Erasmus in his new Latin translation are not corrections of any mistakes of the Vulgate but are purely of a stylistic nature: Erasmus' version is more elegant, more Ciceronian than Jerome's.

NATURE OF TRANSLATION

WP

This is a comparatively easy verse, couched in fairly simple and straightforward language. It would not seem to make special demands upon the skill of the translator. On the face of it, it appears so unproblematical that one would not expect it to yield any evidence of extraordinary ability on the part of Luther or anybody else. And yet this verse contains the material for one of the most striking bits of the Lutheran art of translation.

This phrase is *der new geporne kunig der Juden*. It is the insertion of the little word *new* which turns it into the memorable passage it is. There is nothing in either the Greek original or the Vulgate (or Erasmus' translation for that matter) to explain it philologically. The Greek and Latin have nothing but the unadorned τεχθείς and *natus*. It was a stroke of genius to insert *new* before *geporne*. This one little word adds color, realism, urgency to the narrative. The story receives a quality of immediacy, a sense of the dramatic. The stress is on the event that has just transpired. We are still looking in on the stable of Bethlehem. English and American readers will not find this word in the Authorized Version, which is far too conservative and literal to allow such an exciting insertion. Yet the phrase is familiar to all of us from Charles Wesley's Christmas carol "Hark! the herald angels sing Glory to the newborn King," a phrase just as pleasing and idiomatic in English as it is to German ears. The difference between the staid King James Bible and the more dynamic German Bible is, in part, Luther's readiness to avail himself of all the resources of the German language so as to provide a rendering as fresh and immediate as if it flowed directly from the pen of a German author. Luther was bold and adventurous enough to insert a word when the spirit of a passage called for it as it were, as long as he did not transgress against essential meaning. Far from transgressing, Luther at times by his very boldness brought out meaning, released implied meaning. It was as if he, more than any other Biblical translator, read the mind and intention of the original writer and—one should perhaps not shrink from this formulation—sometimes succeeded in transcending him and his product in quality. Luther could do this partly because he lived in the work he translated, partly because he was one of the greatest masters of language of any age. Only because he identified himself with what he was translating could he achieve such unheard-of feats. In other words, Martin Luther, while translating, occasionally rose to the stature of a fellow-author along with, even beyond the capacities of, the original author. The phrase just discussed testifies to the genius of this incomparable "translator."

Aside from this one superb phrase, there is nothing of importance in the second verse. The word *auffgang* occurs again as it did in the first verse.

ST

It stands to reason that even Martin Luther himself could not really surpass his achievement in WP. What he had done there, in a moment of literary inspiration, just could not be improved on. He still remembered it when he rendered the same verse in ST. It was so perfect that he must have decided to use it again. The critical reader of his New Testament cannot but approve and admire. Short though the phrase is, it is probably one of the immortal passages of the Lutheran Bible.

Two changes from WP should perhaps be noted. The dependent clause *das wyr yhn anbeten* is replaced in ST by the terse infinitive *yhn antzubeten*. The latter is rhythmically superior. It should be pointed out in passing that Luther had anticipated the ST version in the sermon itself.[4] The second change is from *auffgang* to the superb and marvelously rich and resonant *morgenland*.

MATT. 2 : 3 Vulgate, 1509: *Audiens autem herodes rex/turbatus est et omnis hierosolyma cum illo.*

Erasmus' Greek, 1519: ἀκούσας δὲ Ἡρῴδης ὁ βασιλεὺς ἐταράχθη, καὶ πᾶσα ἱεροσόλυμα μετ' αὐτοῦ.

[4]WA 10¹, 1. Hälfte, 565.

Erasmus' Latin, 1519: *Auditis autem his Herodes rex, turbatus est, et tota Hierosolymorum urbs cum illo.*

Erasmus' first edition of 1516 has the following variant: Instead of the longer interpretive phrase of 1519 *tota Hierosolymorum urbs*, he had originally only the literal *tota Hierosolyma.*

WP: *Da das der konig Herodes hörett, ist er erschrocken vnnd mit yhm das gantz Hierusalem.*

ST: *Do das der konig Herodes horte, erschrack er vnnd mit yhm das gantz Hierusalem.*

SOURCE

The only difference between the Greek original and the Vulgate is the latter's use of the present participle *audiens* for the Greek past participle ἀκούσας. Erasmus, in his new Latin version, expressed the Greek tense by employing an ablative absolute, *auditis autem his*. In his *Adnotationes* he took pains to point out that ἀκούσας was the past participle, to be translated literally by *cum audisset*. However, for the actual translation he preferred the ablative absolute as we have seen.

Luther's procedure in this matter is not altogether clear. While there is not the shadow of a doubt that *horte* in ST is the past tense, it is not possible to make the same statement about *hörett* in WP. The latter may be past, but one cannot be sure. ST is definitely based on the Greek. The matter cannot be determined for WP with certainty.

NATURE OF TRANSLATION

WP

It is interesting to note that Luther has abandoned the Latin word order of *Herodes rex*, still observed by him in the first verse, in favor of the more natural German word order, *der konig Herodes.*

ST

It goes without saying that ST retains the German word order of the phrase just discussed. The only change from WP, besides *horte* for *hörett* as indicated above, is the substitution of the simple past *erschrack* for WP's perfect tense *ist . . . erschrocken*. This alteration is in line with ST's preference for the past in straight narrative.

MATT. 2 : 4 Vulgate, 1509: *Et congregans omnes principes sacerdotum et scribas populi: sciscitabatur ab eis ubi Christus nasceretur.*

Erasmus' Greek, 1519: καὶ συναγαγὼν πάντας τοὺς ἀρχιερεῖς καὶ γραμματεῖς τοῦ λαοῦ, ἐπυνθάνετο παρ' αὐτῶν, ποῦ ὁ χριστὸς γεννᾶται.

Erasmus' Latin, 1519: *convocatis omnibus pontificibus, et scribis populi, percontatus est eos, ubi Christus nasceretur.*

WP: *Und hatt vorsamlet alle Fursten der priester und schreyber des volcks, hatt von yhn erforschett, wo Christus sollt gepornn werden?*

ST: *vnd liess versamlen alle hohe Priester vnd schrifft gelertenn vntter dem volck, vnd erforschete von yhn, wo Christus solt geporn werden?*

SOURCE

There is one interesting difference between the Greek and Vulgate texts. The Vulgate uses two nouns, *principes sacerdotum*, for the Greek compound word ἀρχιερεῖς. Erasmus was very much aware of this. He explained the Greek noun by *primarii sacerdotes* and *pontifices* in the *Adnotationes*. In the translation itself he chose the single word *pontificibus*.

This phrase, the first real difference between the Greek and Vulgate in our passage, throws light on the sources followed by Luther in the WP and ST renderings. In WP he translated *Fursten der priester*. This rendering is the first major evidence that the WP version was made on the basis of the Vulgate, which Luther translated very literally: *principes* by *Fursten* and *sacerdotum* by *der priester*. What we have here is a straightforward translation of the Vulgate's free rendering of the Greek original.

In ST Luther abandoned WP's genitival construction so manifestly inspired by the Vulgate. Instead of *Fursten der priester* we now find *hohe Priester*. This would seem to rest on the Greek. Since it is, however, not altogether literal, we cannot make this claim with absolute certainty. But we can say that it goes beyond the Vulgate; it is probably under some debt to Erasmus' new Latin *primarii sacerdotes*. We can safely say that *hohe Priester* is more easily accounted for on the basis of the Greek and Erasmus' Latin translation and *Adnotationes* than on the basis of the Vulgate.

NATURE OF TRANSLATION
WP

Aside from the use of the perfect tense, this translation seems rather awkward with its repetition of *hatt* in *hatt vorsamlet* and *hatt von yhn erforschett*. *Fursten der priester*, in spite of its literalness, is not particularly inferior, though one could hardly claim it to be especially felicitous. The next word, *schreyber*, is just a literal translation of the Vulgate's *scribas*. It grates on our ears in its unrelieved literalism.

The WP version of this verse is a correct, very literal, undistinguished translation of the Vulgate. It gets the basic meaning across to the reader, but it shows no flash of genius. Unrhythmical and monotonous, it cannot be said to represent a special effort on the part of the translator.

ST

The *Septembertestament* version of this fourth verse is, by contrast, a distinguished achievement. It should be stressed that this is not due so much to the almost certain use of the Greek original as to the superb handling of the vernacular as such. Thus the definite superiority of this verse in ST is not primarily a matter of scholarship but a matter of the translator's artistic temperament leading to literary excellence.

The very beginning of the verse shows that we move in a different realm. WP's drab *Und hatt vorsamlet* is replaced by the much better *vnd liess versamlen*. It is not so much the substitution of the past tense for the perfect as it is the insertion of *liess* which converts the phrase into highly idiomatic German.

The words *hohe Priester* are important not only because they are partial evidence that Luther went beyond the Vulgate when he worked on the *Septembertestament*. As stated before, they are not a literal but a free translation. This particular rendering is at least as much a product of Luther's literary genius as of his concern for the meaning of the original. The Greek was clearly difficult to render. Luther emerged with a striking German phrase, definitely superior to WP's *Fursten der priester*. His readers, familiar with such phrases as *hoher Rat* and *hoher Herr*, must have felt immediately at home with *hohe Priester*.

Schrifft gelertenn in place of *schreyber* is another conspicuous improvement. It is in all likelihood not due to Luther's consulting the Greek text. The Greek word by itself could easily be translated as *schreyber*. Though he was not the first to use the expression *schrifft gelertenn* instead, it has become one of the several phrases characteristic of the Lutheran Bible. It is much more specific and expressive of the original meaning of the Biblical term than the colorless *schreyber*.

Luther's free rendering extends to the following genitive, τοῦ λαοῦ, *populi*. In WP he had translated it literally, *des volcks*. Now in ST he replaced it by a prepositional phrase, *vnter dem volck*. This new freedom is a favorite literary device of Luther's. Our passage is one of the earliest occurrences of this "Lutheranism" in the Bible. This added touch enhances the impression of the reader that he is dealing with an original German text.

Finally, Luther avoids, in ST, the unsatisfactory repetition of *hatt vorsamlet . . . hatt von yhn erforschett* found in WP. We now read a smoother phrase: *liess versamlen . . . vnd erforschete von yhn.* This change of the sentence structure in the direction of greater naturalness and easier flow is decidedly for the better.

Taking v. 4 as a whole, we may safely say that the Vulgate-based, unrhythmical translation of WP has been replaced by the rhythmic superiority of ST, which goes beyond the Vulgate for its source and reads as though it had been penned by a master of the German tongue. It was indeed the creation of a master translator.

MATT. 2:5 Vulgate, 1509: *At illi dixerunt ei: in bethleem iude. Sic enim scriptum est per prophetam:*

Erasmus' Greek, 1519: οἱ δὲ εἶπον αὐτῷ. ἐν βηθλεὲμ τῆς Ἰουδαίας. οὕτως γὰρ γέγραπται διὰ τοῦ προφήτου.

Erasmus' Latin, 1519: *At illi dixerunt ei, In Bethleem Judaeae. Sic enim scriptum est per prophetam:*

WP: *Vnnd sie haben gesagt: tzu Bethlehem Jude. Denn alsso ist geschrieben durch den propheten:*

ST: *vnnd sie sagten yhm, zu Bethlehem yhm Judischen land. Denn also ist geschrieben durch den propheten.*

SOURCE

In this comparatively simple verse there is no difference between the Greek original and the Vulgate. The mere fact that Erasmus left the Vulgate rendering practically intact indicates that he was satisfied with what he found there. All he did was to change *iude* into *Judaeae* as he had already done in the first verse.

NATURE OF TRANSLATION

It goes without saying that this straightforward verse presents no major problems and offers no challenge to the translator. The only word that is not too easy to render intelligibly is the name of the country of Judea. It will be recalled that Luther handled it in an undistinguished way in WP in the first verse, where it also occurs. He was satisfied with reproducing the Vulgate's *iude*. He did no better in v. 5. In ST he greatly clarified v. 1 with the excellent phrase *yhm Judischen land,* which he repeated in the fifth verse.

Beyond this crucial change in ST there is only the replacement of the perfect, *sie haben gesagt,* by the past, *sie sagten.* It should perhaps be pointed out in conclusion that in ST Luther supplies, in this very phrase, the pronoun *yhm,* which he had omitted in WP.

MATT. 2 : 6 Vulgate, 1509: *Et tu bethleem terra iuda: nequaquam minima es in principibus iuda. Ex te enim exiet dux qui regat populum meum israel.*

Erasmus' Greek, 1519: καὶ σὺ βηθλεέμ, γῆ Ἰούδα, οὐδεμῶς ἐλαχίστη εἶ ἐν τοῖς ἡγεμόσιν Ἰούδα, ἐκ σοῦ γὰρ μοὶ ἐξελεύσεται ἡγούμενος, ὅστις ποιμανεῖ τὸν λαόν μου τὸν Ἰσραήλ.

Erasmus' Latin, 1519: *Et tu Bethleem terra Juda, nequaquam minima es inter principes Juda. Ex te enim mihi proditurus est dux, qui gubernaturus est populum meum Israel.*

Erasmus' first edition of 1516 has the following variants: *egressurus* for *proditurus* and *reget* for *gubernaturus est.*

WP: *Und du Bethlehem ym land Juda, du bist mit nichten die geringst unter den Fursten Juda. Denn auss dyr soll kommen der Furst, der da regir meyn volck Israel.*

ST: *Und du Bethlehem ym Judischen land bist mit nichte die kleynist vnter den fursten Juda, denn ausz dyr soll myr komen, der hertzog der vber meyn volck von Israel eyn herr sey.*

SOURCE

There is one very interesting difference between the Greek text and the Vulgate: the Greek verb ποιμανεῖ, meaning literally "to feed or to pasture" is rendered by *regat* in the Vulgate. This translation of the Greek verb is nothing new in the technique of the Vulgate. It also occurs, for instance, in one of the most famous verses of the Old Testament Psalm 23 : 1: in the phrase *dominus regit me*, the word *regit* is used to translate the Septuagint's ποιμαίνει, the same word employed in Matt. 2 : 6. The Vulgate prefers the more general *regere* to the more specific, agricultural Hebrew and Greek terms.

One is not surprised at Luther's translation of *regir* in WP. He merely runs true to form here if my general contention is correct that the WP version of Matt. 2 : 1–12 is based on the Vulgate. What is at first surprising, however, is that ST does not produce a change. All it does is to substitute *eyn herr sey* for WP's *regir*. This is little more than the replacement of a "foreign" word by a "German" phrase, apart of course from the superior rhythm and sonorousness of the ST phrase. In other words, Luther does not shift—as one might perhaps have expected— from *regieren* to something like *weiden* or *ein Hirt sein* or a similar phrase.

This passage merits closer examination. A good deal hinges on it for the whole question of the role of the Greek original in ST. On the face of it, Luther seems to disappoint us by failing to present us with a word that would make it crystal-clear that he consulted the Greek original, which in this case is sufficiently different from the Vulgate to allow the critical reader to decide which he used.

One of the factors involved is of course the extent of his knowledge of Greek based on the aids available to him. Chief among these was naturally Erasmus' new edition of the Greek text with the concomitant Latin translation and the rich annotations. Erasmus chose to render ποιμανεῖ by *reget* in the first edition and by *gubernaturus est* in the second. This surely did not of itself suggest the idea of feeding a flock. If anything, it rather reinforced the Vulgate's concept of *regere*. Erasmus further underscored this by using the word *dominatus* in the *Adnotationes*. It is not unlikely that this may even have suggested *eyn herr sey* to Luther. The second aid at his disposal was Aleander's *Lexicon graecolatinum* of 1512. In this important dictionary the verb ποιμαίνω is translated by *rego* and *pasco*, with *rego* listed first. Johannes Lang, Luther's friend who had just translated the Gospel According to St. Matthew from the original Greek, actually chose the second entry in Aleander's dictionary and wrote *weyden*, whereas Luther preferred the first entry (if indeed he had access to Aleander on the Wartburg) and sided with Erasmus and the Vulgate against Lang.

There are at least three reasons why Luther may have given the nod to *rego* over *pasco*. First, the general authority of Erasmus apparently outweighed that of Lang. Secondly, Luther may not even have consulted Lang's rendering when he made his own translation. This is not farfetched at all if one remembers the almost incredible speed with which Luther worked on the Wartburg. Thirdly, Luther may have rejected Lang and Aleander's second entry for literary reasons. Although this aspect of the matter belongs properly to the next heading, it should be considered here also in connection with our effort to establish the sources. It is not inconceivable that Luther, although aware of the literal meaning of ποιμανεῖ, may have decided in favor of its larger meaning of supervising, directing, leading, governing. In this particular passage the subject matter is not that of the Twenty-third Psalm, where a shepherd feeds his flock in green pastures, but rather that of a prince or duke who rules his people. Luther, never a literalist, chose the more appropriate word according to the circumstances in which the term occurs.

If these arguments are valid, Luther's use of *eyn herr sey* does not necessarily point in the direction of the Vulgate. All things considered, the Greek text together with Erasmus' translation and annotation appears to be the source.

NATURE OF TRANSLATION

WP

The Christmas Postil rendering of this verse is a creditable achievement. It bursts the shackles of literalism for the sake of idiomaticalness and greater intelligibility. Two examples of this Lutheran tendency occur. First, Luther is not satisfied with merely saying *Bethlehem land Juda* but he inserts the preposition *ym: Und du Bethlehem ym land Juda*, a wording surely more easily comprehensible to the ordinary reader for whom his Bible was primarily intended. Secondly, Luther changed the preposition *in* in the phrase *in principibus* to *unter*, which is more idiomatic than *in* would be. In fairness it should be pointed out that the printed pre-Lutheran Bibles had anticipated Luther on this point.

ST

ST represents an even greater effort to produce a still better German text. Luther replaced the good German of *ym land Juda* by the rhythmically superior *ym Judischen land*. The word *furst* made way for *hertzog* in ST. This may be due to Luther's desire to avoid repeating the same word in the same verse or to his eagerness to use the expression *hertzog*, so familiar to German ears. It is a fact that Luther endeavored to transplant the New Testament as much as possible to a German milieu. A further change of importance is from *regir* in WP to *eyn herr sey*, a passage already discussed from the point of view of establishing the source for this striking phrase. Stylistically speaking, this is first of all an example of Luther's tendency in ST to replace foreign words by German words. But there is more than that involved in this case, it would seem. Luther had an ear for the ringing, sonorous phrase. On this score alone *eyn herr sey* would easily win out over the somewhat thin *regir*. In addition, Luther may have been anything but indifferent to the alliterative factor in *hertzog* and *herr*. After all, he had ears and eyes for such stylistic niceties.

Finally, there is the special case of the insertion of *myr* in the passage *denn ausz dyr soll myr komen*. At first glance one might think that this was introduced for greater effectiveness, a kind of ethical dative. This would appear to be another indication of Luther's concern that the reader should gain the impression that he was reading a piece of original German rather than a mere translation. This could be the explanation if one takes a modern edition of the Greek text. If one looks, however, at Erasmus' edition of the Greek New Testament, one will find that here the word μοι occurs, reproduced faithfully in Erasmus' new Latin rendering by *mihi*. Thus it might very well be that the use of the original text as accessible to him explains the word *myr*. I wonder whether its introduction could not be due to a combination of circumstances, textual as well as stylistic. This little word bears testimony to the care with which the scholar Luther worked and/or to the sense of style of the writer of highly idiomatic German.

MATT. 2 : 7 Vulgate, 1509: *Tunc herodes clam vocatis magis: diligenter didicit ab eis tempus stellae quae apparuit eis:*

Erasmus' Greek, 1519: Τότε Ἡρώδης λάθρα καλέσας τοὺς μάγους, ἠκρίβωσε παρ' αὐτῶν τὸν χρόνον τοῦ φαινομένου ἀστέρος,

Erasmus' Latin, 1519: *Tunc Herodes clam accersitis magis, accurate perquisivit ab illis, quo tempore stella apparuisset.*

WP: *Da hatt Herodes heymlich tzu sich gefoddert die Weyssager und vleyssig von yhn erlernett die tzeyt des sternes, der yhn erschynen war.*

ST: *Da berieff Herodes die weysen heymlich, vnd erlernet mit vleysz von yhnen, wenn der stern erschynen were,*

SOURCE

There are two minor divergences between the Greek text and the Vulgate. The first is the Vulgate's addition of the last word, *eis*. This is understandable enough. It shows that the Vulgate was by no means a slavishly literal translation. Wherever and whenever its makers thought that the meaning of the original could be brought out more adequately by taking some apparent liberty with the Greek text, they did not hesitate to do so. The second divergence from the Greek is found in the Vulgate's two-word rendering, *diligenter didicit*, of a single-word Greek verb, ἠκρίβωσε. This was an excellent way of trying to express the full meaning of the Greek verb. There is of course no criticism implied in referring to it as a "divergence" from the original. It is recorded here simply as an aid in determining the source Luther followed.

It would appear that the WP version is based on the Vulgate. Luther faithfully reproduced the word *eis* added by the Vulgate to the Greek text, and *der yhn erschynen war* is a literal translation of *quae apparuit eis*. The other phrase under review here, *hatt . . . vleyssig von yhn erlernett*, would seem to stem directly from the Vulgate's *diligenter didicit*.

In the ST version Luther, in full accord with the Greek original and Erasmus' Latin translation, dispenses with the word *yhn* in the final phrase, limiting himself to *erschynen*. It is likely that Luther is indebted to Erasmus' Latin rendering for the structure of his relative clause, which is quite different from that of the Vulgate. There is an agreement between Luther and Erasmus, and decidedly not between Luther and the Vulgate. The other phrase is more elusive. Luther retains in ST the WP verb *erlernet* but substitutes the prepositional phrase *mit vleysz* for WP's adverb *vleyssig*, which had corresponded exactly to the Vulgate's *diligenter*. Luther was obviously aware of the extreme difficulty of rendering the simple verb of the Greek original. He was also, it would seem, very much impressed with the way the Vulgate had solved it. It is rather clear that he was basically satisfied with it, at any rate he himself had no radically new or better solution to offer. The plain fact is that he retained the Vulgate's rendering in substance. The difference between WP's *vleyssig* and ST's *mit vleysz* is minor, perhaps or even probably the product of the moment. *Mit vleysz* is fundamentally a Vulgate derivative. Luther thereby acknowledged, at least implicitly, the literary excellence of the Vulgate. I would still urge, however, that whereas the WP translation of this passage was *directly* from the Vulgate the ST version was only indirectly so. In WP the Greek did not figure at all; in ST the procedure was probably as follows: Greek–Erasmus' Latin–Vulgate–German. Apparently Luther did not find Erasmus' Latin rendering, *accurate perquisivit*, very helpful. He ignored it. Aleander, incidentally, was not very helpful either. He translated the Greek verb ἀκριβόω by *diligenter cognosco*.

NATURE OF TRANSLATION
WP

Although WP adds a short phrase of its own, one not found in the Vulgate, *tzu sich*, it is nevertheless a literal translation, hewing close to the line. This is evident from the second half of the verse. Luther here merely reproduced the Vulgate's structural handling of the Greek genitival phrase τοῦ φαινομένου ἀστέρος. His *die tzeytt des sternes, der yhn erschynen war* is nothing but an exact copy of *tempus stellae quae apparuit eis*. This is hardly the way in which an original German writer would have expressed himself. Luther, in the translation of this passage, had not yet attained the freedom of the German idiom so characteristic of his method only a little later.

ST

Luther reached his full stature in the rendering of this phrase in ST. Few passages show with greater clarity the immense progress toward literary mastery made by Luther in the art of translation once he had made up his mind to undertake the rendering of the Bible as a whole. The casual reader or hearer of our phrase in ST probably pays little attention to this (and many another) passage simply because it poses no problem at all and reads so smoothly and so well. But that is just the point. The new phrase in ST is such superbly idiomatic German that it approximates original German. The achievement of this goal was one of the main criteria Luther set for himself to judge his success as a translator. He had succeeded in his own eyes when his readers did not stumble or shake their heads but read on as if they were reading a master of German prose, which they indeed were.

Luther's success is not primarily due to his use of the Greek original. The fact that the Greek (or Erasmus' Latin for that matter) does not have the equivalent of the Vulgate's inserted *eis* and that Luther consequently drops it from his new rendering has nothing to do with the literary distinction of Luther's German phrase. The German word *yhn* could easily have been retained for all the difference it would have made, that is, none whatsoever. The secret of Luther's success lies elsewhere.

Let us consider first the Greek original: τὸν χρόνον τοῦ φαινομένου ἀστέρος, which means literally "the time of the appeared star." The Vulgate expanded the terse Greek construction. It resolved the participle into a relative clause, adding the pronoun *eis* in the process. Luther followed the Vulgate's handling of this difficult phrase in the Christmas Postil. But this no longer satisfied him when he prepared the ST version. *Die tzeytt des sternes* was simply not the way in which the man in the street and the woman in the house spoke. How did they speak? He probably paused momentarily before setting down his new rendering, so outstanding in its naturalness, *wenn der stern erschynen were*. Instead of the literal *die tzeytt des sternes* we now have the interrogative conjunction *wenn* introducing an indirect question. Although Luther's new rendering is most probably indebted to Erasmus' excellent *quo tempore stella apparuisset*, the further simplification of *quo tempore* to *wenn* is Luther's very own. The final result of Luther's efforts in ST is somehow the ultimate in directness and simplicity, doing away with the strained artificiality of the WP phrase.

However, one should realize that the entire verse does not move on the same high level. The phrase *erlernet mit vleysz*, changed but little and perhaps not even for the better from WP's *vleyssig . . . erlernett*, is far from perfect. It remains a more or less literal translation, heavily influenced by the Vulgate and perhaps Erasmus' *Adnotationes* contain-

Translation in Transition

ing the noun *cura*, in the ablative—*exactaque cura . . . examinate*, not *interrogate*. This may have suggested *mit vleysz* to Luther. Whatever the origin of this phrase in ST, it is at best adequate without attaining the complete naturalness of other parts of the verse.

MATT. 2 : 8 Vulgate, 1509: *et mittens illos in bethleem/dixit: Ite et interrogate diligenter de puero: et cum inveneritis/renunciate mihi: ut et ego veniens adorem eum.*

Erasmus' Greek, 1519: καὶ πέμψας αὐτοὺς εἰς βηθλεὲμ εἶπεν. πορευθέντες, ἀκριβῶς ἐξετάσατε περὶ τοῦ παιδίου, ἐπὰν δὲ εὕρατε, ἀπεγγείλατέ μοι, ὅπως κἀγὼ ἐλθὼν προσκυνήσω αὐτῷ.

Erasmus' Latin, 1519: *et iussis ire in Bethleem, dixit, profecti illuc, accurate inquirite de puero. Ubi vero reperitis, renunciate mihi, ut et ego veniam et adorem illum.*

WP: *und hatt in gen Bethlehem geschickt unnd gesagt: Gehet hyn unnd fragt vleyssig nach dem kind. Unnd wenn yhrss funden habt, sagt myr widder, das ich auch komme und bete yhn an.*

ST: *vnd weyszet sie gen Bethlehem, vnnd sprach, zihet hyn, vnd forsschet vleyssig nach dem kyndlin, vnnd wen yhrsz findet, sagt myr widder, dass ich auch kome vnd es anbete.*

SOURCES

There is but one minor difference between the Greek text and the Vulgate translation. The Greek uses the diminutive in the phrase περὶ τοῦ παιδίου where the Latin has only the regular *de puero*. This is not a very important point to be sure, but being the only distinction between the two versions it assumes greater significance than it would otherwise have.

In WP Luther translates the phrase *nach dem kind*. In ST this is changed to *nach dem kyndlin*. There can be little doubt that the diminutive *kyndlin* can be explained only on the basis of the Greek diminutive παιδίον. Erasmus pointed out in some detail in the *Adnotationes* the difference between the Greek and Vulgate versions: "Graece non παῖς est sed παιδίον diminutiuum, quasi dicas puellum." This philological note, coupled in all likelihood with Aleander's entry of *puerulus* under τὸ παιδίον in his dictionary, is probably the origin of Luther's *kyndlin*. It is interesting to observe that Erasmus did not see fit to use the diminutive in his actual translation. This fact allows us to draw the conclusion that Luther went beyond Erasmus' Latin rendering and consulted the Greek original, Erasmus' *Adnotationes*, and Aleander's *Lexicon*, or at least one of these three.

NATURE OF TRANSLATION
WP

The translation of this verse in the Christmas Postil is adequate, within the framework of the Vulgate of course. The only indication that it was produced in a great hurry is the curious use of the masculine pronoun *yhn* to refer to the neuter *kind*. The tense of the narrative is again the perfect.

ST

The ST version is a decided improvement over the satisfactory translation of WP. It seems that Luther made a conscious effort to elevate the style. *Schicken* is replaced by *weyszen*, *gehet hyn* becomes *zihet hyn*. The reason for the substitution of *forsschet* for *fragt* is perhaps more difficult to establish. It is not unlikely that Erasmus' *Adnotationes* contributed to Luther's preference of *forsschet*. Erasmus interprets the Greek verb to mean *exquirite, examinate* rather than *interrogate*. Aleander's *Lexicon* may also have helped Luther to get away from WP's *fragt*; ἐξετάζω is translated by *exquiro* and *scrutor*.

It goes almost without saying that the pronominal error of the Christmas Postil does not remain uncorrected in SP, and *yhn* is changed to *es*. One should also note the new treatment given the compound verb in the concluding phrase. In WP *anbeten* was still separated in the dependent clause, *das ich . . . bete yhn an*; in ST we read instead *dass ich . . . es anbete*. Finally, the tense of the narrative is changed from the perfect to the imperfect except for the bold use of the present *findet*.

MATT. 2 : 9 Vulgate, 1509: *Qui cum audissent regem/abierunt. Et ecce stella quam viderant in oriente antecedebat eos/usquedum veniens staret supra ubi erat puer.*

Erasmus' Greek, 1519: οἱ δὲ ἀκούσαντες τοῦ βασιλέως, ἐπορεύθησαν, καὶ ἰδοὺ ὁ ἀστὴρ ὃν εἶδον ἐν τῇ ἀνατολῇ προῆγεν αὐτούς, ἕως ἐλθὼν, ἔστη ἐπάνω οὗ ἦν τὸ παιδίον.

Erasmus' Latin, 1519: *At illi audito rege, profecti sunt, et ecce stella quam viderant in oriente, praecedebat illos, donec progressa, staret supra locum in quo erat puer.*

Erasmus' first edition of 1516 has the following variant: *. . . donec venisset, ac staret supra locum . . .*

WP: *Und da sie den kunig haben gehöret, sind sie hyngangen. Und nempt war: der sternn, den sie hatten gesehen ym auffgang, gieng fur yhn her, biss das er kam und stund oben ubir, da das kind war.*

ST: *Als sie nu den konig gehort hatten, zogen sie hyn, vnnd, sihe der stern, den sie ym morgen land gesehen hatten, gieng fur yhn hyn, bisz das er kam, vnd stund oben vber, da das kyndlin war.*

SOURCES

There is only one difference between the Greek original and the Vulgate, the same as in the preceding verse. The Greek has the diminutive τὸ παιδίον instead of the Vulgate's regular *puer*. In WP Luther again follows the Vulgate (*kind*) and in ST the Greek (*kyndlin*).

NATURE OF TRANSLATION
WP

The WP version is informal, produced in a hurry, it would seem. It is an *ad hoc* translation, serving a special purpose, namely, supplying a German text for the sermon to follow. The accent was on the sermon, not on the preliminary textual selection. Our verse has the characteristic feature of the preceding verses in the Christmas Postil. It repeats a number of words already discussed. We find *hyngangen* for *abierunt*, *nempt war* for *ecce*, *ym auffgang* for *in oriente*. There is a mixture of the perfect and imperfect tenses in the narrative: *haben gehöret, sind hyngangen; gieng, kam, stund, war.* As regards word order, the verb is not yet placed at the end of dependent clauses: 1. *da sie den kunig haben gehöret*, 2. *den sie hatten gesehen ym auffgang.*

ST

In ST all the phrases just enumerated were improved. The whole verse was put into more formal German. *Zogen hyn* replaced *hyngangen*, *sihe* replaced *nempt war*, and *morgen land* replaced *auffgang*. The tenses were regularized to the extent that one perfect of WP was eliminated in favor of an imperfect and, in apparent observation of *consecutio temporum*, the other in favor of a pluperfect—*sind hyngangen* became *zogen hyn* and *haben gehöret* became *gehört hatten*. Finally, the word order of dependent clauses is regularized in ST: *Und da sie den kunig haben gehöret* emerged as *Als sie nu den konig gehort hatten*, and *den sie hatten gesehen ym auffgang* as *den sie ym morgen land gesehen hatten*.

What all these changes amount to is more than a mere revision, however careful; the verse in ST is the result of a different principle of translation. The difference is not one of degree but one of kind.

MATT. 2 : 10 Vulgate, 1509: *Videntes autem stellam gavisi sunt gaudio magno valde.*

Erasmus' Greek, 1519: ἰδόντες δὲ τὸν ἀστέρα, ἐχάρησαν χαρὰν μεγάλην σφόδρα.

Erasmus' Latin, 1519: *Cum autem vidissent stellam, gavisi sunt gaudio magno valde.*

WP: *Da sie aber den sternn gesehen haben, sind sie mit sehr grosser freud erfrewett,*

ST: *Da sie den stern sahen, wurden sie hoch erfrawet,*

SOURCES

The Vulgate is a correct translation of the Greek original. There are in consequence no differences between them that could reveal Luther's source.

NATURE OF TRANSLATION

WP

In the Christmas Postil Luther offers a literal translation of the verse. The second half of the verse provided a real challenge to the translator. The question is how to translate the phrase *gavisi sunt gaudio magno valde* in such a way that it is readily understood. It can hardly be claimed that Luther solved this difficult problem in a distinguished manner. All he did was to present an almost painfully literal rendering, *sind sie mit sehr grosser freud erfrewett.* The tense of the narrative is again the perfect.

ST

This verse in ST is an extraordinary achievement on Luther's part. The vexing second half of the verse, handled in WP in little more than mediocre fashion, is treated in ST with consummate skill. The basically unidiomatic *mit . . . freud erfrewett* is replaced by the superbly idiomatic, thoroughly German *wurden sie hoch erfrawet.* In comparison with this translational triumph of Martin Luther, the second point to be mentioned here is far less significant. The perfect tense of WP yields to the imperfect in ST, *Da sie den stern sahen.*

MATT. 2 : 11 Vulgate, 1509: *Et intrantes domum/ invenerunt puerum cum Maria matre eius: et procidentes adoraverunt eum: et apertis thesauris suis/ obtulerunt ei munera: aurum/ thus et myrrham.*

Erasmus' Greek, 1519: καὶ ἐλθόντες εἰς τὴν οἰκίαν εὗρον τὸ παιδὶ ον μετὰ μαρίας τῆς μητρὸς αὐτοῦ, καὶ πεσόντες προσεκύνησαν αὐτῷ καὶ ἀνοίξαντες τοὺς θησαυροὺς αὐτῶν, προσήνεγκαν αὐτῷ δῶρα· χρυσὸν καὶ λίβανον καὶ σμύρναν.

Translation in Transition 73

Erasmus' Latin, 1519: *Et ingressi domum, repererunt puerum, cum Maria matre eius, et prostrati adoraverunt illum, et apertis thesauris suis, obtulerunt illi munera, aurum, et thus, et myrrham.*

WP: *und sind ynn das hawss gangen, habenn funden das kind mit Maria seyner mutter. Und sind nydergefallen, haben yhn anbetet und haben auffthan yhre schetz und yhm geopffert geschenck, golt, weyrauch und myrrhen.*

ST: *vnd giengen ynn das hausz, vnd funden das kyndlin mit Maria seyner mutter, vnnd fielen nyder, vnnd betten es an, vnd theten yhre schetze auff, vnnd legten yhm geschenck fur, gollt, weyrach vnnd myrrhen.*

SOURCES

The difference between the Greek text and the Vulgate is again the Vulgate's failure to express the full meaning of τὸ παιδίον. For the third time the Vulgate lets it go at *puer*. Luther, as before, uses *das kind* in WP and *das kyndlin* in ST. As pointed out earlier, this involves a shift from the Vulgate to the Greek as the sources for WP and ST respectively.

The absolute importance of using Erasmus' edition of the Greek New Testament rather than a modern one can readily be gathered from this verse. Modern editors prefer the reading of εἶδον to εὗρον. A scholar using only the Nestle or some such edition would be forced to conclude that Luther's *funden* in ST is evidence that he based his rendering on the Vulgate rather than the Greek original. This conclusion is unwarranted if one refers to the Greek text available to Luther, and it would obviously be a gross injustice to the Wittenberg master.

NATURE OF TRANSLATION

WP

The verse is rendered acceptably in the Christmas Postil. Being just straight narrative, it does not offer many opportunities for showing particular skill. There is again the little slip of referring to *das kind* by the masculine pronoun *yhn*. The tense used throughout the verse is the perfect.

ST

There are but two actual changes from the WP version. Aside from the consistent replacing of all perfects by imperfects (six in number), Luther corrects the gender of the pronoun from masculine to neuter, from *yhn* to *es*, referring to *kind/kyndlin*. He also has a new rendering for WP's *haben . . . yhm geopffert geschenck*. In ST we read *legten yhm geschenck fur*. This is a definite improvement in the direction of greater naturalness. To what extent this rewording may also be due to Luther's increasing hesitancy to overuse the term *opffern*—so easily misunderstood in his opinion—is difficult to say. Considered solely from the point of view of ready intelligibility, the ST version reads better. Just to indicate that there was still room for further improvement, I should like to point out that in the first revision of 1526 another change was made. *Legten yhm geschenck fur* now became simply *schenckten yhm*. This is perfection itself. The bold contraction, showing his unending effort to find an increasingly better German garb for the Greek text, is but one of a host of passages revealing the mastery in translation attained by Martin Luther.

MATT. 2 : 12 Vulgate, 1509: *Et responso accepto in somnis/ne redirent ad herodem: per aliam viam reversi sunt in regionem suam.*

Erasmus' Greek, 1519: καὶ χρηματισθέντες κατ' ὄναρ, μὴ ἀνακάμψαι πρὸς Ἡρώδην, δι' ἄλλης ὁδοῦ ἀνεχώρησαν εἰς τὴν χώραν αὐτῶν.

Erasmus' Latin, 1519: *oraculo admoniti, in somnis, ne reflecterent se ad Herodem, per aliam viam reversi sunt in regionem suam.*

WP: *Und ym schlaff haben sie eyn antwort empfangen, das sie nitt sollten widder tzu Herodes kommen. Und sind durch eynen andern weg wider heymtzogen ynn yhr landt.*

ST: *Unnd gott bevahl yhn ym trawm, das sie sich nitt sollten widder zu Herodes lencken, vnd zogen durch eynen andern weg wydder ynn yhr land.*

SOURCES

This is perhaps the most interesting and important verse in our entire passage of 12 verses so far as the question of the sources is concerned. There are really major differences between the Greek original and the Vulgate. There is first of all the Vulgate's rendering of the Greek χρηματισθέντες by *responso accepto*. It is quite clear that Luther's translation of this passage in the Christmas Postil was based on the Vulgate: *eyn antwort empfangen* can have no other source than the Vulgate. In ST we have an altogether different version: *gott bevahl yhn*. At first sight this seems a strange translation indeed. Whatever its origin, one thing is certain—this phrase could not have been inspired by the Vulgate. There is no bridge leading conveniently from *responso accepto* to *gott bevahl yhn*. This is clearly a rendering difficult to account for. It would seem that Luther did not arrive at this remarkable version all by himself, without the good offices of Erasmus. It is in Erasmus' *Adnotationes* that we must look for an answer to the riddle of Luther's translation. Even for Erasmus the Greek verb was difficult to explain. He wrestled with it more than once. In the *Adnotationes* he furnished the following information about the Greek word: *oracula, quae redduntur a numine aliquo*. He recommended as a better translation: *oraculo moniti*, which he actually used in his formal translation. Luther's rendering is the result of these interpretative remarks.

To be specific, Luther's word *gott*, not explicitly in the Greek text, could be held to derive from Erasmus' word *numen*. What Luther did was to render specific and to Christianize Erasmus' general and broadly religious term. Erasmus speaks of *numen aliquod,* "some deity," Luther speaks of God, the Christian God, the father of the Lord Jesus Christ. In other words, Luther took his cue from Erasmus, but then boldly struck out on his own. The second significant word in Luther's phrase, *bevahl*, could be related to Erasmus' *monere*. Again, there is no exact correspondence. What we seem to have before us is Luther's alert mind at work, struggling with a difficult Greek verb, looking for help where it could be found. Aleander's dictionary supplied him with *lucror, appello, do responsam*, probably not too useful information. Erasmus' *Adnotationes* were more explicit and detailed. While Luther was looking over what Erasmus had to say on this word, his vivid imagination probably caught fire, translating the great humanist's generally theological note into Christian concepts and emerging triumphantly with *gott bevahl*, a free, ingenious rendering bearing the mark of Luther's individuality. It is anything but an irresponsible translation. The worst—and the best—that can be said about it is that it is creative translating. This unique translator rises on occasion to the stature of a co-author.

The other interesting phrase, from the point of view of running down the source, follows hard upon the heels of the passage just discussed. In Greek it reads κατ' ὄναρ, in the Vulgate *in somnis*. The difficulty arises from the double meaning of the Latin word—it can designate either "sleep" or "dream." *Somnis* can be the ablative either of *somnus* meaning sleep or of *somnium* meaning dream. It would be wrong to charge the Vulgate with a faulty rendering of the Greek text. The ambiguity resides in the structure of Latin, which in some of the oblique cases including the ablative plural does not permit a differentiation between *somnus* and *somnium*. It is just one of those numerous confusions occurring in language as it has grown. *In somnis* can be interpreted either way. This is evident from Erasmus' retention of the word in his new Latin translation. It can mean "dream" as the Greek text clearly has it.

Real confusion arises only when someone unacquainted with the Greek original undertakes to translate the Vulgate using nothing but the Vulgate. This was the lot of the medieval translators in general. Let us look at Luther's performance again. In WP he joins the throng of his predecessors in translating the phrase by *ym schlaff*. This is Luther operating within the framework of the Vulgate. In ST the tables are turned. Fully aware of the Greek word ὄναρ, interpreted to mean *per somnium* by Erasmus in his *Adnotationes*, Luther now has *ym trawm*. Passages like this reveal Luther's transition from a medieval scholar to a Renaissance scholar taking advantage of the change of the intellectual climate which has put new tools at his disposal. Luther was one of the first to avail himself of the new learning.

Thus the 12th and last verse of our pericope contains striking evidence that the WP version is still based on the Vulgate, while ST rests solidly on the Greek original as interpreted by Erasmus. If there were such important differences between the Greek text and the Vulgate in the preceding verses as in the last, the first eleven verses might well also show more clearly Luther's use of the original rather than of the Vulgate in ST.

NATURE OF TRANSLATION
WP

As is to be expected, the final verse of our passage is no exception in the use of the perfect tense for the narrative. In general, v. 12 contains a competent, straightforward rendering of the Vulgate. It is a comparatively simple verse, easy to comprehend in Luther's early WP version.

ST

The *Septembertestament* rendering of this verse, besides the two important changes pointed out above as inspired by the Greek original, replaces all perfects by imperfects, thus bringing the final verse into line with the preceding 11 verses. As for further actual differences from the Christmas Postil translation, there is really only one. WP reads *das sie nitt sollten widder tzu Herodes kommen*. ST substitutes *das sie sich nitt sollten widder zu Herodes lencken*. A major reason for the change is doubtless Luther's endeavor to attain a higher tone, more formal and elevated language in his official version. The relative informality and what might be called naturalism of WP are abandoned or rather overcome by what appears to be a conscious striving toward a classical rather than a more or less happy-go-lucky version. It is not impossible that a contributory reason for the use of *lencken* could be found in Erasmus' word *reflecterent* occurring in both the translation and the *Adnotationes*.

All things considered, the 12th verse is probably more important for us for the clear light it throws on Luther's use of the Vulgate in WP and of the Greek original in ST than for any particularly noteworthy literary distinction of the official version. The verse as it now stands in ST is a worthy literary achievement to be sure. But, in the nature of the verse in the original Greek itself, it did not call for any extraordinary effort in this respect. It represents a greater scholarly than artistic accomplishment on Luther's part.

By way of a quick summary we may state two major conclusions: First, the WP version is based on the Vulgate, the ST version on the Greek original with the concurrent aid of Erasmus' Latin translation and *Adnotationes*. This result of our investigation is in flat opposition to Walter Köhler's[5] and Albert Freitag's[6] view that WP is based on the original Greek. Secondly, the WP version of Matt. 2 : 1-12 cannot in any responsible way be regarded as a "substitute" for the lost manuscript of ST. The two versions are separated by an unbridgeable gulf. The WP translation is an *ad hoc* translation, made for the express purpose of furnishing a more adequate rendering of the text than that found in any German translation accessible to Luther. It was not made for its own sake, as an end in itself, but merely as the necessary introductory German text for the sermon based on it. It does not aspire to literary distinction, though it certainly is, within its own frame of reference, satisfactory, workmanlike, adequate for the goal the translator had in mind. The ST version on the other hand is almost everything that the WP version is not. It is an independent translation, to be judged by itself on both scholarly and literary grounds. It is an integral part of the official Bible translation. It is a major achievement resulting from new methods and principles of translation. In WP what matters is the ensuing sermon; the translation is but a prelude. In ST what matters is the translation itself. The two versions have little to do with each other except that they were made by one and the same man, working, however, with different sources and toward different goals.

[5] WA 10¹, 2. *Hälfte*, p. LXXIII.
[6] WA, *Deutsche Bibel* 6, 603 and 616.

Chapter 4

Translating the Twenty-third Psalm

a. THE PREDECESSORS

(1) The Printed High German Bibles

ALTHOUGH the literature on the pre-Lutheran German Bibles is fairly extensive, practically all of it deals either with the Bible as a whole or with a relatively comprehensive portion of it such as the Gospels or the Psalter. Here an attempt will be made to examine what must appear to be an infinitesimal part of the Scriptures, a single psalm, the well-known and beloved twenty-third. Generally speaking, there are two reasons which prompt a self-imposed limitation of this sort. First, it is my belief that some of the current ideas on the nature and particularly on the relative merit of the various redactions of the High German Bible before Luther may have been arrived at rather too hastily and on the basis of too cursory an acquaintance with what is really an unusually long book. It is my definite impression that the study of a specific psalm, the twenty-third in our case, may make us less sure that the prevailing view of the several stages of the earlier German Bible is valid. Secondly, a somewhat detailed analysis of the evolution of Luther's version of the Twenty-third Psalm led me to investigate more closely than I had originally planned the nature of the translations of this psalm contained in the printed German Bibles which, whether or not he actually consulted them, were at least theoretically available to him.

It is not necessary to examine all 14 editions of the printed High German Bible before Luther. After dealing with the first of them, the Mentel Bible of 1466(?), we need discuss only those later redactions in which revisions of, or at any rate deviations from, the Mentel text occur, i.e., the Pflanzmann, Zainer, and Koberger Bibles; the changes made in the other editions are so few and unimportant that they will be merely listed for the sake of gaining a complete picture of the translations of the Twenty-third Psalm found in the printed High German Bibles from 1466 (?) to 1518, the date of the last High German Bible to appear before Luther's translation began to come out in 1522.

Mentel[1]

Der herr der richt mich vñ mir gebrast nit: vnd an der stat der weyde do satzt er mich. Er fūrtte mich ob dem wasser der widerbringung: er bekert mein sel. Er fūrt mich aus auf die steig der gerechtikeit: vmb seinen namen. Wañ ob ich ioch gee in mitzt dez schatē dez tods ich vörcht nit die vbeln dinge: wann du bist mit mir. Dein rūte: vnd dein stab sy selb habent mich getröst. Du hast bereyt den tisch in meiner bescheude: wider die die mich betrūbent. Du hast erveystent mein haubt mit dem öl: vñ mein kelch der macht truncken wie lauter er ist. Vnd deī erbermbd die nachuolgt mir alle die tag meins lebens. Das auch ich entwele in dem haus des herrn in die leng der tag.

This translation is, on the whole, far from unsatisfactory. With the exception of some matters in the rendition of tenses, it can fairly be held to be a reasonably acceptable, certainly an accurate, version of the Vulgate. To anticipate any possible misunderstanding, let it be said emphatically at the outset that it rests squarely on the Vulgate and not on the Hebrew original. In order to proceed as carefully as possible, we shall divide the psalm into verses as has become customary since the middle of the 16th century and take up each verse individually.

V. 1

Der herr der richt mich vn mir gebrast nit:
Dominus regit me et nihil mihi deerit.

Aside from the resumptive *der* after *herr*, rather peculiar to the Mentel Bible throughout, it is chiefly the tense of the second verb that needs discussion. Why should the translator, who was by no means devoid of a considerable knowledge of Latin (as is sufficiently evidenced by his rendering of the psalm as a whole), choose to translate an obvious future, *deerit*, by the preterit *gebrast?* There are at least two explanations, in my opinion. First, all students of the Mentel Bible have been struck by the fact that the anonymous translator, while possessing a certain acquaintance with Latin, was not a highly accomplished scholar. Thus it might be possible, even though only remotely, to charge the above grammatical mistake to his inadequate mastery of Latin. However, in view of the fact that this is the only serious error in the entire psalm under review, this explanation, although not inconceivable to be sure, does not really satisfy, I believe. There must be

---

[1] Quoted from the copy in the Pierpont Morgan Library in New York City.

another reason for this singular slip in an otherwise correctly rendered psalm. The second explanation that occurs to me and that seems much more likely is derived from two observations made by Wilhelm Walther, a pioneer in the scholarly study of the medieval translation of the Bible into German. He points out first that the copy of the Vulgate used by the translator was not free from errors that were often fatal and, secondly, that the German manuscript used by the printer may not always have been clearly legible.[2] Without wishing to rule out the latter possibility—that the printer misread as *gebrast* the translator's possible *gebrist*—I am somehow more inclined to assume that the Latin manuscript used by the translator had an erroneous *deerat* for *deerit* or that the translator may have misread *deerat* for the correct *deerit*. At any rate, it seems to me that a not improbable explanation might very well be that *deerat* was misread for or, what appears to me to be somewhat less likely, actually stood in lieu of, *deerit*.[3]

Of some interest is the translation of *regit* by *richt*, especially inasmuch as it occurs only in the first two printed High German Bibles, Pflanzmann starting the employment of *regiert*, which then recurs throughout the remaining 11 editions of the pre-Lutheran High German Bible and which is familiar to the casual student of the Twenty-third Psalm in any of the more accessible redactions of the German Bible before Luther.

V. 2

vnd an der stat der weyde do satzt er mich. Er fürtte mich ob dem wasser der widerbringung:
in loco pascuae ibi me collocavit. Super aquam refectionis educavit me.

With the exception of the introductory *vnd* added by the translator, this is a fairly literal rendering of the Vulgate text. The fact that our unknown translator had at best only an average knowledge of Latin is again shown by his inattention to subtle shades of meaning. He apparently did not distinguish between *educare* and *educere*, translating them indiscriminately by *furen*. Aside from this point, our verse needs no comment beyond our calling attention again to the important question of the tenses; one should note that the two Latin perfects, *collocavit* and *educavit*, are rendered by German preterits, *satzt* and *fürtte*.

[2] Wilhelm Walther, *Die deutsche Bibelübersetzung des Mittelalters* (Braunschweig, 1889-92), p. 84.
[3] Eduard Brodführer, *Untersuchungen zur vorlutherischen Bibelübersetzung* (Halle, 1922), p. 89.

V. 3

er bekert mein sel. Er fūrt mich aus auf die steig der gerechtikeit: vmb seinen namen.
animam meam convertit. Deduxit me super semitas iustitiae propter nomen suum.

Apart from the tense used in this verse of the Mentel Bible, the translation is literal enough and correct. It is fairly easy to account for the present *bekert* (if it *is* a present); the Latin *convertit* may, by itself, be taken for a present. It is considerably more difficult to explain the rendering of the perfect *deduxit* by the present *fūrt*. One could hold that the translator, having begun with a present in the first part of the verse, blithely went on with the same tense in the second part. It seems more reasonable, however, to assume that the manuscript which he used may have contained *deducit* for *deduxit*. Whatever the cause, the fact remains that Mentel has the present tense in the two verbs that are quite certainly, even the former, in the perfect.

V. 4

Wañ ob ich ioch gee in mitzt dez schatē dez tods ich vörcht nit die vbeln dinge: wann du bist mit mir. Dein rūte: vnd dein stab sy selb habent mich getröst.
Nam et si ambulavero in medio umbrae mortis, non timebo mala, quoniam tu mecum es. Virga tua et baculus tuus ipsa me consolata sunt.

Again, little need be said about this literal translation beyond calling attention to the tenses—for the two futures *ambulavero* (future perfect!) and *timebo* Mentel used the presents *gee* and *vörcht*. It should also be noted that it is in this fourth verse that, for the first time in our psalm, a Latin perfect is rendered by a German perfect: *consolata sunt* becomes *habent . . . getröst*.

V. 5

Du hast bereyt den tisch in meiner bescheude: wider die die mich betrübent. Du hast erveystent mein haubt mit dem öl: vñ mein kelch der macht truncken wie lauter er ist.
Parasti in conspectu meo mensam adversus eos, qui tribulant me. Impinguasti in oleo caput meum, et calix meus inebrians quam praeclarus est.

It is again the tenses that should be noted in this literal translation of the fifth verse: As in the preceding verse, Latin perfects are rendered by German perfects, *parasti* by *du hast bereyt* and *impinguasti* by *du hast erveystent*. Although the present participle *inebrians* is rendered rather skillfully by the finite verb *macht truncken*, this unexpected display of freedom from Latin usage is somehow spoiled by the disturbing obscurity of the phrase as a whole, for which lack of intelligibility and perspicacity the Vulgate bears no small responsibility. Finally, we should not overlook the resumptive *der* after *mein kelch*, a construction characteristic of the pre-Lutheran German Bibles down to the Koberger redaction.

V. 6

Vnd dei erbermbd die nachuolgt mir alle die tag meins lebens. Das auch ich entwele in dem haus des herrn in die leng der tag.
Et misericordia tua subsequetur me omnibus diebus vitae meae. Et ut inhabitem in domo domini in longitudinem dierum.

One should note here as before the resumptive use of the article: *erbermbd die*. Aside from this customary phenomenon, our attention is necessarily focused again on the tenses. The future *subsequetur* is rendered by the present *nachuolgt*. If one were not aware of the widespread employment of the present to express the future in most of the pre-Lutheran High German Bibles, one might be tempted to account for the present verb *nachuolgt* in the sixth verse from the fact that the *Psalterium Romanum*, rather frequently used by medieval translators, actually has the present tense *subsequitur*. Convincing as this fact appears to be at first sight, it loses a great deal of its force upon the realization that the Mentel Bible invariably, at least so far as our Twenty-third Psalm is concerned, renders the Latin future by the German present. Thus it is not necessary in my opinion to call upon the *Psalterium Romanum* for an explanation of the present tense in this instance. The general observation that the present also stands for the Latin future is sufficient.

Summarizing our examination of the Twenty-third Psalm in the Mentel Bible, we may say that it is translated literally and, in the main, correctly. So far as word order is concerned, this translation is considerably superior to the older interlinear versions with their slavish adherence to Latin word order. While the Mentel Bible's rendering is still a far cry from the relatively free word order of a later day, it is no longer wholly bound by its Latin model but moves with some measure of ease according to a German pattern, however stiff and rigid it may sound to our ear. In the light of these considerations it is almost superfluous to remark that this translation of the Twenty-third

Psalm is practically devoid of literary merit; it is decidedly not a work of art in any sense of that word. No less an authority than Wilhelm Walther[4] saw fit to observe that the aim of the translator of the Mentel Bible was not a literal rendering but one intelligible to everybody and easily readable. He even went so far as to assert that the translator reached his goal in several respects. But it seems to me that, even if Walther's contention about the author's striving for an intelligible and readable text should be essentially correct, it is next to impossible to agree with Walther's claim that he did succeed in carrying out this laudable purpose. I for one cannot bring myself to differ materially with Luther's charge that the German Bible before him was not distinguished by clarity, perspicuity, and ready comprehensibility.

Aside from these general conclusions a brief summarizing remark about the tenses of our psalm is in order. There are some actual mistakes: In the first verse the future *deerit* is rendered by the preterit *gebrast*, and in the third verse the perfect tenses *convertit* and *deduxit* are translated by the German present. We also noted some peculiarities: The Latin perfect is rendered both by the German perfect (vv. 4, 5) and by the German preterit (v. 2); the Latin future (perfect as well as simple) is expressed by the German present (vv. 4, 6). While these peculiarities are by no means idiosyncrasies of the translator but apparently characteristic of much of older German literature, it can be said at the end of our discussion of the Mentel Bible's version of our psalm that one of the chief advances made by later redactions of the pre-Lutheran German Bible consists in the relatively closer attention paid to the very question of tenses. Although all the major revisions of the Mentel text make some improvement in this respect, they are not equally extensive or systematic. As a matter of fact, the best-known of the later editions of the German Bible, the Zainer and Koberger redactions, are rather inferior in this important matter to the somewhat neglected Pflanzmann Bible, to a consideration of which we shall now turn.

Pflanzmann[5]

Der herre regiert mich vn̄ mir wirt nichtz gebresten vnd an der stat der weide do hat er mich gesetzt Er hat mich ernert auff

---

[4]Walther, p. 84.

[5]Quoted from the copies available in the Pierpont Morgan Library and the New York Public Library. My principal reason for consulting these extremely rare copies was that I had great difficulty in understanding the fifth verse as found in W. Kurrelmeyer's indispensable edition of the first German Bible and the variants occurring in the succeeding thirteen editions. Upon consulting the New York copies I discovered that Kurrelmeyer omits a vital phrase. See page 87.

dē wasser der widerlabūg. er hat bekert mein sel Er hat mich vssgefürt an die steig der gerechtigkeit. vmb seinē name Wiewol ich würd wādeln in mittē des schatē des tods. ich fürcht nit die übeln dinge. dān du bist mit mir Deī růt vñ deī stab sy habē mich getröst Du hast bereit den tisch in meinē angesicht. wider die die mich betrübēt Du hast veisst gemacht mein haupt mit öl. vnd wie garlauter ist mein kelch der do truncken machent ist Vnd dein barmhertzigkeyt die wirt mir nachuolgen alle die tag meins leben. das ich wone ī dē hauss des hern. in der lenge der tag

The translation of the Twenty-third Psalm contained in the Pflanzmann Bible, the first illustrated German Bible and generally held to be the third among all printed German Bibles, underwent more extensive and significant revisions than those found in the far better-known Zainer and Koberger redactions, the fourth and ninth German Bibles, respectively. In contradistinction to these later, considerably more famous editions the changes occurring in the Pflanzmann version of the Twenty-third Psalm are of so important and striking a nature that one may very well wonder whether the word "revision" is not an understatement in the last analysis. However that may be, the fact remains that every single verse is different in the Pflanzmann Bible from what it had been in the first and second German Bibles.

As suggested above in the concluding paragraph of our discussion of the Mentel version, one of the first things to catch the eye of the careful reader of the Twenty-third Psalm in the Pflanzmann Bible is probably the surprisingly and unusually accurate translation of the Latin tenses. Markedly differing from the first printed German Bible (the Mentel Bible), the Pflanzmann redaction, besides avoiding the actual mistakes occurring in the former, renders the Latin perfect by the German perfect and, with one exception, the Latin future by the German future.

V. 1

Der herre regiert mich vñ mir wirt nichtz gebresten

It is important to note that the word *regiert,* which is to remain throughout the following pre-Lutheran Bibles, puts in its first appearance in the Pflanzmann Bible, Mentel and Eggesteyn having *richt.* One should also observe that the resumption of the subject by the article, a frequently employed device of the first two Bibles, is dropped in the Pflanzmann redaction; instead of the Mentel version's phrase, *Der herr der richt mich,* Pflanzmann reads, *Der herre regiert mich,* without the repeated article *der.* Furthermore, the third German Bible, rigidly observing the tenses of the Vulgate, corrects the Mentel Bible's erroneous *gebrast* to *wirt . . . gebresten,* a more accurate rendering of the Latin *deerit* than is found in the Zainer and Koberger redactions.

V. 2

vnd an der stat der weide do hat er mich gesetzt Er hat mich ernert auff dē wasser der widerlabūg.

There are several major changes to be noted in this verse over against the first two Bibles. First, the Latin perfect tenses *collocavit* and *educavit* are rendered by the exactly corresponding German forms of *haben* plus the past participle, *hat . . . gesetzt* and *hat . . . ernert.* Secondly, the noun *widerbringung,* for the Latin *refectio,* is replaced by the more expressive and imaginative—so it seems to me at least— *widerlabung.* Thirdly, the Pflanzmann Bible changes the verb *furen* as used by Mentel and Eggesteyn to *erneren.* This significant substitution is altogether in keeping with the general principle of painstaking accuracy so manifestly adhered to by whoever is responsible for the version of the Twenty-third Psalm in the Pflanzmann Bible. Fully aware of the difference between *educare* and *educere,* the translator of the third German Bible uses the rather more accurate *erneren* in lieu of the less accurate *furen,* thereby indicating an appreciation and perception of nuances quite foreign not only to the Mentel and Eggesteyn Bibles but also to all other redactions, including the well-known Zainer and Koberger revisions.

V. 3

er hat bekert mein sel Er hat mich vssgefürt an die steig der gerechtigkeit. vmb seinē name

The differences between this version and that of the two preceding Bibles are only those of tense. Whereas the earlier Bibles erroneously use the present for what is clearly the perfect in Latin, the Pflanzmann Bible has the correct perfect in German: . . . *hat bekert* and . . . *hat . . . vssgefürt* replace *bekert* and . . . *furt . . . aus* as translations of *convertit* and *deduxit.* What we had observed before is evident also here—the third German Bible's meticulous adherence to the tenses of the Vulgate.

V. 4

Wiewohl ich würd wādeln in mittē des schatē des tods. ich fürcht nit die übeln dinge. dān du bist mit mir Deī růt vn̄ deī stab sy habē mich getröst

Suggestive of the greater richness of language and expression at the disposal of the translator of the Pflanzmann Bible is his interesting revision of the introductory clause of the fourth verse: *Wiewol ich würd wädeln* instead of the older *Wan ob ich ioch gee*. Noteworthy is first of all the substitution of *wandeln* (also used by as great a stylist as Luther later on!) for what appears to me to be a fairly colorless word, *gee*, of the preceding (as well as, for that matter, of all the following) Bibles. Secondly, the omission of a German word for the initial Latin *nam* may very well be due in part to the third German Bible's attempt to limit the use of *wann*, which was so frequent and indiscriminate in the first two Bibles.[6] In this connection it is important to point out that the place of the Mentel and Eggesteyn Bibles' second *wann* in this single verse is taken by the synonymous and, incidentally, slightly more modern *dann*. Thus both procedures of the Pflanzmann Bible, the omission of one *wann* and the substitution of another less obsolescent word for the other, indicate at least some incipient concern with matters of German style, a concern that seems to have been largely if not wholly nonexistent for the translator of the Mentel Bible and its mechanical copy, the Eggesteyn redaction.

There is one other omission, the reason for which is not a little baffling so far as I can see. In the last phrase of the verse the Pflanzmann Bible drops the preceding versions' *selb* or, if we assume the former to be an independent rendering of its own, chooses to omit to translate the Vulgate's *ipsa*. Two explanations are possible in my opinion. Rejecting the idea that it is merely an oversight as not being in accord with the general carefulness evinced by the translator of the third German Bible, I am inclined to believe either that he felt the *sy* to be an adequate translation of *ipsa* or that he thought it wise to retain the resumptive *sy* and drop the intensive *ipsa*.

With reference to the tenses in this fourth verse, an uncommonly interesting situation prevails. On the face of it and on first sight, Pflanzmann's employment of the present *ich fürcht* for what is indisputably the future in Latin, *timebo*, would seem to strike a serious blow to our contention that the translator observes the tenses of the Vulgate with truly astonishing accuracy unequalled by any other pre-Lutheran Bible in the German language. Perhaps the charge that our translator slipped in this instance is correct and, if so, his mistake should be duly recognized and held against him. It appears to me, however, that, in view of his amazing reliability in all other instances throughout this psalm, there may conceivably be a definite reason for his rendering this particular Latin future by the German present. Inasmuch as he

[6]Brodführer, p. 133.

had translated the future perfect *ambulavero* by the first conditional (or could it be the simple future?) *würd wandeln*, a translation not at all strange if one remembers the relatively late emergence of the future perfect and second conditional in German, he may have wished to indicate the proper temporal relation between *ambulavero* (future perfect) and *timebo* (simple future) by translating the latter by the present tense. In other words, the Pflanzmann Bible's employment of the present *fürcht* for the future *timebo* may have been inspired by the desire to maintain in German something of the relationship that exists in the Vulgate between the future perfect of the protasis and the simple future of the apodosis.

V. 5

Du hast bereit den tisch in meinē angesicht. wider die die mich betrübēt Du hast veisst gemacht mein haubt mit öl. vnd wie garlauter ist mein kelch der do truncken machent ist

This is the verse which causes those who limit themselves to Kurrelmeyer's immensely helpful edition of the High German pre-Lutheran Bibles much grief and literally no end of trouble until they decide to take a look at a copy of the Pflanzmann Bible itself. The reason for the difficulty is that Kurrelmeyer does not print the entire verse but omits a very important part of it.[7] While an omission in a critical edition of this significance and magnitude is always regrettable and unfortunate, it is absolutely fatal in this particular case.

In order to make this clear it is necessary to see the medieval translation of the Psalter into German in a somewhat larger frame. Although the overwhelming majority of the pre-Lutheran German translations of the Psalms are made from the *Psalterium Gallicum* (i.e., the Vulgate) with an occasional preference for the older *Psalterium Romanum*, there are one or two which, at least partially, went beyond these sources to Jerome's final revision of his version of the Psalter, the so-called *Psalterium iuxta Hebraeos*, translated as the name implies directly from the Hebrew rather than from the Septuagint as the earlier *Psalteria Romanum et Gallicum* had been. It so happens that our verse has a different reading in the *Psalterium iuxta Hebraeos* from what it has in the preceding *Psalteria*, which in their turn are not wholly identical with each other. The three versions read as follows:

---

[7]At least on the basis of the two copies of the Pflanzmann Bible consulted by me in the Pierpont Morgan Library and the Public Library in New York City. It is of course not impossible, though it seems improbable to me, that the copy used by Mr. Kurrelmeyer may read differently.

Psalterium Romanum: *Parasti in conspectu meo mensam adversus eos qui tribulant me. Impinguasti in oleo caput meum, et poculum tuum inebrians quam praeclarum est.*

Psalterium Gallicum: *Parasti in conspectu meo mensam adversus eos qui tribulant me. Impinguasti in oleo caput meum, et calix meus inebrians quam praeclarus est.*

Psalterium iuxta Hebraeos: *Pones coram me mensam ex adverso hostium meorum. Impinguasti oleo caput meum; calix meus inebrians.*

Ignoring all of the minor differences between the *Psalterium Romanum* and the *Psalterium Gallicum* and most of the considerable divergences between these two *Psalteria* and the *Psalterium iuxta Hebraeos*, let us, for our present purposes, dwell on one of the chief departures of the third *Psalterium* from the first two—the absence, in the third version, of the last phrase of the first two versions, *quam praeclarum* (*praeclarus*, respectively) *est*. It is at just this juncture that Kurrelmeyer's edition threatens to lead us into a dangerous pitfall. Is it not a pity that in this work of patient and painstaking scholarship, held in the highest esteem by all those who have ever used it, this crucial phrase is conspicuous by its absence? The mind of the investigator, on the lookout for possibilities of this sort, begins to toy with the idea that the anonymous translator of the Twenty-third Psalm in the Pflanzmann Bible may have intentionally left behind the Vulgate in this instance and boldly made his way to a version decidedly closer to the Hebrew original. It seems to me that this is a legitimate reaction to the fifth verse reading as follows in Kurrelmeyers edition:[8]

Du hast bereyt den tisch in meinem angesicht: wider die die mich betrubent. Du hast veisst gemacht mein haubt mil ol: vnd mein kelch der do truncken machent ist.

Although it is true that this reading does not quite make sense and that consequently one's suspicions as to its genuineness are aroused, it is also true that the earlier (and later) editions of the pre-Lutheran German Bible translating the words *quam praeclarus est* do certainly not offer what may seriously be called a clear and easily understandable German rendering. Thus the mere fact that Kurrelmeyer's version of the Pflanzmann redaction is not distinguished by ready comprehensibility does not by itself deter the student from entertaining the notion that a source other than the Vulgate may be responsible for the curious omission of so critical a phrase.

[8]Wilhelm Kurrelmeyer, *Die erste deutsche Bibel* (Tübingen, 1904–15), VII, p. 272.

However, before assuming that this omission is due to the translator's consulting Jerome's *Psalterium iuxta Hebraeos,* the investigator, by this time fascinated by the passage, recalls that there are many variants in the several editions of the Vulgate. It is not impossible therefore that the edition which the translator used may conceivably have lacked the words in question. Although one should realize that the translator might have made his rendering from a manuscript of the Vulgate, which would obviously be inaccessible in this country even if it could be located, it seems more likely in view of the relatively late date of the Pflanzmann Bible (1473–1475) that a printed Vulgate was his source. Upon perusing the printed Vulgates available in the superb Copinger Collection in the Library of General Theological Seminary in New York City I found that not a single copy from the Gutenberg Bible to 1476 omitted the phrase *quam praeclarus est.* The possibility remains of course that there may have been an edition, unavailable in America or even lost entirely, which did not have the words in question.

It is a clear indication of the high repute in which Kurrelmeyer's edition of the pre-Lutheran Bibles is held that only after checking the various editions of the Vulgate did I take seriously the idea, which of course had suggested itself earlier, of collating our verse in the two copies of the Pflanzmann Bible accessible in the New York libraries. Here I discovered that Kurrelmeyer's reading is incomplete and that the phrase *quam praeclarus est* was actually translated, at least in the two New York copies.

After sketching this Odyssey of running down our pivotal but elusive phrase, we resume the discussion of the general characteristics of the Pflanzmann version of Ps. 23 : 5. The chief result of looking the verse up in the two copies referred to above is of course the conclusion that it is not influenced by the *Psalterium iuxta Hebraeos,* a theory that may reasonably be held as long as one restricts oneself to Kurrelmeyer's edition. Consultation of the original volumes shows that the opposite is true—verse five is wholly explicable on the basis of the Vulgate.

The principal lexicographic differences between the Mentel and Eggesteyn Bibles on the one hand and the Pflanzmann redaction on the other are the substitution in the latter of the more modern *angesicht* for the obsolete *bescheude* and of *du hast veisst gemacht* for *du hast erveystent.* The most interesting change is doubtless the stylistic one occurring in the very phrase that we have been discussing at some length. Instead of Mentel-Eggesteyn's *vnd mein kelch der macht truncken wie lauter er ist,* Pflanzmann reads *vnd wie garlauter ist mein kelch der do truncken machent ist.* It seems to me that the translator of the Pflanzmann Bible surpassed himself in this particular rendering. He accomplished nothing less than to make sense out of the Latin phrase which is anything but readily intelligible. Whereas the previous German Bibles contented themselves with a mechanical reproduction of the Vulgate text leaving it still more obscure than it already was, the translator of the third German Bible, by changing the elements of the sentence around, succeeded in turning it into a German phrase which, whether or not it expresses the somewhat puzzling intention of the Vulgate, is at least meaningful to a certain degree. The position of honor which our translator of the Twenty-third Psalm holds among the translators or revisers of all 14 printed High German Bibles before Luther is in no small measure due to such happy renderings as the one just discussed. If one bears in mind that 12 of the German Bibles express tacit approval of the Mentel Bible's original phrase by leaving it unchanged throughout, the boldness and ability of the unknown translator of the third Bible stand out all the more clearly. Besides observing the Latin tenses more closely than any other translator of the Twenty-third Psalm, he also rendered what is perhaps the most difficult, certainly the most tantalizing phrase of the entire psalm more idiomatically and more felicitously than even the Zainer and Koberger redactions. It is distressing to think that Kurrelmeyer's unfortunate misreading of just this verse might have prevented us from paying fair tribute to this man.

V. 6

Vnd dein barmhertzigkeyt die wirt mir nachuolgen alle die tag meins leben. das ich wone ī dē hauss des hern. in der lenge der tag

In accordance with his pronounced tendency to render the Latin tenses accurately, the translator of the Pflanzmann Bible translated the Vulgate's *subsequetur* not by the present *nachuolgt* as the Mentel and Eggesteyn Bibles had done but by the future *wirt . . . nachuolgen.* Apart from this meticulous attention to tense, the Pflanzmann redaction replaces obsolescent words like *erbermbd* and *entwelen* by the more modern *barmhertzigkeyt* and *wonen.* Finally, although this is a very minor point, it should be stated that the third German Bible drops the *auch* inserted by the first two Bibles between *das* and *ich* in the second half of the verse; Kurrelmeyer's edition, incidentally, does not indicate this omission in the third German Bible.[9]

[9]Loc. cit.

Since it is in connection with the changes in the sixth verse made by the Pflanzmann Bible that Kurrelmeyer cautiously revised or at least modified his original estimate of this Bible, it may not be out of place to say a few words about this well-known scholar's remarks on the third German Bible in 1904 and in 1915. In the introduction to the first volume of *Die erste deutsche Bibel,* published in 1904, Kurrelmeyer expressed himself as follows on the Pflanzmann redaction: "Die änderungen in der sprache sind unerheblich, und beschränken sich gewöhnlich auf einzelne wörter, die dann konsequent durch andere ersetzt werden. So, z.b. . . . wonen—entweln. Auf satzgefüge oder textinhalt erstrecken sich diese neuerungen nie. Zuweilen sind dieselben äusserst verstandlos und mechanisch durchgeführt. . . . Die veränderungen sind jedoch verhältnismässig selten. MEP sind folglich als gruppe für sich zu betrachten in welcher der überlieferte text ohne erhebliche abänderungen wiedergegeben wird. Die folgende ausgabe leitet eine neue gruppe ein: Z Ausgabe von Günther Zainer, Augsburg ca. 1475."[10] In 1915, when the concluding tenth volume of Kurrelmeyer's monumental undertaking appeared, the introduction again touches upon the Pflanzmann Bible. We are first informed that what he has to add in 1915 to what he wrote in 1904 on this German Bible is inconsiderable: "Die nachträge über die Pflanzmannsche ausgabe sind unerheblich."[11] After this broad and fairly sweeping statement Kurrelmeyer proceeds in the following way: "Im allgemeinen folgt der drucker mechanisch seiner vorlage, ab und zu jedoch, und zwar besonders im Psalter, macht er änderungen, die nur auf vergleichung des lateinischen textes zurückzuführen sind. In diesen fällen hat dann P oft einen korrekteren oder moderneren text als die folgenden drucke Z–Oa: . . . Ps. 23, 6 dein erbermbd die nachuolgt mir MEZ–Oa, dein barmherzigkeyt die wirt mir nachuolgen P . . ."[12]

Now I am in no way competent to speak about the pre-Lutheran Bibles as a whole. Inasmuch as Kurrelmeyer in 1915 points out that the Psalter occupies a special place in the Pflanzmann Bible, he thereby suggests that his earlier generalizations of 1904 certainly do not apply to the Psalter *in toto.* It seems to me that he might have expressed himself a little more strongly in this direction if he had been more fully aware what significant changes the Twenty-third Psalm underwent in the third German Bible. Instead of referring only to v. 6 as he does he might have referred to the entire psalm, especially vv.

---

[10]*Die erste deutsche Bibel,* I, xiv.
[11]Ibid., X, xxxvii.
[12]Ibid., X, xxxviii.

2, 4, and 6, in which the changes are even more considerable than in v. 6. If Kurrelmeyer had realized what the Pflanzmann Bible did to vv. 4, 5 in particular, he would have been compelled to revise his original estimate of 1904 somewhat more materially in 1915 than he did. As matters stand now, the reader of Kurrelmeyer's two introductions—of which the earlier, through no fault of the author to be sure, is far better known than the slightly modified later one—is in no way prepared for what I believe I have found, namely, that the Twenty-third Psalm in the Pflanzmann Bible is so thorough a revision of the version contained in the Mentel and Eggesteyn Bibles that one is strongly tempted to regard it as an original translation considerably superior to the preceding one and also, for that matter, to all those that were to follow before Luther.

I do not wish to give the impression that it is only Kurrelmeyer who has stressed the significance of the Zainer Bible, the fourth German Bible, at the total expense of the third. As a matter of fact, Wilhelm Walther, long before him, sang the praises of the fourth Bible over against the third. In a special article, written as early as 1887, on "Die Psalmenübersetzung der vier ersten hochdeutschen Bibeln" Walther also insisted that it is the fourth Bible that counts.[13] While recognizing that there are changes in the third Bible, he maintained that the changes in the fourth Bible are far more considerable.[14] It is important to remember that this straightforward statement occurs in an article especially devoted to an examination of the Psalter. Several years later, in his great work *Die deutsche Bibelübersetzung des Mittelalters*, Walther unhesitatingly reiterates this view, no longer restricting it to the Psalter but extending it to the whole Bible: "Ganz unabhängig von der vierten, müht sich die dritte Bibel, wenn auch in zaghafterer Weise, um die Modernisierung des Textes."[15] With Walther and Kurrelmeyer thus clearly extolling the merits of the fourth Bible and unmistakably detracting from the third, though Walther rather less so than Kurrelmeyer, it is small wonder that practically all later publications on this subject invariably speak of the first and fourth German Bibles, generally relegating the third, the Pflanzmann redaction, to the background.

It is not my intention to question our present picture of the pre-Lutheran Bibles on the basis of my altogether inadequate knowledge

---

[13]*Zeitschrift für kirchliche Wissenschaft und kirchliches Leben*, VIII (1887), pp. 513–27.
[14]Ibid., p. 516.
[15]*Die deutsche Bibelübersetzung des Mittelalters*, p. 72. Cf. also pp. 46, 47.

of them. What I do wish to emphasize, however, is that the translation of the Twenty-third Psalm in these Bibles does not fit very well in this general picture. So far as this particular psalm is concerned, the third German Bible contains a version of it that is at once materially different from that of the Mentel and Eggesteyn Bibles (as well as all later redactions) and markedly superior. Walther's and Kurrelmeyer's judgments of the third German Bible as a whole do not do justice to the version of the Twenty-third Psalm found in this Bible. Kurrelmeyer's partial modification of his original estimate does not go far enough either. The psalm investigated in this chapter calls for a rather more radical reconsideration of the Bible as a whole, unless it should be found that it constitutes a single exception, in which event further suggestive questions appear on the horizon.

In view of the singular, somewhat unexpected importance of the Pflanzmann Bible's version of the Twenty-third Psalm, a very brief summary of our findings will be given before we proceed to a discussion of the Zainer redaction. The most striking thing about the Pflanzmann version is probably the painstaking, almost meticulous attention paid to the accurate rendering of the tenses. By this fact alone this version differs greatly from its predecessors. However, the care manifestly expended by its translator does not end here. In general, he translates both more carefully (*erneret* in verse 2) and more imaginatively (*widerlabung* in the same verse) than the Mentel and Eggesteyn versions. Contrary to Kurrelmeyer's statement that he could find no change in sentence structure in the third Bible, I believe there are such changes in vv. 4, 5. Stylistically the Pflanzmann Bible's version of our psalm is rather superior to what went before. Finally, there are a number of conscious lexigraphic modernizations in v. 4, 6, some of which are also pointed out by Kurrelmeyer in his introduction to the last volume of his *magnum opus*.

Zainer[16]

Der herr regieret mich. vnd mir gebrist nichts. vñ an der statt der weyde da satzt er mich. Er hat mich gefüret auff dem wasser der widerbringung. er bekeret mein seel. Er füret mich auf die steig der gerechtigkeyt. vmb seinen namen. Wan ob ich ia gee in mitt des schatten des tods. ich fürcht nit die übeln ding. wañ du bist bei mir. Dein rut vnnd dein stab. die selb haben mich getröst. Du hast bereyt den tisch in meinem angesicht. wider die die mich betrübent. Du hast erueystet mein haubt in dem öl. vnnd mein kelch der macht

[16]Quoted from the copy of the Pierpont Morgan Library in New York City.

trücken wie lauter er ist. Vnd dein erbärmbd die nachuolget mir all die tag meins lebens. Das auch ich inwone. in dē haus des herren. in die länge der tag.

In spite of many prevalent opinions to the contrary, the Zainer redaction of the Twenty-third Psalm is considerably more like Mentel and Eggesteyn than the Pflanzmann version is. In fact, compared with the almost timid changes made by Zainer, the third German Bible can practically be held to contain an independent rendering of our psalm.[17] The least that can be said in view of the important differences between the Pflanzmann and Zainer versions is that they are separate, unassociated revisions of varying degrees of intensiveness as well as extensiveness of the text of the first two German Bibles. At any rate, Zainer does not appear to have consulted the slightly earlier Pflanzmann, since the differences between these two versions far outweigh the similarities.

V. 1

Der herr regieret mich. vnd mir gebrist nichts.

It is interesting to observe that Zainer uses *regieren* as Pflanzmann does in place of the earlier Bibles' *richten*. With reference to the tenses, Zainer changes Mentel's and Eggesteyn's erroneous preterit *gebrast* to the present *gebrist*. One should note that the Pflanzmann Bible's exactitude is not attained by the Zainer redaction. Zainer still makes the present tense do double duty as both present and future.

V. 2

vn̄ an der stat der weyde do satzt er mich. Er hat mich gefüret auff dem wasser der widerbringung:

The first half of the verse is in complete agreement with the Mentel and Eggesteyn Bibles. It differs in tense (preterit) from the Pflanzmann Bible (present perfect). The second half of the verse departs in tense (present perfect) from the first two Bibles' preterit but agrees in the use of the verb *furen*. While employing the same *tense* of the verb as the Pflanzmann Bible, the Zainer redaction does not use the same verb as Pflanzmann (*erneren*) but reverts to the first two Bibles' *furen*. The Zainer Bible also reverts to the noun *widerbringung* used by Mentel and Eggesteyn. Looking at v. 2 as a whole, the reader is convinced that the Zainer redaction all but ignores the changes made by the Pflanzmann Bible.

---

[17] I am aware that this statement, naturally made about our psalm only, is the very opposite of what Walther says about the relation of the third and fourth Bibles. Cf. footnote 15.

V. 3

er bekeret mein seel. Er füret mich aus auf die steig der gerechtigkeyt vmb seinen namen.

Although it seems incredible, it is a fact that the Zainer Bible left the faulty tenses of Mentel-Eggesteyn wholly uncorrected. The Latin perfect tense is still rendered by the German present. Pflanzmann alone (of *all* High German pre-Lutheran Bibles!) translates *convertit* and *deduxit* properly.

V. 4

Wan ob ich ia gee in mitt des schatten des tods. ich fürcht nit die übeln ding. wañ du bist bei mir. Dein rut vnnd dein stab. die selb haben mich getröst.

There is no trace of Pflanzmann's bold new translation of the important first phrase; the only change is the unessential substitution of *ia* for *ioch* and *mitt* for *mitzt*. The ubiquitous *wann*, changed to *dann* by Pflanzmann, is also left untouched. By and large, Zainer is practically identical with Mentel-Eggesteyn. It is again the Pflanzmann Bible alone which diverges sharply from the rest of the pre-Lutheran Bibles. Zainer is quite conservative compared with Pflanzmann.

V. 5

Du hast bereyt den tisch in meinem angesicht. wider die die mich betrübent. Du hast erueystet mein haubt in dem öl. vnnd mein kelch der macht trücken wie lauter er ist.

Beyond substituting *angesicht* for the obsolete *bescheude* and writing *in* for *mit (dem öl)*, the Zainer version does not change this verse from what it was in Mentel-Eggesteyn. There is no suggestion of the audacity of the Pflanzmann Bible's major revision of the difficult final phrase. Zainer, supposedly the most thorough revision of the first German Bible, turns out to be far less radical than the all too often underestimated Pflanzmann version.

V. 6

Vnd dein erbärmbd/die nachuolget mir all die tag meins lebens. Das auch ich inwone. in dē haus des herren. in die länge der tag.

With the exception of using the more modern *inwone* for Mentel-Eggesteyn's *entwele*, Zainer is exactly like the first German Bible. Contrary to Pflanzmann, the Zainer redaction retains the obsolete *erbärmbd*. As regards the problem of tense, Zainer keeps the present *nachuolget* for the Vulgate's *subsequetur;* Pflanzmann, it will be recalled, employed, more accurately, the German future.

Summarizing the chief results of our survey of the Zainer Bible's version of the Twenty-third Psalm, we may state that it is far less thoroughly revised than the Pflanzmann redaction. The lexigraphic modernizations are fewer; the tenses are only partially corrected and revised; of stylistic improvements over Mentel-Eggesteyn there is none so far as I can see. In short, as regards the Twenty-third Psalm, the Zainer version is a very conservative, almost timid, revision of the text of the first German Bible. It does not, in this instance, rank with the Pflanzmann version.

Koberger[18]

Der herr regieret mich vnd mir gebrist nichts. vnd an der stat d'weyde da satzt er mich. Er hat mich gefuret auff dem wasser der widerbringung. er bekeret mein seel. Er furet mich aus auf die steyg der gerechtigkeit. vmb seinē namē. Wañ ob ich gee in mitt des schatten des todes. ich furcht nit die vbeln ding. wan du bist bey mir. Dein rut vnnd dein stab. die selb haben mich getrostet. Du hast bereitet den tysch in meinē angesicht: wider die die mich betruben. Du hast erueystet mein haubt in dem ol. vnnd mein kelch macht truncken wie lauter er ist. Vnd dein erbermbd nachuolget mir. Alle tag meins lebens. Das auch ich inwone in dem haus des herren in die lenge der tag.

Since the Koberger version of the Twenty-third Psalm is practically identical with the Zainer redaction, it is not necessary to take up each verse by itself. A few general remarks will do. Besides omitting *ia* in v. 4 and the second *die* in v. 6, the only change of note made by Koberger is the systematic dropping of the resumptive article: *der* in v. 5 and the first *die* in v. 6. It should be pointed out that in this matter Koberger excels even Pflanzmann. Aside from this definite modernization, the Koberger redaction is little more than a reproduction, with orthographic differences to be sure, of the Zainer text.

The Post-Koberger Redactions[19]

Apart from fluctuations between *die selb* and *die selben* (v. 4), the later redactions show no differences from Koberger with one exception—the Augsburg Bible of 1487 inserts the word *auch* before *erveystent* in v. 5.

In order to give a definite idea of how our psalm reads in the last of the printed High German Bibles to appear before Luther's Bible, it

---

[18] Quoted from the copy in the Yale University Library.

[19] With the exception of the Augsburg Bible of 1518, which is quoted from the copy of the Yale Library, I have consulted for the post-Koberger redactions only the Kurrelmeyer edition.

may not be amiss to quote at the end of our investigation the version contained in the rare Augsburg Bible of 1518:

Der herr regieret mich und mir geprist nichts / und an der stat der wayde da satzt er mich. Er hat mich gefuret auff dem wasser der widerpringung / er bekeret mein sel: Er furt mich aus auff die steyg der gerechtigkait umb seinen namen. Wañ ob ich gee in mitte des schatten des todes / ich furcht nit die ublen ding / wann du bist bey mir. Dein rut und dein stab / die selben habn mich getrostet. Du hast beraytet den tisch in meinē angesicht / wider die die mich betruben. Du hast erfaystet mein haubt in dem ol / und mein kelich machet truncken wie lauter er ist. Und dein erparmbde nachuolget mir / alle tag meines lebens / Das auch ich innwone in dem haus des herren / in die leng der tag.

The results of this investigation are very briefly as follows: While it is true that the first printed High German Bible was revised by the fourth Bible, and the fourth Bible in turn was further, though very little, revised by the ninth Bible, it is the third Bible which represents the most thorough revision of the first Bible so far as the Twenty-third Psalm is concerned. It is not Zainer, or Koberger, or any of the other 11 redactions, but Pflanzmann that constitutes the most complete revision of the original Mentel text, a revision so elaborate in character that it is at times difficult to refrain from calling the Pflanzmann version of the Twenty-third Psalm an independent translation. Yet, in order to avoid any possible misunderstanding, let it be said emphatically that, despite its relative merit when compared with the other editions of the printed High German Bibles, even the Pflanzmann version is immeasurably inferior to Luther's superb rendering. There is a difference of *degree* between the Pflanzmann and its sister versions; there is a difference of *kind* between the Pflanzmann and the Luther renderings of the Twenty-third Psalm.

(2) The Printed Low German Bibles

There are 18 printed Bibles prior to Luther, the last of which was published on July 8, 1522, a little more than two months before Luther's *Septembertestament*. Of these 18 Bibles 14 are High German and only four Low German. The High German Bibles are readily available in modern editions. The four Low German Bibles unfortunately are not. They can be used only in the original editions of 1478, 1494, and 1522.[1]

---

[1] Happily, a beginning has been made. Cf. Gerhard Ising, *Die niederdeutschen Bibelfrühdrucke* (Berlin, 1961 and 1963). Only two volumes have appeared thus far, covering Genesis to First Kings.

This is probably the chief reason why they are much less widely known and used than the High German Bibles. Only very few libraries have all four of them.

After examining Psalm 23 in the High German Bibles in the preceding chapter, let us now turn to the version(s) of this famous psalm in the printed Low German Bibles. The first two appeared in the same year, 1478, in Cologne. We shall refer to them as Cologne I and Cologne II. The third came out in Lübeck in 1494 and the fourth in Halberstadt in 1522.

V. 1

Vulgate: *Dominus regit me, et nihil mihi deerit.*
Cologne I, 1478: *De hé ŕgeret my vn̄ my en schal nicht ghebreken:*

This is a correct translation of the Vulgate. It is a rendering in no way dependent upon the first two High German Bibles, which have *richt* instead of *ŕgeret* and the incorrect imperfect *gebrast* for *schal . . . ghebreken*. Cologne I has more in common with the Pflanzmann Bible of 1473, which is the first printed German Bible to replace the Mentel and Eggesteyn Bibles' *richt* by *regiert*, destined to remain in effect down to the last High German Bible of 1518 and, for that matter, to the fourth and last Low German Bible of 1522. Pflanzmann also was the first to correct the past tense *gebrast* by changing it to the future *wirt nichtz gebresten*. Cologne I is just as accurate as Pflanzmann in the use of the future.

These two fundamental facts, the foreign word *ŕgeret* and the future *en schal nicht ghebreken*, do not mean, however, that Cologne I is necessarily dependent on Pflanzmann. As I see it, they merely mean that the anonymous translator of Cologne I was just as accurate and conscientious as the equally anonymous translator of Pflanzmann. It will not do to claim more. The post-Pflanzmann Bibles removed Pflanzmann's future and substituted the present tense *gebrist nichts*. It is manifest that Cologne I did not follow them.

Cologne II, 1478: *Der here regieret mich ind myr en sal neyt gebrechen.*

This is, apart from purely linguistic differences, the same text as that found in Cologne I.

Lübeck, 1494: *De here regeret my: vn̄ my enscal nicht ghebrekē.*

Again, the same basic text as Cologne I and II, except for dialect divergencies.

Halberstadt, 1522: *De here regeret my vnd my schal nicht gebrekē /*

This is clearly the same text as that of the preceding three versions, with one interesting difference: Halberstadt modernizes the language to the extent of dropping the negative particle *en* before the *schal* and limiting itself to the simple *nicht*.

V. 2

Vulgate: *In loco pascuae ibi me collocavit. Super aquam refectionis educavit me,*
Cologne I, 1478: *in der stede der weyde he my satte. He ledde my vth vppe dat water der weddermakinghe:*
This is an independent rendering, independent at least of the preceding High German versions. It is at once more exact and more inexact. It follows the Vulgate closely by not having the introductory *vnd* characteristic of all High German versions from Mentel to Silvanus Otmar, including, surprisingly enough, the very careful Pflanzmann. On the other hand, Cologne I does not translate the *ibi* of the Vulgate, which occurs as *do* in all High German Bibles.

The verb *educavit* is translated by *ledde . . . vth;* none of the High German Bibles expressed the prefix *e [x]*. But Cologne I does not differentiate between *educere* and *educare*. It does not attain the distinction of the Pflanzmann Bible, which alone among all the High German Bibles recognizes and expresses the difference. The Pflanzmann Bible remained unique among all 18 High and Low German Bibles in paying attention to the fact that the Vulgate has *educavit* and not *eduxit*. Finally, Cologne I renders *refectionis* by *weddermakinghe*, similar to but yet distinct from the High German Bibles' *widerbringung*. Cologne I does not follow the Pflanzmann Bible's *widerlabung*, a departure from all other High German versions.

It is clear that Cologne I, accurate and independent as it is, is not so good as Pflanzmann. The third High German Bible remains the high-water mark of the pre-Lutheran printed translations, both High and Low German, in this particular verse. Cologne I is rather on the level, respectable enough, of the Zainer redaction of 1473, which remained the basic text for the subsequent High German Bibles down to Silvanus Otmar.

Cologne II, 1478: *in der stad der weydē dair he mich satte. He leyte mich vs vp dat wasser der weder maching.*

This version is practically identical with Cologne I except that it inserts *dair* between *weydē* and the first *he*. It seems that this was to be a correction of the omission in Cologne I, *dair* translating the Vulgate's *ibi*.

Lübeck, 1494: *in der stede der weyde he my sette de He ledde my vth vppe dat water der weddermakinghe.*

Again an only slightly modified version of Cologne I. Lübeck also expresses the Latin word *ibi* by *de*, thus agreeing in principle with Cologne II rather than Cologne I (unless *de* is part of the verb *settede*). Halberstadt, 1522: *yn der stede der weyde dar he my satte. He ledde my vth vp dat water der weddermakinghe /*

This agrees almost completely, except for minor orthographical changes, with Cologne II. It cannot be looked upon as an independent version.

V. 3

Vulgate: *Animam meam convertit. Deduxit me super semitas justitiae, propter nomen suum.*

Cologne I, 1478: *he bekerde myne sele. He ledde my vth vppe dē wech d'rechtuerdichait dorch sinen namen.*

This is a correct rendering of the Vulgate. Interesting is the substitution of the word *rechtuerdichait* for the High German Bibles' *gerechtikeit*. Surprising, in view of the overall exactitude of Cologne I, is the use of the singular *dē wech* for the Latin plural *semitas,* rendered as *die steig* by the High German Bibles. This appears to be an independent version.

Cologne II, 1478: *he bekerde mȳ sele. He leyte mich vs vp dē wech der gerechtheyde durch sinen namen.*

Almost identical with Cologne I except that the word *rechtuerdichait* is not used, but the High German Bibles' *gerechtikeit.*

Lübeck, 1494: *he bekerde mine sele He ledde my vt vppe dē wech der rechtuerdicheyt durch sinen namen.*

This is fully identical with Cologne I down to the "restoration" of *rechtuerdicheyt.*

Halberstadt, 1522: *he bekerde myne sele. He ledde my vth vp den wech d'rechtferdicheyt durch synen namen.*

Ignoring orthography, this is the same version as Cologne I and Lübeck.

V. 4

Vulgate: *Nam, etsi ambulavero in medio umbrae mortis, non timebo mala, quoniam tu mecum es. Virga tua, et baculus tuus, ipsa me consolata sunt.*

Cologne I, 1478: *Wente efft ick ga in dem middel des schemen des dodes ick en schal myn quat vruchten: wente du bist myt my. Din rode vnde din staff: de hebben mȳ getrost.*

This is an accurate translation of the Vulgate, uninfluenced, it would seem, by the preceding High German versions. In particular, Pflanzmann's splendid introductory clause is not followed in any way. It cannot be held that Cologne I is superior to its High German predecessors and rivals.

Cologne II, 1478: *want off ich gae in deme midden deme schemē des dodes ich en sal geyn quait wirten. wā du bist myt myr. Dyn roide ind dyn staff. Dese hant mich getroist.*

The differences between Cologne I and II are minor. It is essentially the same translation. The second dative *deme schemē* is surprising. Is it just awkward, or an error, or merely a misprint? The genitive of Cologne I is surely a more accurate rendering.

Lübeck, 1494: *Wēte efte ick gha in deme middel des schemē des dodes ick enscal nen quaet vruchten. wēte du bist myt my Dine rode vn din staf de hebbē mi ghetrost.*

Again the same basic rendering. The genitive *des schemē* has been "restored." Lübeck is identical here with Cologne I rather than with Cologne II.

Halberstadt, 1522: *Wente effte ick ga yn dem middel des schemen des dodes ick schal nein quat forchten / wente du byst mit my. Dyn rode vnd dyn staff / de hebben my getrost.*

The version of the last Low German printed Bible is still basically the same as that of the first. Only a slight modernization has taken place, one we have noticed before—the enclytic negative *en* has been abandoned. Otherwise there is no real change beyond the orthography, which varies as is to be expected in these centuries of chaotic spelling.

V. 4 has remained essentially the same from the first to the last of the Low German Bibles. Influence from the High German Bibles is apparently absent. The Low German Bibles are accurate but just as little distinguished as the High German ones.

V. 5

Vulgate: *Parasti in conspectu meo mensam, adversus eos qui tribulant me. Impinguasti in oleo caput meum. Et calix meus inebrians quam praeclarus est!*

Cologne I, 1478: *Du hest beret in myne angesichte en tafel en teghen de de my bedrouent. Du hast mȳ houet vet gemaket in olye vnde mynen kelik de drunckende maket de is seer clar.*

This is an essentially independent version. It is less close to the first two Low German than to the later High German Bibles. The first part is a correct literal translation, all the way to *in olye*. Then the real difficulty of this verse begins. The trouble is that the Vulgate reading is obscure. The first Cologne version puts *calix meus* in the accusative, *meynen kelik*, which would mean that the translator made it somehow dependent on the verb *parasti* (*impinguasti* seems less likely). He then ignores the Vulgate's *quam* and substitutes a demonstrative article *de*. *Praeclarus* itself is rendered, not unskillfully, by *seer clar*. It cannot be held that Cologne I succeeded in providing an intelligible translation of the difficult second part of the verse. The painfully literal translation of the High German Bibles (with the exception of Pflanzmann) is probably preferable: *vnd mein kelch der macht truncken wie lauter er ist*. Only Pflanzmann, as presented in detail in the preceding essay, produced an imaginative rendering, which is intelligible though so free that it is hardly a translation at all.

Cologne II, 1478: *Du hais bereyt in myne angesichte eyn taffel intgain die die mich bedrouent. Du hais myn houfft vet gemacht in oley ind mȳ keylch de drückēde machet wye clair he is.*

Only the difficult second part of the verse differs from the Cologne I version. In the second part Cologne II changes Cologne I's wrong accusative *mynen kelik* to the correct nominative *mȳ keylch*. Cologne II also substitutes a literal rendering of the final phrase, *wye clair he is*, for Cologne I's free translation. In other words Cologne II approximates the literal rendering of most of the High German Bibles. But by retaining Cologne I's inverted word order *de drückēde machet* instead of the High German Bibles' *der macht truncken* it achieves more intelligibility than the obscure versions found in the High German Bibles (always excepting the Pflanzmann Bible).

Lübeck, 1494: *Du heft beret in minē anghesichte ene tafelen te ghen de de my bedrouen. Du heft min houet vet ghemaket in olie vnde min kelk te drunken maket de is sere klar.*

The long first part of the verse is identical with Cologne I and Cologne II. The second part is essentially the same as Cologne I, save that it corrects the error of the accusative *mynen kelik* by using the nominative *min kelk*. That makes it a relatively free and intelligible rendering of an exasperating Vulgate passage.

Halberstadt, 1522: *Du hest beret yn minem angesichte eine tafelē / entegē de de my bedrouen. Du hest myn houet vet gemaket yn olye / vnnd myn kelik de drunken maket de ys seer klar.*

This last of the Low German Bibles agrees *in toto* with its predecessor, the Lübeck Bible. What was said about that above applies to the Halberstadt Bible.

None of the four Low German Bibles approaches the third High German Bible, the Pflanzmann redaction, in the clever handling of the admittedly difficult final portion of the verse. The Low German Bibles are rather on the level of the first two and the last 11 High German

Bibles. None of course comes close to the Luther Bible or the Authorized Version, which are based on the Hebrew original. The Low German Bibles could merely make the best of a bad situation, the corrupt text of the Vulgate. They wrestled valiantly with an obscure Latin translation.

V. 6

Vulgate: *Et misericordia tua subsequetur me omnibus diebus vitae meae. Et ut inhabitem in domo Domini, in longitudinem dierum.*
Cologne I, 1478: *Unde dine barmherticheit schal my volghen, alle dage mynes leuendes. Unde vppe dat ick wane ī dē huse des heren in der lanckheide der daghe.*

This is a correct literal translation. It is more exact, as far as the tense is concerned, than the first two High German Bibles of Mentel and Eggesteyn and the last 11, from Zainer to Silvanus Otmar. Only the Pflanzmann Bible uses the future for the Vulgate's *subsequetur*. Cologne I is perhaps not very felicitous in translating the Vulgate's *Et ut inhabitem* by *Unde vppe dat ick wane*. The High German Bibles did better to translate it by *Das auch ich inwele;* the verb became *wone* in the Pflanzmann Bible and *inwone* from the Zainer redaction on.
Cologne II, 1478: *Ind dine barmhertzijcheit sal mir volgen alle de daige myns leuēs Inde vp dat ich woynē in dē huyse des heren in der lāckheide der dage.*

Cologne II is, aside from the usual orthographic differences, identical with Cologne I.
Lübeck, 1494: *Uñ dine barmherticheit schal my volghen. alle daghe mines leuēdes. Uñ vppe dat ick wane in dem huse des heren in der lankheyde der daghe.*

This third Low German Bible is also identical with Cologne I and II. There are naturally the customary differences in spelling.
Halberstadt, 1522: *Uñ dyne barmherticheit schal my volgen / alle dage mynes leuendes. Und vp dat ick wone yn dem huse des heren / yn der lank heyde der dage.*

Halberstadt too is identical with the preceding Low German versions, apart from matters of orthography.

By way of a brief summary, we can draw the following conclusions:
1. All four Low German Bibles contain practically the same translation of Psalm 23. Besides major orthographical divergencies there are a few minor differences in the actual text. The fourth Bible presents a refined text of the first. There is, as a matter of fact, something approaching constant refinement from Cologne I via Cologne II and Lübeck to Halberstadt.

2. The Low German Bible, regarding all four as fundamentally one, is an independent rendering, independent, that is, of the preceding High German versions. The first two High German Bibles are on the whole inferior to the Low German Bibles in that they are less accurate. The post-1478 High German Bibles neither influenced the Low German Bibles nor were influenced by them. The Low German Bibles are not derivatives, either wholly or in part, of the High German versions.

3. They are, as a translation, more or less on a par with the High German Bibles from Zainer (1475) on. They are not so good as the third High German Bible, the Pflanzmann version. They did not copy the Pflanzmann Bible either.

4. Like the High German Bibles, the Low German Bibles are based on the Vulgate.

5. They are no closer to Luther than the High German Bibles are. In other words, for Psalm 23 at any rate, if Luther consulted the Low German Bibles at all, he got no more help from them than from the High German Bibles.

b. THE EVOLUTION OF LUTHER'S MASTERPIECE

There is universal agreement that the Psalms are among the most excellently rendered parts of Luther's Bible, probably even the most excellently rendered part. Luther certainly expended more time and effort on the Psalter than on any other single book of the Bible. Still, while his rendering of the Psalms has received the widest acclaim, there exists no more than one close analysis of Luther's translation of one Psalm so far. Psalm 46 was investigated by Hans Schmidt, one of the most eminent of German Old Testament scholars, almost half a century ago.[1] Schmidt's article has been quoted over and over again as the only one of its kind. As a student of Hebrew, he—perhaps naturally—paid more attention to the relation of Luther's translation to the original text than to the development of the German rendering and to its artistic aspects.

In this essay the emphasis will be on the literary and aesthetic phase of Luther's work; we shall study primarily the artistic evolution of Luther's translation of the Twenty-third Psalm. Since we are fortunate enough to possess the manuscript version of Luther's rendering, we can begin our investigation at the very beginning. Although Psalm 23 is perhaps the most famous, surely the most beloved, of all psalms, it is curiously enough not found among the small number of psalms that

---

[1]Hans Schmidt, "Luthers Übersetzung des 46. Psalms," *Jahrbuch der Luther-Gesellschaft*, VIII (1926), 98–119.

Luther had translated prior to the undertaking of the formal translation of the Psalter in 1524. Aside from a few scattered renderings of individual verses of this psalm before 1524, the manuscript of the "official" rendering is the earliest version we have of a Lutheran translation of this best-known of all the psalms.

If we look closely at the manuscript, we can clearly differentiate at least two stages of Luther's translation within the framework of the manuscript itself: the first draft, with its corrections, deletions, and additions, written in black ink; and what appears to be the printer's copy, i. e. the black-ink text gone over, more or less extensively, in red ink, representing in general the final corrections made by Luther before the manuscript was rushed to the printing office. Since there are considerable differences between the first draft and the printer's copy, it is worthwhile to examine both stages separately. In order to do so it is best to reproduce, as accurately as we may, each major phase of the evolution of Luther's translation.

The First Draft[2]

Der herr ist meyn hirtte
myr wirt nichts mangeln
(Er hatt mich lassen)[3]
Er lesst mich weyden ynn der wonug des grases
vnd neeret mich am wasser gutter ruge
Er keret widder meyne seele
er furet mich auff rechtem pfad vmb seyns namens willen
Vnd ob ich schon wandert ym finstern tal. furcht ich keyn
    vngluck
denn du bist bey myr
Deyn stab vnd stecken[4] trosten mich
Du bereyttest fur[5] myr eynen tisch zu gegen meynen
    verfolgern
Du machst meyn heubt fett mit ole, meyn kilch ist satt
    hatt die fulle[6]
Gutts vnd barmhertzickeyt werden myr nach lauffen meyn
    leben lang
vnd werde wonen ym hause des herrn so lange zeyt

[2] See frontispiece for reproduction of Luther's first draft of Psalm 23 in his own handwriting.
[3] This line is crossed out in black ink.
[4] Here the word order was changed, in black ink, to "stecken vnd stab."
[5] "Fur" is written above the line.
[6] "Fulle" is written below the line.

If we consider the first draft as a whole, only two verses, the first and the fourth, remained unchanged not only in the printer's copy but all the way from the first printed editions of 1524 through the last revision of 1531. Looked at from the opposite point of view, as many as two verses of the total of six were held good enough by Luther to be incorporated literally into the final, great version of 1531. Aside from this general observation, what are the chief characteristics of the first draft?

To begin with, Luther's rendering is based on the Hebrew original as he understood it with the aid of the Christian scholarship of his day. This does not mean of course that Luther ignored completely or broke radically with the long tradition of the Greek and Latin renderings of the Psalm; especially the Vulgate version, with which he had been thoroughly familiar for practically two decades, must always be assumed to have been automatically present in the great translator's mind. Though Luther often departed from the Vulgate where it obviously deviated from the original, he never quite freed himself from the general spirit that underlay and pervaded the Greco-Roman translations, or, to put it more positively, he was ever under the influence of the ethos that shaped the famous post-Hebrew versions. No matter how conscientiously he tried to base his rendering, verse by verse and phrase by phrase, on the Hebrew text; no matter how religiously he abandoned a long-accustomed word when its Vulgate form did not check with the original; the fact remains that Luther's rendering as a whole is still tinged with the spirit of the Septuagint and of the Vulgate. In other words, Luther changed many details but retained, mostly unconsciously, the whole religious and spiritual tenor of the highly influential and all-pervasive versions that had reigned supreme for more than a thousand years.

Moreover, in trying to determine whether a relatively early version, such as Luther's is after all, is based on the Hebrew or on one or several Latin translations, one must not lose sight of the fact that the Vulgate is, on the whole, a better and more reliable version than is sometimes assumed. There are differences from the Hebrew to be sure, but in general their number is not too great. So far as Psalm 23 is concerned, we do not find many divergences. It is therefore not easy to point to various definite instances that prove beyond the shadow of a doubt that Luther used the Hebrew text accessible to him as his primary source and ultimate authority. Moreover, we must be careful not to measure Luther's knowledge of Hebrew by the standards set by modern critical Hebrew grammars and dictionaries. It is necessary rather to consult contemporary 16th-century works: Reuchlin's famous Hebrew-Latin

Dictionary of 1506 is probably the most important single source of information to which Luther turned especially in the earlier years. This dictionary, epoch-making and authoritative in Luther's day, is naturally a far cry from a modern critical work. Its Latin equivalents for the Hebrew terms are often strongly suggestive of the all-pervasive influence of the Vulgate. Especially its rendering of Yahweh by *dominus* or *deus* is one of the clearest examples of its vain struggle to throw off the shackles of traditional meaning. With these major difficulties besetting Luther's path in his heroic efforts at translating the original text, it is perhaps not too surprising that he should not always have succeeded perfectly. The wonder is really that he did as well as he did from a purely philological point of view.

In Psalm 23 there are at least two cases where the Vulgate departs sufficiently from the Hebrew to allow us to arrive at a rather definite conclusion. These occur in verses one and five. In verse one, Luther's rendering, *meyn hirtte*, would seem to be explicable only on the basis of the Hebrew text. Quite apart from the fairly important matter of *regere* (*dominus regit me*), the use of the noun instead of the traditional verb (Vulgate: *regit. Psalterium iuxta Hebraeos: pascit*) is almost certainly due to the Hebrew original. In verse five, Luther's translation *meyn kilch ist satt* or the alternate phrase *hatt die fulle* could scarcely have been arrived at on the basis of the Vulgate's quite different reading: *Et calix meus inebrians quam praeclarus est.* Jerome's *Psalterium iuxta Hebraeos* cannot be considered a source for Luther either since it is identical with the Vulgate except that it omits the last three words. The fact that the pre-Lutheran German Bibles were based on the Vulgate can be clearly seen from the awkward way in which all but the Pflanzmann redaction translated this passage: *vnd mein kelch der macht truncken wie lauter er ist.*[7]

Leaving behind the difficult problem of Hebrew versus Latin sources let us now turn to our main problem which is to determine not so much what Luther translated from as how he translated. The first draft is a strange mixture of painstakingly literal and astonishingly free renderings. Those parts which were done best in the first draft were retained, without appreciable change, throughout the revisions to come. As a matter of fact, the important revisions that were to follow are in a sense a very successful effort to raise the rest of the psalm to the high level of the verses or phrases especially well rendered from the very start.

We shall first examine those passages which were done literally,

[7] In: *Die erste deutsche Bibel,* ed. W. Kurrelmeyer (Tübingen, 1910), VII, 272.

chiefly in verses two and five. In the second verse, *ynn der wonug des grases* is perhaps the most literally translated phrase. Neither the Greek τόπον nor the Latin *loco* or *pascuis* is as painfully literal as Luther's *wonug*. The claim can scarcely be made that Luther's phrase *ynn der wonug des grases*, indubitably based on the Hebrew, is in any way an artistic rendering. It merely translates, as literally as is humanly possible, the Hebrew words. The parallel phrase, *am wasser gutter ruge*, seems on first sight to be quite similar to *ynn der wonug des grases*. Upon closer inspection, however, it turns out to be rather above the unrelieved literalness of the latter phrase. By virtue of inserting the adjective *gutter*, which is not found in the Hebrew, Greek, or Latin texts, Luther has already departed from the dull literalness of what the text really calls for: *am wasser der ruge*. The felicitous addition of *gutter*, probably suggested by Luther's innate tendency to express himself in good German, is an indication of the peculiar nature of the first stage of the evolution of his translation of the Twenty-third Psalm—its range all the way from utter literalism to superb freedom. *Am wasser gutter ruge*, while still near the bottom of the ladder, is already moving up.

In verse five there is another fairly literal phrase: *meyn kilch ist satt*. It is instantly obvious that Luther was not quite satisfied with this translation. An alternate version appears to have occurred to him almost immediately, and he jotted it down next to his first attempt: *hatt die fulle*. He could not make up his mind at the moment and consequently left both versions in his manuscript, the issue to be decided when he would prepare the printer's copy. This phrase, long familiar to English-speaking readers from the Authorized Version's "my cup runneth over," is by no means easy to render; it is made up, in the Hebrew, of two nouns, "my cup" and "abundance." Luther tried his best to translate them. What emerged is the two phrases mentioned above. Luther himself left the matter open at the time of the first draft. There is a second phrase in verse five which strikes the reader as being glaringly literal: *Du machst meyn heubt fett mit ole*. This is absolutely correct but scarcely aesthetically satisfactory.

Let us now look at the passages that were rendered well and even very well as early as the first draft. Two kinds of good translations are to be distinguished here: those that are literal and yet superb, and those that are clearly free in order to attain literary excellence. The first verse of the psalm is probably the best example of a passage rendered literally and exquisitely at the same time: *Der herr ist meyn hirtte/ myr wirt nichts mangeln*. This is incidentally one of the two verses in the entire psalm which Luther left untouched in the various revisions to which he subjected his translation. What he put down in the first draft remained unaltered even to the extent, rarely found in Luther, that nothing was corrected, added, or deleted within the framework of the first draft itself. There can be no doubt that Luther himself was fully satisfied for once with his handiwork. Perhaps we can best appreciate the superiority of this translation by remembering how the first of the pre-Lutheran German Bibles had rendered the verse: *Der herr der richt mich vnd mir gebrast nit*.[8] Compared with this obvious translation from the Vulgate, Luther's is first of all based on the Hebrew original as we have already observed. From a strictly literary point of view, Luther's employment of the device of alliteration is probably one of the most interesting aspects of this verse:

Der herr ist meyn hirtte,
myr wirt nichts mangeln.

So far as alliteration is concerned, there is another noteworthy instance in the fourth verse: "Deyn stecken vnd stab." This is doubtless Luther's own contribution. The pre-Lutheran German Bibles and other translations of the Psalter do not have it.

Among the best examples of how he achieved excellence by a free rendering are verses three and four. In the third verse there is the line: *er furet mich auff rechtem pfad*. Luther here substitutes an adjectival construction, *auff rechtem pfad*, for what would be literally *Pfad der Gerechtigkeit*. In verse four he follows the same technique: *Vnd ob ich schon wandert ym finstern tal*. The phrase, *ym finstern tal*, for the literal *im Tal der Finsternis* corresponds in structure exactly to *auff rechtem pfad*. It is hard to conceive of a translation of these phrases reading more like an original German composition. They are thoroughly and delightfully idiomatic.

The first draft of Luther's translation of the Twenty-third Psalm is a highly interesting product. It is clearly the work of a master translator passionately concerned with rendering his text correctly and idiomatically at the same time. While trying to the best of his ability to base his translation on the original, he endeavors to use the best natural German he can muster. The first draft as a whole is full of promise. There are great possibilities in it, some of them already actualized. As it stands, it is a curious combination of painfully literal and superbly idiomatic passages. It is anything but a finished product, but the partial perfection it has already attained assures the reader that greater things are to follow.

[8]Ibid.

Luther, an indefatigable worker on his translation of the Bible, did not turn the first draft that we have just examined over to the printer. Before doing so, he went over his manuscript with a fine comb and made, in red ink, a number of significant changes. We shall single out the most important ones for special consideration. In order to see the printer's copy as a further stage in the evolution of Luther's translation, it seems best to reproduce it here in its entirety.

The Printer's Copy

Der herr ist meyn hirtte
myr wirt nichts mangeln
Er lesst mich weyden da viel gras steht
vnd furet mich ans zum wasser das mich erquickt erkület[9]
Er erquickt meyne seele
er furet mich auff rechter strasse vmb seyns namens willen
Vnd ob ich schon wandert ym finstern tal.
furcht ich keyn vngluck denn du bist bey myr
deyn stecken vnd stab trosten mich
Du bereyttest fur myr eynen tisch gegen meyne feynde
Du machst meyn heubt fett mit ole/vnd schenckest myr voll eyn
Gutts vnd barmhertzickeyt werden myr nach lauffen meyn leben lang
vnd werde bleyben ym hause des herrn die lenge.[10]

So far as individual passages are concerned, it appears that in the second verse Luther was no longer satisfied with the first-draft phrases *ynn der wonug des grases* and *am wasser gutter ruge*, of both of which we were critical when discussing the first draft. In the printer's copy he crossed them out and replaced them by two relative clauses; *ynn der wonug des grases* became *da viel gras steht*, and *am wasser gutter ruge* emerged as *zum wasser das mich erkület* via the interesting intermediary *ans wasser das mich erquickt*. The new relative-clause formulations are definitely superior to the old literal and semiliteral genitival constructions. They are both imaginative and highly idiomatic. In the third verse Luther removed *er keret widder meyne seele,* replacing the basic phrase *keret widder* by the delightful word *erquickt*. This decided improvement on the first draft was probably suggested to Luther by the changes he had just made in the preceding verse, especially by the

---

[9] *Ans* and *erquickt* are crossed out in red ink.
[10] See footnote 2 above.

phrase *zum wasser das mich erkület.* The new word *erquickt* is most apt in this context. A still more interesting change occurred in the fifth verse. In the first draft Luther had put down alternate renderings: *meyn kilch ist satt* and *hatt die fulle.* Both of them he now eliminates and substitutes for them the magnificent phrase *vnd schenckest myr voll eyn,* long since quite familiar to all acquainted with the Lutheran Bible. This new rendering is superb for at least two reasons. First and quite obviously, the phrase as such is excellent idiomatic German. The image of filling the cup to the brim is splendid. Secondly, Luther changed the construction of the whole line by ingeniously turning the second half into a sentence of the same basic structure as the first half. Instead of having as heretofore two different subjects, *du* and *meyn kilch,* and consequently two different verb forms, Luther now has but one subject, *du,* for the two halves of the line and therefore both verbs in the second person: *Du machst meyn heubt fett . . . vnd schenckest myr voll eyn.* The result of this syntactical change is the felicitously formulated line we now have.

The printer's copy has seen the elimination of the more awkward phrases of the first draft. It has become in the process of this revision a definitely superior version. Though it is not yet fully representative of the highest flowering of Luther's literary genius, it is assuredly far along on the road toward that final goal. The printer's copy is unquestionably better than the good version of the first draft, but it is not yet the finished masterpiece that was to emerge a few years later.

The actual text of the editions that appeared in 1524 was practically identical with the copy Luther had sent to the printer. Only one change was made. In verse six the second expression of time had undergone an interesting development. The first draft had *so lange zeyt,* and the printer's copy read *die lenge.* Neither is really very good, though neither is a literal translation; literally rendered, the verse would be *alle Tage meines Lebens.* In the printed editions of 1524 a much better rendering is found: *ymmerdar.* This is the only change I have been able to discover between the printer's copy and the earliest printed text.

The revision of the Psalter in 1528 left the Twenty-third Psalm completely unchanged. It seems that Luther was sufficiently content with what he had produced so far to allow it to be reprinted in the form of 1524. At any rate he had nothing better to offer in 1528.

It was only in connection with the thorough revision of the entire Psalter in 1531 that Luther's rendering of Psalm 23 received its final shape, which has indelibly impressed itself upon all who have ever used the German Bible. We shall again confine our remarks to the most important changes. These occur, in my opinion, in verses two and five.

In the second verse, on the proper translation of which Luther had already expended so much fruitful labor, he now came forward with alterations that are noteworthy in every respect. The two phrases *da viel gras steht* and *zum wasser das mich erkület* are abandoned in favor of adjectival constructions of great beauty and captivating simplicity; *da viel gras steht* is replaced by *auff einer grünen awen*, and *zum wasser das mich erkület* yields to *zum frisschen wasser*. Both are incomparable not only by the criterion of simple, idiomatic German but also because they merge so beautifully with the other adjectival phrases dating back to the first draft or the printer's copy—*auff rechter strasse* and *ym finstern tal*. These superb phrases, arrived at so astonishingly early, are now joined by the equally superb *auff einer grünen awen* and *zum frisschen wasser*. In the version of 1531 a perfect concinnity of all these phrases has been attained.

Besides this fundamental improvement of verse two there is another fairly significant change to be recorded for verse five. Here the somewhat crude phrase *Du machst meyn heubt fett mit ole* is surrendered in 1531 for the much more elegant formulation *Du salbest mein heubt mit öle*. Perhaps one more change should be noted, a change along the same line of greater refinement as the substitution of *salbest* for *machst . . . fett*. The sixth verse had read from the first draft through the revision of 1528 as follows: *Gutts vnd barmhertzickeyt werden myr nach lauffen*. The verb *nach lauffen* is finally dropped in 1531 in favor of the much simpler and more subdued *folgen*. This means that it, too, is brought into line with the prevailing elevated tone characteristic of the version of 1531 as a whole.

Luther's translation of the Twenty-third Psalm is, in the final version of 1531, a consummate work of art. Though it is and remains but a translation of course, it was artistically reborn in the gradual process of its complete vernacularization. It is still similar to, but no longer wholly identical with, the original Hebrew poem, the Twenty-third Psalm. One could hold that it has become a German poem of almost independent artistic significance. The least one can claim for it is that it is integrally "new," having a structure of its own which is perhaps not inferior to that of the marvelous original. The final product of Luther's long struggle to find an adequate German garb for this great psalm is somehow beyond the limits of even creative translation. It is somewhere in the borderland between creative translation and "original" composition. Whatever it is ultimately adjudged to be, it is clearly a work of art of high order. This is how it appeared in the German Psalter of 1531:

DEr HERR ist mein hirte/mir
wird nichts mangeln.
Er weidet mich auff einer grünen awen/vnd füret mich
zum frisschen wasser.
Er erquicket meine seele/er
füret mich auff rechter strasse/vmb seines
namens willen.
Und ob ich schon wandert im finstern tal/
fürchte ich kein vnglück/Denn du bist bey
mir/Dein stecken vnd stab trösten mich.
Du bereitest fur mir einen tisch gegen meine
feinde/Du salbest mein heubt mit öle/
vnd schenckest mir vol ein./
Gutes vnd barmhertzigkeit werden mir
folgen mein leben lang/vnd werde bleiben im hause des HERRN imer dar.[11]

[11]From a copy in the Library of the Hartford Seminary Foundation. In the original, all umlauts are expressed by a tiny *e* over the *u* and *o*.

PART II. INTERPRETING THE TRANSLATOR'S TASK

Chapter 5

Responsible Freedom: The New German Psalter

WHEN Luther published his thoroughly revised version of the Psalter in 1531 he saw fit to append a brief but important postface in which he stated simply and boldly that this was a free rendering. By this clear and unequivocal announcement Luther tried to forestall the attacks on his translation which he knew were only too likely to be forthcoming.

He had been in the public eye as a translator for almost a decade, since 1522 to be exact. His work had been enthusiastically received in the Reformation camp and severely criticized by the opposition. The attacks had been so bitter that Luther finally decided to defend himself in his *Sendbrief vom Dolmetschen* of 1530, long since become one of the best-known of his vernacular popular writings. Here he had recorded the main principles which had been guiding him in the performance of his arduous task. The *Sendbrief* revolves around Luther's extraordinary rendering of Rom. 3:28, with a few other examples, chiefly from the New Testament, as further illustrations of the procedures followed by the eminent translator.

The *Sendbrief* was written and published several months before Luther began work on the most thoroughgoing revision he ever undertook of an important book of the Bible. This was the great edition of the German Psalter of 1531, the preparation of which occupied Luther and his learned Wittenberg and Leipzig colleagues for the first three or four months of the year. The student of this incomparable version of the Psalter soon realizes that the principles of translation laid down in the only slightly earlier *Sendbrief* still apply by and large to the Psalter of 1531. In fact, this epoch-making edition cannot be fully appreciated without some understanding of the principles announced in the *Sendbrief*. But the *Sendbrief* had been written in connection with Emser's attack on Luther's *New* Testament. Now the New Testament had not yet been rendered by Luther with the breathtaking degree of freedom with which he moved in the 1531 edition of the Psalms. Not until much later was he to render the New Testament with anything like the freedom shown in this Psalter; only in the last years of his life, from around 1544 on, did he undertake a radical revision of some of the major Pauline Epistles. By 1530, the year of the *Sendbrief*, he had not yet made bold to embark on such a venture.

But what he was not to do for the New Testament until 1544, and then only partially, he did for the Psalter, in its entirety, as early as 1531. This revision was so startling that even Luther felt it required a special explanation beyond what he had already written in defense of his New Testament. He therefore provided a restatement and even an extension of the general principles first systematized in the *Sendbrief* of the preceding year.

Instead of waiting for the attack of his opponents to descend upon him, Luther took the offensive this time and appended two significant announcements to his new, astonishing version of the Psalter. He first told his readers that this Psalter represented a new stage in his art of translation. In addition to this brief characterization of his new enterprise he promised to give in a forthcoming publication a more detailed presentation of the principles underlying his Psalter. I shall examine in this essay both the short postface to the 1531 German Psalter and the longer statement of principles in the book referred to in the postface, *Ursachen des Dolmetschens*.

Let us first turn to the important postface with its preliminary proclamation of the translator's stand. Luther states bluntly that this Psalter is in no way a literal translation. In the face of the critical avalanche he fully expects to fall upon him, he takes pains to point out that the freedom of the new Psalter is quite intentional: "wir habens wissentlich gethan."[1] The unusual liberties he has allowed himself are bound to cause concern. Luther, fully realizing this, insists that he and his fellow scholars approached and carried out their self-appointed task with a high degree of responsibility and with all the care of which they were capable, singly and jointly: ". . . wir haben . . . freilich alle wort auff der gold wage gehalten, vnd mit allem vleis vnd trewen verdeudschet."[2]

Following this straightforward announcement of the nature of the rendering contained in the edition of 1531, Luther makes another statement which must have aroused almost as much comment as the preceding words. The new Psalter is not to displace his older translations altogether. The older translations, chiefly the first edition of 1524 and the revised edition of 1528, are not to vanish completely.

Only in the case of the Psalter did Luther advocate the retention of

[1] WA, *Deutsche Bibel* 10¹, 590.   [2] Loc. cit.

an older version once a new or at least greatly revised version had been put out and made generally available. The fact is that Luther spent rather more time and energy on the Psalter than on any other book of the Bible. The version of 1531 represents a stage of translation not attained in the bulk of the Scriptures. The Psalter of 1531 thus occupies a special place. The Psalters of 1524 and 1528 are more nearly comparable to the level of the translation of the Bible as a whole. It is largely for this reason that Luther can seriously suggest that his previous versions of the Psalter be retained. If we bear in mind that these are both major achievements on the high plane of his German Bible at large, we shall not be surprised at what would ordinarily have to be considered a strange suggestion indeed.

Now Luther does not of course give an equal rating to the old and new versions. The new version of 1531 he regards as definitely superior without any doubt. But it represents such a startling departure—even for him—from his usual methods of translation that he is quite willing to have the older versions around, for a while at any rate. In fact, Luther has a special function in mind for the older versions. They are to show his critics, friendly and otherwise, how the Psalter of 1531 has evolved. Luther may have felt that the new Psalter, taken by itself, would seem surprisingly free. It goes without saying that he is proud of the new work; it represents, he is convinced, his best achievement thus far. There has been nothing like it in the long history of the translation of the Bible. Neither the Septuagint nor the Vulgate can in any way be considered a precursor. That is why Luther is not averse to preserving his translations of 1524 and 1528. By comparing these with the new Psalter, the more discerning of his readers will be enabled to grasp the extraordinary significance of the undertaking. They will be in a position to trace the gradual evolution of the Psalter of 1531: "Doch lassen wir vnsern vorigen deudschen Psalter auch bleiben, umb der willen, so da begehren zu sehen, vnser Exempel und fustapffen, wie man mit Dolmetschen neher vnd neher kompt."[3] Luther himself sums up the essential difference between the earlier and the new edition: "der vorige deudsche Psalter, ist an vielen orten dem Ebreischen neher, vnd dem deudschen ferner, Dieser ist dem deudschen neher und dem Ebreischen ferner."[4] Luther adds that he will treat of these matters at greater length in a forthcoming publication: "Dauon weiter (ob Gott wil) jnn den Summarien." It is to this work that we now turn.

In contrast to the famous *Sendbrief* of 1530, *Summarien über die Psalmen und Ursachen des Dolmetschens*[5] (henceforth referred to as

[3]Loc. cit.   [4]Loc. cit.   [5]1532. WA 38, 9-69.

Ursachen) is rather more systematic and subdued in tone. The crisis which called forth *Ursachen* was far less acute than had been the case for the *Sendbrief*. Nobody had plagiarized Luther's Psalter in the way that Emser had appropriated his New Testament. All Luther is doing in *Ursachen* is to give an account of why he had translated the Psalter as he did. Moreover, *Ursachen* discusses more than twice as many examples as does the *Sendbrief*.

Ursachen was probably written in as much of a hurry, if not in the same white heat of passion, as the *Sendbrief*. It has all the earmarks of a typical Luther publication in the vernacular. It is vivid, picturesque, to the point, absorbingly interesting; there is never a dull moment in its pages. What it lacks is careful organization. It was apparently not written on the basis of an outline. The reader feels that it just grew. Luther obviously had plenty of exciting ideas, but he did not take the trouble to arrange them beforehand. One can easily visualize the author, filled with ideas, sitting at his desk and just writing them down as they came to him.

Luther apparently chose his examples quite arbitrarily. They are in no way the best he could have found. He simply put down those he could remember without looking at his own copy of the new Psalter. His readers of today might well wish he had given us a more closely organized treatise. In the absence of that we must make the best of what we have—an informal discussion, with a number of illustrations, of the special nature of the new version.

Let us concentrate on what we might call Luther's general *defense* of his rendering. What are the principles at the bottom of the new Psalter? We have to cull them from the entire body of the essay.

Luther begins by declaring that he and his colleagues have just finished ("umb diese Ostern des 1531. jars"[6]) revising the German Psalter. The revision must have been both thorough and satisfactory because Luther adds that this is the final "improvement" he has in mind and that he contemplates no further change in the future. This was an essentially correct prediction, for the differences between this Psalter of 1531 and that contained in the Bibles of 1545 and 1546 are few and minor. What he has to say on translation at this time comes from a man who has just completed the most exhaustive revision to which he ever subjected any section of the Bible, a task that was both arduous and, in his opinion at least, quite successful. Luther the theorist enlarges upon what he has recently practiced. Theory and practice go hand in hand in his case. The theory comes from the fullness of

[6] WA 38, 9.

rich experience in actual translating, and the practice was performed by a man able and willing to formulate the principles underlying his distinguished translation. What Luther has to say at this time and in this place is said in the flush of realized achievement and victory.

Luther starts out with a major reservation. He states flatly that he is not interested in the reaction of his opponents to his new Psalter. The opinion of "meister klügling"[7] does not concern him, he insists. He is not writing this particular essay for the man in the street either. True, the unlettered Christians who constitute the main body of Luther's readers have put their stamp of approval upon Luther's translation by buying it in large numbers. Luther's rendering has manifestly pleased them, and they have used it very widely ever since the New Testament was first published, on September 21, 1522. There can be no question about the enthusiastic reception of Luther's German Bible among the people at large. But the people do not have the learning to pass upon its scholarly merits. The common man, for whom Luther has such a high regard, is ruled out simply because he is not scholarly enough to benefit from the discussion. Luther respects the common man enough to put his magnificent Bible into his hands. But when it comes to giving an account of the nature of his translation, he can and does address himself only to men of sufficient linguistic equipment to follow his argument intelligently.

However, Luther is writing not merely for the men of his own immediate generation. Though he clearly has these men in mind, he is thinking even more of future generations, who, he implies, will still be using his German Bible. All these people, whether of his own or of later generations, may quite understandably wonder about his unusual manner of translating. It is these educated people whom he wishes to help by providing them with something like a key to his translation. In the nature of the case, Luther's audience is restricted to such as are, in his own words, "der sprachen kündig."[8] Upon close examination of his translation, linguistically qualified readers now and in the future are bound to question Luther's procedure in translating. Luther in fact uses a much stronger expression than questioning. The words he deliberately employs are "sich stossen und ergern."

Luther fully recognizes that there are other expert linguists besides himself. What he fears is that these men may very well be inexperienced and incompetent translators: "der sprachen kündig und doch des dolmetschens ungeübt."[9] He is conscious of his status as a master translator, and it is on this score that Luther feels a distinct superiority.

[7] Loc. cit.   [8] Loc. cit.   [9] Loc. cit.

Knowledge of the sacred languages alone does not suffice, though it is a prerequisite. But equally indispensable is the ability to express in the vernacular the meaning of the material to be translated. Learning the necessary languages is a more or less scientific process, attainable by almost anybody of sufficient intelligence. But to render a passage adequately in another language, even though the passage is well understood, is more of an art. In this essay Luther tries to explain, as far as he can, the artistic process at work in a great translator. It is clear that this artistic process, while present from the beginning of the effort of translating, reaches its height only after the hard and humble work of understanding the text has been done. In other words, art raises its head fully only after "science" has finished its task. It is primarily but not exclusively the artistic process about which Luther proposes to speak. It is the *art* of translating that Luther stresses—an art that should rest on as firm a scientific foundation as the translator may command with the tools at his disposal.

The secret of the real translator is the idea of freedom. Freedom, within reason to be sure, Luther considers the basic and inalienable right as well as the bounden duty of any translator worthy of the name. This at any rate has been one of the major reasons for his own success and for the instantaneous and wide acceptance of his rendering.

Luther says simply that many passages of the new Psalter were rendered very freely: "frey an vilen orten von den buchstaben gangen."[10] On the face of it this might not seem to require such an elaborate defense as Luther feels called upon to provide. It is primarily the *degree* of freedom which needs an explanation. At times his rendering is so free that he surrenders the Hebrew words altogether and merely expresses the meaning of a passage in his own words: "zu weilen allein den sinn gegeben."[11] What Luther wants wholly understood by his learned readers is that these liberties were not taken irresponsibly or irreverently. Above all, they were not taken because he and his colleagues did not know the literal meaning of the text they rendered with such astonishing freedom ("nicht aus unverstand der sprachen").[12] On the contrary, they are thoroughly at home in the original Hebrew, and their free translation was intentional and fully planned: "wir . . . wissentlich und williglich so zu dolmetschen furgenommen haben."[13]

However, freedom is not the only characteristic of the new rendering. Luther also followed another principle—a seemingly quite contradictory one: literalism, even extreme literalism. From time to time Luther kept strictly to the Hebrew words: "zu weilen die wort steif

[10]Loc. cit.　　　[11]WA 38, 17.　　　[12]WA 38, 9.　　　[13]Loc. cit.

behalten."[14] Whenever a fundamental point of theology was involved, Luther insists, he adhered to the text very closely. In order to maintain the full flavor of the original, Luther, to whom German idiomatic expressions meant so much, was willing to surrender the appropriate German idiom and to translate verbatim. What this means is that Luther's highest set of values was not aesthetic or literary but definitely and unalterably theological and religious.

Yet the places where there was a clash between theology and art are relatively few. It did not too often happen that Luther felt constrained to sacrifice the genius of the German language to theological criteria. But it is important to bear in mind that the great translator, the unsurpassed master of the German language, made it abundantly clear that his ultimate standards were theological and religious. To these considerations his final allegiance was due. However, by and large he did not have to appeal to these ultimate commitments, for most of the Bible could, without sacrifice of content, be rendered in a totally different idiom and within the reasonable limits of the other language. In general, though there are notable exceptions to be sure, Luther's basic principle holds throughout, that the Jews of old must be made to deliver their message in as idiomatic German as possible. That is why Luther's Bible is so thoroughly German in language and expressions.

Luther is far from insisting that his rendering is free from mistakes. It is impossible, he says, to avoid all errors. What he objects to is that some of his critics have played up the few mistakes to the exclusion of everything else. Luther is plainly angry at critics who have no word of recognition for a job well done on the whole and who single out a few errors. If these men were at least respectable translators in their own right, Luther would be far less incensed than he is. He admits that he has made mistakes, but he suggests that he might be given some credit for having produced a rendering which is by and large a good piece of work.

Luther wonders why he alone should be attacked so bitterly for occasional mistakes. He asserts that the Septuagint and Vulgate Psalters, Jerome's *Psalterium iuxta Hebraeos*, and other translations of the Psalters into Latin contain many more mistakes than his: "aus der massen viel mehr gefeilet . . . denn wir."[15] The same critics who have been very hard on him ("gifftig und unbarmhertzig")[16] have shown themselves considerate ("geduldig und gütig")[17] toward other translators.

[14] WA 38, 17.   [15] WA 38, 16.
[16] Loc. cit.   [17] Loc. cit.

Luther's chief grievance is this. Contemporary critics are exceedingly easy on the pre-Lutheran versions with their many mistakes, and excessively severe on his version, which is a superior piece of work. Luther does not expect that his strong remonstrance against his critics will do any good. But he appeals to history and states confidently that time will work for him and show the value and superiority of his own version. There is a strong feeling in Luther that he has given the world a rendering of the Psalter better than all previous versions. It is important to add that Luther does not even mention earlier translations into German. He is aware that his own German Psalter stands in a far larger, in an international, tradition; the German Psalter is a greater achievement than the Septuagint, Vulgate, and final Jerome versions. This is a proud but justified statement.

Chapter 6

The Original's Intent and the Modern Idiom

a. "ALLEIN DURCH DEN GLAUBEN"

MANY passages in Luther's German Bible called forth the ire of his opponents, but perhaps none more than his translation of Rom. 3 : 28: "So halten wyrs nu, das der mensch gerechtfertiget werde, on zu thun der werck des gesetzs, alleyn durch den glawben"[1] (1522 to 1527[1], except that in 1526[2] "wyrs" was changed to "wir es"). In the major revision of 1530[1] this famous verse received its final Lutheran form: "So halten wir es nu, Das der Mensch gerecht werde, on des Gesetzes werck, alleine durch den Glauben."[2]

The attacks on Luther's rendering of this passage assumed such violence that even some of his friends were made uneasy. They had no ready answer when confronted with the plain fact that the word "alleyn" does not occur in the Greek text, not to speak of the Vulgate at all. It was for the benefit and enlightenment of his friends rather than as an answer to his foes[3] primarily that Luther undertook in 1530 to explain and defend his extraordinary and astonishing translation, in the famed *Sendbrief vom Dolmetschen,* a vigorous and spirited, even boisterous piece, the very tone of it expressive of the immense and irrepressible superiority the true *defensor fidei* felt over his detractors and enemies.

Luther was fully aware of the pivotal position occupied by this single verse in the bitter controversy in which he was engaged. He begins and ends the main body of the *Sendbrief* with discussions of this key verse. Although four other examples of how to translate properly are introduced for illustrative purposes, they clearly play a more or less subordinate role in the economy of the whole essay. After dealing with them parenthetically as it were, he reverts to the core of it all, Rom. 3 : 28. The analysis of this basic verse takes up almost twice as much space, 140 lines to be exact, as the other four passages together with their 84 lines. It is Rom. 3 : 28 around which the essay really revolves, no matter how interesting and even exciting the other verses may be and actually are in their own right.

[1] WA, *Deutsche Bibel* 7, 38.   [2] Ibid., 39.   [3] WA 30[2], 635-636.

Without a formal introduction, Luther begins *in mediis rebus*. He states simply enough that he will give an account of the reasons that prompted him to render Rom. 3 : 28 as he did. As one would expect, he starts out by quoting the verse. What is surprising, however, is that he does not quote it in the original Greek. This fact has always been disappointing to scholarly readers of this great treatise. Whatever the reasons may have been, whether hurried composition or the practical purpose of the essay, or both, one cannot help wishing that Luther had seen fit to quote so important a verse in the original, all the more because the essay, though the common man looms large in it, is nevertheless scarcely addressed to the man in the street but rather to the learned. It is true of course that a knowledge of Greek was still comparatively rare, and Luther may have thought it useless to refer to the Greek original. Whatever the ultimate reason or reasons, the fact remains that he is content to quote the verse in Latin only.

The Latin text he cites raises new problems in itself: *Arbitramur hominem iustificari ex fide absque operibus*. This is not the Vulgate text. According to the authoritative edition of Wordsworth and White this reads as follows: *Arbitramur enim iustificari hominem per fidem sine operibus legis*. Two variants are recorded by Wordsworth and White—the omission of *enim* and the substitution of *fide* for *per fidem*. While these do not fully account for Luther's version, they offer some help. If we turn to the new Latin translation which Erasmus furnished along with the Greek text in his edition of the New Testament, we receive more help, especially on one major point. Erasmus' Latin version of this verse, which remained unchanged throughout all five editions of 1516, 1519, 1522, 1527, and 1535, reads as follows: *Arbitramur igitur fide iustificari hominem absque operibus legis*. It is probably to Erasmus that Luther is indebted for his own *absque*. There can be little doubt why Erasmus replaced the Vulgate's *sine* by *absque—absque* is stronger than *sine*. He tried to express by *absque* the basic meaning of the Greek χωρίς. It is interesting to note in this connection that the Revised Version of the King James Bible replaced the original edition's "without" by "apart from."

Luther's quotation of Rom. 3 : 28 is apparently not taken from any single source. As a matter of fact, it is not even the whole text of the verse. Luther has stripped the verse of all nonessentials, keeping only the most important words. Thus *enim* or *igitur* and even *legis* fall by the wayside. What is left is the irreducible structure of the verse, its basic meaning remaining intact. It is even brought out more effectively and vigorously than in the Vulgate. Luther's quotation, for all its condensation, or perhaps just because of it, expresses the fundamental meaning of the original. The quotation is in fact inconceivable without Luther's awareness of the Greek original, whether acquired directly or indirectly with the aid of Erasmus' new Latin rendering. What is really important is that Luther's quotation, albeit in Latin, goes beyond the Vulgate and fully catches the spirit and intent of the original. It is an independent, personal rendering, probably made on the spur of the moment, jotted down as he was composing the essay, without looking up either the Greek text or Erasmus' Latin translation or even the Vulgate for that matter. This procedure is in no way surprising to anyone acquainted with his method or, better, manner of quoting from the Bible. Constantly living and moving in the Scriptures as he was, he had the habit of quoting from memory. His memory was a rich storehouse of the verses that had affected him deeply. Few verses, it almost goes without saying, had stirred him more profoundly than Rom. 3 : 28. He had appropriated this great verse with all his mind and heart.

The Latin quotation of St. Paul's text in the *Sendbrief* is followed by the German translation which had been so vitriolically attacked and which Luther proposes to defend to the death in this essay: "Wir halten, das der mensch gerecht werde on des gesetzs werck, allein durch den glauben." It will be noted that the introductory phrase is somewhat abbreviated from his final official version. The principal section of the verse, however, agrees fully, except for orthography and punctuation, with his formal translation from 1530 on. The *Sendbrief* quotation is thus a slightly simplified text. This he sets out to uphold with every argument at his disposal.

The assault of his opponents is centered, according to Luther's own presentation of the case, on the word *allein*, which is not found in St. Paul's text: "und sey solcher zusatz von mir nicht zu leiden ynn gottes wortenn."[4] The enemy is utterly unwilling to tolerate such unwarranted addition to the words of God, Luther says with perceptible irony.

Before proceeding to a detailed defense of his rendering, Luther makes an important general statement about the spirit in which he undertook the tremendous task of the translation of the Bible into the vernacular. He insists he did his very best, always guided by his Christian conscience: ". . . das ich das Newe Testament verdeutscht habe, auff mein bestes vermügen und auff mein gewissen."[5] Luther readily admits the possibility of occasional error though he suggests he is not aware of any at this time. It would trouble him deeply if he could be justly accused of willful falsification of a single letter of the

[4]Ibid., 633.   [5]Loc. cit.

text: "und freilich ungern einen buchstaben mütwilliglich wolt unrech verdolmetschen."[6] Among the basic qualifications of a good translato: he singles out sound learning and great industry, always undergirded by reason and understanding: "was fur kunst, fleisz, vernunft, verstand zum gutten dolmetscher gehöret."[7] Without saying so specifically Luther implies strongly that he possesses these prerequisites in no small measure. It is only after these general observations on the char acter of his translation as a whole and on what it takes to be a good translator that Luther is ready to embark on a full discussion of his rendering of Rom. 3 : 28.

He begins by asserting that his translation has not been read very closely. In this particular passage, which has called forth such an up roar, he protests vigorously that he did not even use the word *sola* as he had been accused of doing. The phrase under attack, "allein durch den glauben," is not, he insists, a translation of *sola fide*, as appears to be the common interpretation or rather misinterpretation. Luther main tains he did not use an adjective in this instance but an adverb. He did not say *sola* but "solum odder tantum."[8] In other words, *allein* is not an adjective modifying *glaube* but really an adverb, the equivalen of *nur*.

After this basic clarification of the grammatical nature of the word *allein* in this connection Luther freely admits that the word *solum* does not occur in the Latin and Greek texts: "Also habe ich Roma. 3 fast wol gewist, das ym Lateinischen und krigischen text das wor 'solum' nicht stehet."[9] But while it is perfectly true that the word itself is not there, he asserts that the idea is implicit in the fundamenta meaning of Paul's text.

This is a highly significant statement. It is tantamount to saying that Luther the translator cannot be divorced from Luther the exegete and interpreter. He had achieved eminence as an exegete years before he undertook, or was persuaded to undertake, the translation of the Bible into German. It so happens that one of his earliest lecture courses at the University of Wittenberg had been on Romans. This was in its way almost as remarkable an accomplishment as the translation of the New Testament. Thus when Luther was ready to translate the Epistle to the Romans he did so on the basis of an intimate knowledge of the text and of an impressive portion of the history of its interpretation Besides, he somehow identified himself more with Paul than with any other New Testament author. There is an almost incredible spiritual and intellectual affinity between the two men.

[6]Loc. cit.　　　[7]Loc. cit.　　　[8]WA 30^2, 636.　　　[9]Loc. cit.

After speaking briefly as an experienced and successful exegete on the meaning of Rom. 3 : 28, he reemphasized some of the basic principles that guided him as a translator. One has the feeling that Luther the translator set out to rival Luther the interpreter. Once he had fully made up his mind to translate the Scriptures as a whole, he followed quite definite rules of procedure. He states as one of his principal goals the achievement of idiomatic and clear German: "Ich hab mich des geflissen ym dolmetzschen, das ich rein und klar teutsch geben möchte."[10]

When in the course of his translation he came upon so central a verse as Rom. 3 : 28, of the basic meaning of which he was perfectly sure, he naturally strained every nerve to put it into intelligible German. The translator in him was not willing to be outdone by the interpreter. The question before him was simply how to express in the best and most adequate manner, in his own native tongue, the full meaning of Paul's Greek phrase. In accordance with his principles of translation, Luther, after establishing the essential meaning of his text, proceeded to render it in the best German he was capable of writing. And the best German, he maintained, required the insertion of *allein:* "wo mans wil klar und gewaltiglich verteutschen, so gehoret es hinein."[11] It is Luther's contention that German can and does use *allein* when two statements are made, one of which is put in the affirmative and the other in the negative. He gives three striking examples and maintains that countless others are in daily use.

It is important to bear in mind that Luther does not assert that *allein* is *absolutely* necessary. It is possible to omit it. One may of course say in German "Der Baur bringt korn und kein geld" instead of "Der Baur bringt allein korn und kein geldt," meaning "Nein, ich hab warlich ytzt nicht geldt, sondern allein korn."[12] The other examples are: "Ich hab allein gessen und noch nicht getruncken. Hastu allein geschrieben und nicht uberlesen?"[13]

All that this greatest master of the German language maintains is that the inclusion of *allein* makes a statement of this type "volliger und deutlicher." He for one prefers what he calls "ein vollige Deutsche klare rede" to something that, to him, is "nicht so vollig und deutlich."[14] Thus it is not a matter of absolute right and absolute wrong, but rather of a clearer expression versus a less clear one.

Such argument inevitably leads to the question of who decides what is the best German. What is the criterion? For Luther there was no

[10] Loc. cit. [11] WA 30², 637. [12] Loc. cit.
[13] Loc. cit. [14] Loc. cit.

doubt about where the living language is to be found: in the house and in the marketplace. The language of daily life, as used by the common man unspoiled by Latin idiom, is the yardstick by which Luther measures real, natural German. Whatever other scholars may do and believe, he has, linguistically speaking, cast his lot with "die mutter jhm hause," . . . "die kinder auf der gassen, den gemeinen man auff dem marckt."[15] It is their language he listens to, it is their mouths he watches in order to determine the nature of truly idiomatic German. If a translation of the Bible is to reach the people, it must be couched in their language. Since his translation was most definitely made for the people, Luther did his utmost to put it in the language they used in their everyday life. Thus the ultimate *linguistic* reason for the addition of the controversial word *allein* is that in his considered opinion and judgment it corresponds to the way in which the ordinary man speaks. The full impact of the passage is greater, its full meaning becomes clearer if *allein* is inserted. That is the real issue so far as Luther is concerned. He thought it was his task to make the Word of God as readily understandable as he could to the masses. That's why he translated as he did.

Luther's procedure as a translator is clear. First he establishes, to the best of his ability and upon his conscience, the meaning of the text before him. Then he tries hard to find the most suitable, idiomatic German garb for it. This is the order in which he works. Luther takes great pains to point this out again and again. He is convinced that his translation does not take undue liberties with the text. The text is king, the translation only a humble but faithful handmaiden bent upon serving her master. But this handmaiden insists on the privilege of talking in her own idiom, "wie ihr der Schnabel gewachsen ist."

There are definite limits to the freedom with which a translator may move. If the original text contains a word or phrase which would lose its essential religious meaning should too familiar a German expression be used, the flavor of the original Greek should be retained even if the resulting German does not fully measure up to the requirements of the German idiom: "wo etwas an einem ort gelegenn ist, hab ichs nach den buchstaben behalten."[16] In other words, language must never interfere with meaning: "ich hab ehe wöllen der deutschen sprache abbrechen, denn von dem wort weichen."[17] It is very important to stress this major reservation Luther is making. The liberties which he allows himself do not, in his opinion, exceed a well-defined range. Luther insists that he is a responsible translator: "Das kan ich mit

[15] Loc. cit.   [16] WA 30², 640.   [17] Loc. cit.

gutem Gewissen zeugen, das ich mein höchste trew und fleisz drinnen erzeigt, und nye kein falsche gedanken gehabt habe."[18]

It is in the light of these sober remarks and reflections that Luther's insertion of *allein* must be seen. This addition to the text of Rom. 3 : 28 is not the act of an irresponsible translator, Luther protests emphatically. He takes great pains to point out in detail that Paul's meaning and German usage together practically clamor for the translation he has provided.

In accordance with his own principle that a translation must in no way tamper with the text, Luther shows that he merely expressed, in the best German at his disposal, the intention of the original author. He contends that whoever wishes to make Paul's full meaning perfectly clear in German cannot but say "allein der glaube."[19] Luther regards this translation as really inevitable: "das zwinget die sache selbs neben der sprachen art."[20] The very substance of Paul's thought is at stake. Luther leaves no doubt that he believes he has penetrated to the very core of Paul's teaching. In impassioned language he bursts out: "Es mus . . . allein der ewige glaube ym hertzen sein, der selbige allein, ja gar allein. . . ."[21] If this is indeed the heart of Paul's message, Luther sees no reason why one should not express this in adequate German: "Warumb soll man denn nicht auch also reden?"[22] Fervently he exclaims that it is not heresy to announce in unmistakable form that it is faith alone which takes hold of Christ. He states emphatically that he is neither the only one nor the first to say that faith alone justifies man before God. Proudly he asserts that he has distinguished predecessors in this understanding of Paul's central message; St. Ambrose, St. Augustine, and many others hold this view, according to Luther.[23] One wishes that he had mentioned the "vil andere" by name. It is perhaps not superfluous to bear in mind that the foremost contemporary Roman Catholic student of Luther and the Reformation, Joseph Lortz, points out in his *Die Reformation in Deutschland* that Thomas Aquinas also maintained that *sola fide* was Paul's ultimate meaning.[24]

The reader cannot escape the impression that Luther is proud and happy that such great authorities as Ambrose and Augustine agree with his interpretation of Paul. But is is also very plain that Luther would not budge from his view even if there were no important predecessors in this matter. By 1530 he is sure he can stand on his own feet against anybody if need be. He has read Paul carefully and pene-

[18]Loc. cit. [19]WA 30^2, 641. [20]Loc. cit.
[21]WA 30^2, 642. [22]Loc. cit. [23]Loc. cit.
[24]3 ed. (Freiburg: Herder, 1949), I, 292.

tratingly, and he is fully convinced that no other interpretation is possible: "wer S. Paulum lesen und verstehen sol, der mus wol so sagen, und kan nit anders. Seine wort sind zu starck, und leiden kein, ja gar kein werck. Ists kein werck, so mus der glaube allein sein."[25] Naturally, Luther is glad he is not alone in this interpretation, but he would still hold his view even if he were all alone. He is not afraid to side with Paul against the whole world.

Since, however, Augustine and many others share his conviction as to the basic meaning of Paul, it is somewhat easier for Luther to state with the greatest emphasis at his disposal that his reading of Paul's mind is in no way heretical: "Es ist nit ketzerey, das der glaube allein . . . das leben gibt."[26] He is glad to be able to point out that there are contemporary scholars in the Church of Rome who also agree with his interpretation: "die sachen bekennen sie fur recht."[27] So far as his translation of Rom. 3:28 is concerned, Luther continues to insist that the insertion of *allein* simply *renders* "klar und gewaltiglich" this Pauline passage *interpreted* by him in the orthodox tradition of Ambrose, Augustine, and many others, including men of his own age who have remained in the Roman Church.

Luther ends his presentation with an excellent summary of the argument:

1. The matter itself—what Paul really meant—demands the translation he made.
2. The nature and usage of the German language call for this rendering.
3. Great fathers of the church have interpreted Paul as he does.

To these three more or less theoretical considerations he adds a fourth, which is perhaps of a more practical kind: There is always the danger that the people at large may not rise to the height of the religion of faith; they are apt to rest content with works and fall short of faith. This great danger, ever present to be sure, has been especially threatening in his own age, "sonderlich zu diser zeit."[28] The religion of works has been preached so long, almost to the exclusion of faith, that it is absolutely necessary to set the time, which is out of joint, right again.

Luther concludes that it is therefore not only theoretically correct but also practically imperative to express as clearly and as fully as possible the fundamental view of Paul on the dominating place of faith in the Christian dispensation. In the white heat of his passionate defense of his translation Luther adds that he is really sorry he did not put the matter still more strongly. What he would actually like to do is

[25] WA 30², 642. [26] WA 30², 642.
[27] Loc cit. [28] WA 30², 643.

to add two more words, which, together with the *allein* already in his rendering, would make it impossible ever again to misunderstand Paul. This is how he would really like to have Rom. 3 : 28 read in German: "Wir halten, das der mensch gerecht werde, on alle werck aller gesetz, allein durch den glauben."[29]

Luther did not see fit to incorporate what is doubtless the boldest rendering of Paul's words ever made, into his official Bible. But he did retain the word *allein* and he announced vigorously that it was to remain in his German New Testament. It has remained thus far. Luther's New Testament, revised by himself many times, has been revised by others repeatedly since his death. But Rom. 3 : 28 has not been altered. It should not be. It is likely to remain as long as Luther's translation will endure. It is woven into its very texture.

After this brief presentation of the principal aspects of Luther's defense of his translation we are ready to examine his position more closely and in greater detail. Let us first look at Luther's claim that the addition of *allein* was inspired by German idiom. The essential question is whether or not the *allein* of this verse is really an adverb as Luther emphatically asserts. Is it really the German equivalent of *solum* or *tantum?* That is the crucial question.

In order to be considered a bona fide adverb, it must, as Luther's argument runs, occur in connection with a negative. All three of Luther's examples illustrating German usage fulfill this basic requirement he makes:
1. "Der Baur bringt allein korn und kein geldt, Nein, ich hab warlich ytzt nicht geldt, sondern allein korn."[30]
2. "Ich hab allein gessen und noch nicht getruncken."[31]
3. "Hastu allein geschrieben und nicht uberlesen?"[32]

In all these cases two things are mentioned, of which one is affirmed and the other negated (". . . ein rede . . . von zweyen dingen, der man eins bekennet, und das ander verneinet").[33] This situation applies in the case of Rom. 3 : 28: "on des gesetzs werck, allein durch den glauben." Luther's contention that the word *allein* in this verse is an adverb is wholly acceptable.

If Luther had added the word *allein* without some word of negation occurring in the same sentence, he could have been accused of willful addition, unwarranted by linguistic usage. It is a matter of record that he did not. The simple fact that he did not add *allein* where it was not required by his own definition of German idiom is a sure indica-

[29]Loc. cit.   [30]WA 30², 637.   [31]Loc. cit.
[32]Loc. cit.   [33]Loc. cit.

tion of the essential soundness of his argument and of the sincerity of his position.

There are two cases in Romans where Luther, had he not lived up to his own principle, might very well have added *allein*. In Rom. 5 : 1 he could have inserted it easily. But he wrote instead: "Nu wyr denn sind rechtfertig worden durch den glawben, so haben wyr fride mit Got." If Luther had added *allein* before *durch den glawben*, he could justly have been accused of an improper insertion. But the word *allein* is conspicuous by its absence. This verse remained intact throughout the several revisions made in the course of the years; the only change, made in 1530, was the substitution of *gerecht* for *rechtfertig*. No *allein* was added at any time, from the first edition of 1522 to the last of 1546. However much Luther may have wished to do so, no linguistic usage of which he was aware could either suggest or permit it. Similarly in Rom. 1 : 17 he could have added *allein* if he had been motivated by other than linguistic reasons. The verse reads as follows in the *Septembertestament*: "Der gerechte wirt leben aus seynem glawben." In the second edition, the *Dezembertestament* of the same year 1522, an interesting change was made, but one that does not affect what concerns us here: "Der gerechte wirt seynes glawbens leben." This rendering, long familiar to all readers of the German Bible, was not changed again by Luther.

If Luther had in any way been reckless about adding *allein*, he certainly could have added it here as well as in the other verse just discussed. He obviously did not for the simple reason that these are two passages containing single affirmative statements on faith. Luther manifestly held himself in check. In Rom. 3 : 28 he had proceeded differently because other linguistic conditions prevailed, conditions which he had argued so eloquently called for the insertion of *allein* in order to produce the best idiomatic German of which he was capable and which he felt it his duty to supply.

Rom. 1 : 17 is of unusual interest in this connection. There are several casual quotations of this verse prior to the *Septembertestament*. In one of these Luther did insert *nur*. In the world-famous treatise *Von der Freyheyt eynisz Christen menschen* of 1520 the following passage occurs: "Wie S.Paulus sagt Ro.1. 'Ein rechtfertiger Christen lebt nur von seynem glauben.'"[34]

We may conclude from this fact that Luther allowed himself a certain latitude in a casual quotation, even if that occurred in an important essay. However, when he undertook the formal and official

[34] WA 7, 23.

translation of the Bible late in 1521, there was a major change in his fundamental approach. He did not take any liberties with the text unless German linguistic usage, as he knew it so extraordinarily well, allowed or even called for some modification. Once he had become something like a designated or even commissioned translator of the Bible into German, he adhered closely to the text, rendering it faithfully and responsibly. Luther's translation of Rom. 1 : 17 is a superb example of his loyalty to his supreme task. The freedom of the casual quotation of Rom. 1 : 17 in 1520 yields to the considered restraint exercised by Luther in the official Bible.

There is one more passage which should be examined carefully. It presents some new and unexpected difficulties. It may even undermine all that Luther has said in his own defense and our own argument as well. Gal. 2 : 16 reads as follows in the *Septembertestament:* "doch weyl wyr wissenn, das der mensch durch die werck des gesetzs, nicht rechtfertig wirt, sondern durch den glawben an Jhesu Christ, so haben wir auch an Jhesum Christ geglewbet, auff das wyr gerechtfertiget werden, durch den glawben an Jhesu Christ, vnd nicht durch die werck des gesetzs . . . ."[35]

This verse underwent a number of changes, resulting in this final form contained in the German Bible of 1546: "Doch weil wir wissen, das der Mensch durch des Gesetzes werck nicht gerecht wird, Sondern durch den Glauben an Jhesum Christ, So gleuben wir auch an Christum Jhesum, Auff das wir gerecht werden durch den glauben an Christum, Vnd nicht durch des Gesetzes werck . . ."[36]

Here we seem to be up against an extraordinary inconsistency on Luther's part. In this passage we expect, perhaps by this time even demand, the addition of *allein*. If Luther ran true to form, the word *allein* prefixed to *durch den Glauben* would appear to be all but inevitable. For did Luther not defend the *allein* of Rom. 3 : 28 in just this way? "Das ist aber die art unser deutschen sprache, wenn sie ein rede begibt, von zweyen dingen, der man eins bekennet, und das ander verneinet, so braucht man des worts 'solum' (allein) neben dem wort 'nicht' oder 'kein' . . . ."[37]

The rules set down by Luther apply fully in the case of Gal. 2 : 16:
1. ". . .wir wissen, das der mensch durch des Gesetzes werck nicht gerecht wird, Sondern durch den Glauben. . . ."
2. "Auff das wir gerecht werden durch den glauben an Christum, vnd nicht durch des Gesetzes werck. . . ."

What explanation can possibly be given for this procedure besides

[35]WA, *Deutsche Bibel* 7, 178.   [36]Ibid., p. 179.   [37]WA 30², 637.

downright inconsistency? Let us frankly admit that there is here a certain degree of inconsistency, though perhaps not nearly so much as seems to be the case on first sight.

It should first of all be remembered that Luther had never claimed that the addition of *allein* was *absolutely* necessary. He had said that it is possible to get along without it. What he had maintained, vigorously enough, to be sure, was that the insertion of *allein* would convert good German into better German. Without *allein* the phrase would not be as "vollig, deutlich, klar"[38] as with it.

But why should Luther in one place (Rom. 3 : 28) insist on what he considered the best possible German and in another place be satisfied with what he would call something less than the best and the clearest? There is at least one good reason for Luther's behavior.

In the structure and economy of the chapter and even the whole epistle, the first passage, Rom. 3 : 28, occupies a place totally different from that of the other passage, Gal. 2 : 16, in its context. Rom. 3 : 28 is the concluding and climactic verse in a whole series of verses. It is the final link in a chain of reasoning. This single verse contains the gist of the matter, it is the grand summary of all that has preceded, even anticipating all that is to follow. Luther himself goes even further than that. In one of his famed marginal notes he calls the entire passage, of which v. 28 is the capstone, "das hewbtstuck vnd der mittel platz diszer Epistel und der gantzen schrifft."[39] That is exactly the reason why he admonished the reader to pay particular attention to this passage. Small wonder then that Luther went out of his way to render this crucial verse in the clearest and strongest way consonant with the genius of the language into which he was translating.

We must ever bear in mind that Luther was deeply stirred by Paul's thought and argument. He was not a detached, unconcerned translator. Moreover, having lectured on Romans and doubtless reflecting on Romans all the time anyway, he was fully aware of the peculiar place of this particular verse in the larger whole of which it was so prominent a part. There is every indication that his every nerve was strained when he was rendering this key passage, this summary of the religious insight of Paul. Extraordinarily profound and sensitive religiously, and marvelously endowed artistically, he reacted spontaneously and magnificently to the power of Paul's presentation and re-created in his own language what he was deeply persuaded was the heart of Paul's message. Luther's version of Rom. 3 : 28 is manifestly the creation of a mind at once aflame with one of the greatest self-

[38] Loc. cit.   [39] WA, *Deutsche Bibel* 7, 38.

revelations of Paul and at the same time wondrously able to express what he felt at the moment of affective reading.

In Gal. 2 : 16, on the other hand, the translator Luther was, for good reason, not so thoroughly stirred as in Rom. 3 : 28. He consequently rendered this passage less powerfully than Rom. 3 : 28. The latter passage, quite understandably and legitimately, moved him much more profoundly and made him produce, of inner religious and artistic necessity, one of the most excitingly rendered lines of the German Bible, possibly the most superb translation or rather rebirth of a key Pauline verse anywhere, in any language.

So far as his defense of this striking rendering is concerned, one should not forget that it is after all only an attempt to account logically, *post eventum* as it were, for an artistic statement born in the white heat of inspiration. The translator's process from within can perhaps never be wholly revealed from without, in logical language, even by the translator himself, be he as articulate as Martin Luther.

In this man interpretation and translation went hand in hand. His interpretation of Rom. 3 : 28 is surely correct. Augustine and Thomas Aquinas interpreted Paul in the same way. Among recent interpreters of Paul's greatest epistle few are more distinguished than Karl Barth. He goes so far as to entitle the entire passage, of which Rom. 3 : 28 is a part, "allein durch den Glauben."[40] There cannot be any reasonable doubt of the essential correctness of Luther's interpretation.

None of the other interpreters mentioned achieved distinction in the field of translation in addition to that of interpretation. Luther alone did. A sound interpreter of Paul, he was also a masterful, unsurpassed translator of Paul. This distinction is still unique. His superb rendering of Rom. 3 : 28 is bound to endure. It is *monumentum aere perennius*. So far it has survived practically four centuries and a half. It is indestructible and impregnable.

As long as Paul is read, Luther's rendering of what he wrote will last. Luther is the translators' translator as he is the theologians' theologian. In sheer mastery of language, he is easily the equal of Jerome. In religious insight, he is at least the equal of Augustine. The wonder of it all is that it takes both a Jerome and an Augustine to equal one Martin Luther, to put it the other way for once. But why underestimate so astonishing a genius as Martin Luther? He is greater than Jerome as an artist and greater than Augustine as a Christian thinker. Far from being an *enfant terrible* as he has all too often been presented, he is *un homme incroyable et prodigieux*.

[40] *Der Römerbrief*, 81.

b. "WES DAS HERZ VOLL IST"

Among the many well-rendered verses of the German Bible few are better known than Matt. 12: 34b: "Wes das hertz voll ist, des geht der mund vbir." This translation has received high praise from virtually all writers on Luther's Bible. In his *Sendbrief vom Dolmetschen* Luther pointed to it as one of the best examples of his method of rendering the Bible in German.

Not only is this verse one of the best-rendered in Luther's Bible, it also has an interesting, even exciting history. This history, however, has not been known very long. As recently as the 20s and 30s of our century it was taken for granted that Luther coined this remarkable phrase himself, establishing it at once on the level of a fully accepted proverb. Archer Taylor, one of the foremost living authorities on the proverb, asserted in 1931 that Luther is the father of this saying: "Occasionally we trace the origin of a Biblical proverb to a single version. Thus Luther translated 'Ex abundantia cordis os loquitur' . . . as 'Wes das hertz voll ist, des geht der mund vbir.' . . . Luther's form drove out the others . . . which were struggling to establish themselves. . . . There is . . . no question that Luther's version has fixed itself in tradition."[1] Georg Büchmann's *Geflügelte Worte* implied, as late as the 27th edition of 1926, that Luther was the creator of this excellent rendering: ". . . von Luther volkstümlich gefasst . . ." (p. 49). In the light of Taylor's and Büchmann's pronouncements it is not too surprising that Karl Wander's *Deutsches Sprichwörter-lexicon* (1863–80) listed as the first entry for *Wes das hertz voll ist* Luther's German Bible. M. Lenschau in her detailed investigation of Grimmelshausen's proverbs[2] was in full agreement, designating Luther's translation a "biblisches Lehnsprichwort."

Now these views, held till the 1930s it would seem, are definitely wrong. *Wes das hertz voll ist* existed before Luther both as an independent proverb and even as a translation of Matt. 12 : 34 or Luke 6 : 45.

It does not seem to be a very old German proverb, however. It is not mentioned in Samuel Singer's *Sprichwörter des Mittelalters* (1944–47), which lists proverbs through the 14th century. It appears to have originated in the 15th century. At least I have so far been unable to

---

[1] Archer Taylor, *The Proverb* (Cambridge, Mass.: Harvard University Press, 1931), pp. 56, 57.

[2] Martha Lenschau, *Grimmelshausens Sprichwörter und Redensarten* (Frankfurt am Main: Diesterweg, 1924), p. 86.

The Original's Intent and the Modern Idiom 139

trace it beyond that century. Its earliest occurrence known to me is in Hans Rosenplüt's (c.1420 to c.1460) *Ein disputatz eins freiheits mit eim Juden:*

> "Des mündes red gang von dem hertzen
> Vnd welcherlay das hertz vol stee
> Das des der münd vbergee."[3]

If we make allowance for the rhyme, which obviously required *stee* for *ist*, and for the rhythm, which called for a longer word *welcherlay* for *wes*, there can be little doubt that we are here dealing with the proverb familiar to us primarily from Luther's Bible.

Its second occurrence is also well before Luther's translation. It is found in an anonymous Colmar manuscript of a tract on political and ecclesiastical reform to be dated between 1490 and 1510. H. Haupt first published it in 1897[4] as one of a longer list of *Oberrheinische sprichwörter und redensarten des ausgehenden 15. jahrhunderts*. It reads as follows: ". . . der gemein spruch: was daz herz voll ist, louf der munt uber." The substitution of *louf* for *geht* is not a major matter. It is basically the same proverb, occurring in this form also in Luther: "da leufft der mund gar uber." (WA 16, 194,31f.)

These two passages found in 15th-century texts show quite definitely that *Wes das hertz voll ist* was by no means coined by Luther but existed before him. Taylor and Lenschau are wrong in their assumption that it is a Biblical "Lehnsprichwort" going back to Luther.

Still, it could be urged, even if Luther did not actually coin this phrase, it was he at least who first had the imagination and boldness to make use of it as a "translation" of Matt. 12 : 34 and Luke 6 : 45. Let the record speak for itself. We shall trace the translation of this passage from the Gothic Bible to Johann Lang's version of Matthew in 1521, i.e., from the fourth century to the very year in which Luther began his official rendering.

Before examining these translations, however, we should present the verse in the Greek original and in the most famous and influential Latin version, the Vulgate.

Greek: ἐκ γὰρ τοῦ περισσεύματος τῆς καρδίας τὸ στόμα λαλεῖ.
Vulgate: *Ex abundantia enim cordis os loquitur.*
No variants are recorded. The Vulgate is a correct, practically literal translation of the original Greek.

[3]Adalbert Keller, *Fastnachtsspiele aus dem fünfzehnten Jahrhundert* (Stuttgart, 1853), III, pp. 1122, 23.
[4]In *Zeitschrift für deutsche Philologie*, XXIX, 109, 110.

Gothic: (Matt. 12 : 34 has not come down to us, but Luke 6 : 45 has) *uzuh allis unfarfullein hairtins rodeit munþs (is).*
The Monsee Fragments: *fona ganuhtsamemo muote sprihhit munth.*
Tatian: *Fon ginuhtsami thes herzen sprihhit thie mund.*
Mentel Bible: *Wann vor der begnugsam des hertzen redt der mund.*

This version of c. 1466 remains unaltered in the Eggensteyn and Pflanzmann redactions, the second and third printed German Bibles of c. 1470 and c. 1473. Only in the fourth German Bible, the famous Zainer redaction of c. 1475, are a few minor changes introduced. There is no further alteration to record after that in the entire subsequent history of the printed High German Bibles, the last of which came out in Augsburg in 1518, only four years before Luther's epoch-making *Septembertestament.*

Zainer Bible: *Wann auss uberflussigkeit des hertzens redt der mund.*
Johann Lang: *dan der mundt redet aus der uberflussigkeyt des hertzes.*

The picture is the same so far as the printed Low German Bibles are concerned.

Cologne I, 1478: *Wēt vth auerulodicheit des hertē spreckt de munt.*
Cologne II, 1478: *Want vyt auervlodicheyt des hertē spreeckt dye munt.*
Lübeck, 1494: *wēte vt auervlodicheit des hertē spreket de mūd.*
Halberstadt, 1522: *wente vth ouerflödicheyt des herten sprickket de munt.*

With the exception of the rendering found in the Monsee Fragments, all these translations from the Gothic down to Luther's own day are more or less strictly literal. Only the Monsee manuscript can be said to depart from the pattern: It resolves the genitive construction (*abundantia cordis*) into an adjectival construction, *fona ganuhtsamemo muote*. But even this successful effort to provide a somewhat smoother version really remains within the general framework of a fairly literal translation. There is clearly nothing remotely resembling an anticipation of Luther in the Gothic and Old High German renderings or in the printed pre-Lutheran German Bibles. It would be highly interesting to know whether the Plenaria might contain a freer version. Unfortunately Pietsch did not include this passage in his *Ewangely und Epistel Teutsch* (1927).

In addition to these formal translations of the Middle Ages there is another source of Biblical material: the rich field of informal casual quotations found throughout medieval literature. So far as our verse is concerned, two highly important occurrences have been noted by previous investigators.

In 1935 William Kurrelmeyer[5] called attention to the following passage in Johann Geiler von Kaiserberg's *Evangelibuch*, first published by Johannes Pauli in 1515, five years after Geiler's death, and again in 1517 and 1522: "(ex habundantia cordus os loquor) was das hertz vol ist, des loufft der mund vber (fol. 152 verso, col. 2)." Kurrelmeyer suggested that the reader not take seriously the obvious misprints (*cordus, loquor, was*), attributing them largely to the way in which the text has come down to us.

What is exciting about this discovery is not so much that it is another pre-Lutheran occurrence of our proverb but that this proverb was used to render Matt. 12 : 34 (or Luke 6 : 45, for that matter). It is not easy to determine whether Luther ever saw Geiler's book and specifically this phrase. All we can say is that Geiler's name does not occur in the recently published index of names in the Weimar edition of Luther's works. But whether Luther knew it or not, we are faced with the indisputable fact that Luther was not the first to link the proverb to the Biblical verse. Geiler clearly anticipated Luther in the rendering of Matt. 12 : 34 by an already existing German proverb.

Incidentally, it is of some interest that Kurrelmeyer's discovery apparently found its way into the 28th edition (1937) of Büchmann's *Geflügelte Worte*. It will be recalled that the 27th edition (1926) had credited Luther with coining this proverbial phrase himself. In 1937, as a result of Kurrelmeyer's important article, it would seem, the editors of Büchmann revised their earlier statement as follows: "Luther entscheidet sich bei der Übersetzung von Matthäus 12, 34 . . . für Wiedergabe der volkstümlichen Redeweise: 'Wes das Herz voll ist, des geht der Mund über.' Er hat damit ein altes Sprichwort aufgenommen. Das lässt sich daraus erschliessen, dass schon in dem 'Evangelibuch' (1515) des Johann Geiler von Kaiserberg (Bl. 152 v., Sp. 2) begegnet: 'Was das hertz vol ist, des loufft der mund vber' " (p. 50).

This thoroughly revised statement in Büchmann does not do full justice to Kurrelmeyer's discovery, however. It fails to take cognizance of the fact that *Wes das Herz voll ist* occurs in Geiler not only as a proverb but as the translation of a Biblical verse, Matt. 12 : 34 or Luke 6 : 45. This is the more important aspect of Kurrelmeyer's noteworthy contribution. As we were able to point out earlier in this essay, the phrase as such occurred as early as the 15th century in Germany.

If Kurrelmeyer's discovery of 1935 was extraordinary, Arno Schirokauer's discovery of 1944 was still more startling. He reported in *Modern Language Notes* (March, 1944, p. 221) that none other than

[5] *Modern Language Notes*, L (1935), 380-382.

Hieronymus Emser, one of Luther's worst enemies, also used *Wes das Herz voll ist*, both as a common proverb and, above all, as the translation of Matt. 12 : 34. In Emser's *Quadruplica auf Luthers Jungst gethane antwort, sein reformation belangend* we find the following passage: "Sihe, Luter, dem . . . Goliath bistu . . . tzuuorgleychen . . . gleych wie der selbig Riss vnbeschnitten was, also hast du ouch gar ein vnbeschnitten mund, Wolches ein tzeichen ist eins vnbeschnitten hertzen, dann wie Christus vnd das gemeyn sprichwort sagt, was das hertz vol ist, gehet der mund vber, ex cordis enim abundantia os loquitur, Mathei XII."[6]

We do not know exactly when Emser wrote this piece. All we know is that it was forwarded from Wittenberg to Luther at the Wartburg and that he received it there at the beginning of July 1521. We may safely assume that it was written not too long before the date of delivery to the "exiled" Luther. What is most important to remember in this connection is that it reached Luther at a time when, so far as we know, he did not yet entertain any idea of translating the Bible into German. It was in fact more than five months before we have the first indication that Luther had made up his mind to undertake this immense task, largely at the insistence of his friends and colleagues.

Luther must have read Emser's *Quadruplica* almost immediately upon receiving it, because he outlined the fundamental ideas for a reply to Emser in a letter to Amsdorf July 15 (WA, *Briefwechsel* 2, 361ff). The full-length reply, entitled *Eyn widderspruch D. Luthersz seynis yrrthumsz, erczwungen durch den aller hochgelertisten priester gottis, Herrn Hieronymo Emser, Vicarien tzu Meysen*, was in print by early October (WA 8, 245). What one would like to know more than anything else from our present point of view is of course what impression Emser's remarkable rendering of Matt. 12 : 34 made on Luther. Unfortunately we have no direct evidence in this matter. The fairly extensive correspondence with Amsdorf and Melanchthon concerning the *Quadruplica* does not mention the passage in question. The emphasis in these letters is on matters of content throughout. Luther's failure to refer to the translation of Matt. 12 : 34 does not of course preclude the possibility that he may have made a mental note of it and stored it in his prodigious memory.

There is some indirect evidence, however, that this may not have been the case. It is fairly likely that Emser's noteworthy rendering did not register with Luther at all. At about the same time that Emser

---

[6]Ludwig Enders, *Luther und Emser* (Halle, 1892), p. 131.

The Original's Intent and the Modern Idiom 143

furnished his excellent translation of our verse, Luther himself had occasion to refer to Matt. 12 : 34 in one of the sermons of his *Weihnachtspostille* of 1521. In the sermon on John 1 : 1-14, probably written soon after Luther got hold of Emser's work (WA 10¹, 2. Hälfte, LXVI), we find the following quotation: ". . . Christus sagt: Auss ubirfluss des hertzen redet der mund" (WA 10¹, 1. Hälfte, 187). This is obviously a literal translation. Whatever else it may reveal about Luther's early casual Biblical quotations, it certainly shows no influence of Emser's free rendering. If the latter had actually made any impression at all on Luther, one would have expected him to shy away from this painfully literal translation and to avail himself—he was never squeamish in such matters—of the superior rendering supplied by his adversary.

But the case is still more involved. A few lines after quoting the verse "Auss ubirfluss des hertzen redet der mund" Luther saw fit to introduce a German proverb to drive home further his main point that words express what is in the human heart: "durchs wortt wirtt des hertzen meynung erkennet" (187). Now the proverb that he used to illustrate this truth is none other than *Wess das hertz voll ist, des geht der mund ubir* (188). This creates a most interesting situation indeed. When quoting the Bible Luther translated the well-known *ex abundantia cordis os loquitur* very literally. To develop his basic point still more he employed the German proverb *Wess das hertz voll ist*. What is of crucial importance to realize in this connection is that Luther used both, the Biblical verse and the proverb, *independently of each other*. When he wrote this sermon in 1521 he did not yet relate the reading of Matt. 12 : 34 and the German proverb. The proverb was not yet called upon to render the Biblical verse under review.

In other words, Luther had not yet taken the decisive step of associating proverb and New Testament verse in 1521. Emser on the other hand had, as had Geiler even before Emser. The latter, it will be recalled, used *Wes das Herz voll ist* not only as a *gemein sprichwort* but also as the translation of Matt. 12 : 34! And several years before that, in 1515, Pauli's edition of Geiler's *Evangelibuch* contained the proverbial rendering of this Biblical passage.

It is quite clear then that Luther was by no means the first German to render Matt. 12 : 34 by the famous phrase that has for centuries been associated with his name. His predecessors known to us at this time were Geiler and Emser; perhaps there were others in addition. As a matter of fact, Luther started out by differing with these men: in the pre-*Septembertestament* sermon quoted above, he unmistakably translated Matt. 12 : 34 as literally as it is possible to translate this verse.

Now this was not done in ignorance of the proverb as such. Luther knew it, quoting it even in the same paragraph in which he gave the literal translation of Matt. 12 : 34. Nor is this the only place where he quoted the proverb prior to his official translation of the New Testament. We read in *Eyn trew vormanung Martini Luthers tzu allen Christen . . .*, written between Dec. 10 and 15, 1521 (WA 8, 673), a slightly different version of our proverb: "sie mussen . . . das maul ubir gehen lassen, des das hertz voll ist" (WA 8, 682). Thus it is rather certain that Luther was well acquainted with this phrase by itself. It is equally certain that, up to the end of 1521, he did not make use of it as a translation of Matt. 12 : 34 or of Luke 6 : 45.

A very short time after this second occurrence of the German proverb, probably in the same month of December, Luther embarked on his translation of the New Testament. In the beginning of January, if indeed not in the last days of December, Luther must have reached Matt. 12 : 34. Knowing his literal German quotation of this verse earlier in the year, we should like to find out as much as we possibly can about the origin of the official rendering. We feel more keenly than ever the loss of the manuscript of Luther's new translation. All who have worked with the still extant manuscripts of Luther's translation of parts of the Old Testament know how gradually many a passage since become famous actually evolved. There are words crossed out, written over the line, under the line—all this before the phrasing we now have came into being. We should be eager to examine the manuscript for the light it might throw on the evolution of Matt. 12 : 34. But all we have is the printed version that saw the light of day in September 1522. We do not know more than the accomplished translation reading as follows: "Wes das hertz voll ist, des geht der mund vbir." We are thus faced with this simple and straightforward fact: The familiar proverb, used twice by Luther in the course of the year 1521 independently (not as a translation of Matt. 12 : 34), emerges in September 1522 as the official German rendering of the Greek original. The Vulgate, we may repeat, contains an exact, literal translation of the Greek. Erasmus, whose new Latin translation of the original often departs radically from the Vulgate, saw no necessity to revise the official Latin text materially in this particular verse. All he did was to replace the Vulgate's *enim* by *siquidem*, changing the word order at the same time.

Vulgate: *ex abundantia enim cordis os loquitur.*
Erasmus: *Siquidem ex abundantia cordis, os loquitur.*
This Erasmus version, contained in the first edition of the *Novum*

Instrumentum of 1516, remained unchanged in all editions published during his lifetime: 1519, 1522, 1527, and 1535.

Luther's version also survived in all editions whether of the New Testament alone or of the Bible as a whole. It is scarcely necessary to point out that it has also been left intact by the successive revisions made of the German Bible throughout the centuries down to the present day. It is obviously such a marvelous example of the underlying spirit of Luther's Bible that it is likely to remain unaltered in the foreseeable future.

There cannot be any doubt that all the editions of Luther's New Testament which Emser ever saw contained the proverbial rendering of Matt. 12 : 34. There was no other. Emser was the first important non-Lutheran to undertake both a criticism of Luther's translation and, a few years later, a "new" rendering.

On Sept. 21, 1523, exactly one year after the appearance of Luther's *Septembertestament*, Emser brought out, at the request of Duke George, a major work containing the results of his detailed examination of Luther's translation:

Ausz was grund vnnd vrsach Luthers dolmatschung, vber das nawe testament, dem gemeinē man billich vorbotten worden sey. Mit scheynbarlicher anzeygung, wie, wo, vnd an wölchen stellen, Luther den text vorkert, vnd vngetrewlich gehandelt, oder mit falschen glossen vnd vorreden ausz der alten Christelichen ban, auff seyn vorteyl vnd whan gefurt hat.

It is a relief to be able to report that the second edition of 1524 changed this cumbersome title to one more readable: *Annotationes Hieronymi Emser vber Luthers naw Testamēt gebessert vnd emēdirt.* This title was not changed again in the editions of 1528, 1529, and 1536. In the preface Emser speaks of as many as 1400 heretical errors which he asserts he has discovered in Luther's New Testament. The number of "errors" criticized in the actual body of the book is considerably smaller but still very large.

What interests us primarily in this connection is Matt. 12 : 34 and Luke 6 : 45. Emser has nothing to say on Luther's free rendering. Apparently he can see nothing wrong with it. This is of course what one would expect in the light of his own casual quotation of this verse in 1521!

The next matter we have to take up concerns Emser's own "translation" of the New Testament. This came out in 1527 under the title: *Das naw testament nach lawt der Christlichē kirchen bewertē text, corrigirt, vn widerumb zu recht gebracht.* We are naturally interested at this time only in the fate of our passages. Here is how they read in Emser's New Testament of 1527:

Matt. 12 : 34—*denn aus fölle des hertzen / redt der mund.*
Luke 6 : 45—*Denn aus vberflus des hertzen redet der munde.*

It is manifest that Emser departed both from Luther's New Testament and from his own casual quotation of 1521. This extraordinary situation raises a number of interesting questions. Had Emser forgotten his own early free rendering? This would seem to be unlikely in view of the fact that Luther's official rendering must certainly have reminded him of his own phrase of 1521. Did his intense hatred of Luther blind him to such an extent that he was ready to ignore or even suppress his own past achievement? Or was he just embarrassed because he had been guilty of using a phrase that now came up in Luther's Bible? One would also like to know why he did not claim proprietary rights in the matter of this particular verse.

It would seem that something more fundamental is at stake here. Emser did not shrink from employing a very free rendering in an occasional quotation of this verse. But when it was a matter of rendering it in his own official translation of the New Testament, Emser saw fit to supply a literal version. What he did not mind doing casually and informally he could not bring himself to do formally and officially. Luther on the other hand left all undue conservatism behind when he entered upon the task of putting the Bible into German. He was bold and enterprising in this undertaking. In fact what makes his German Bible the exciting and successful book it was and still is is just this accent on the venturesome, this stress on the delightfully and daringly idiomatic!

Here, then, is the difference between the two men. Emser, highly gifted linguistically, did not take the step of incorporating a superb German phrase—even one that he himself had employed before Luther— in a formal translation of the Bible. Luther, about whose extraordinary linguistic endowment nobody, not even Emser, entertained any doubt, took this very step, using the best German he could find even though it came from an opponent. What mattered to him, above and beyond general accuracy to be sure, was idiomatic excellence. This requirement he put very high. Had he actually remembered this phrase from Emser's essay of 1521, he would not have hesitated to employ it just because one of his worst enemies had used it first. Moreover, he was dealing here with a common proverb, the property of any man

The Original's Intent and the Modern Idiom 147

who cared to avail himself of a treasure open to all. It is to Emser's credit that he used this proverb as a casual translation of Matt. 12 : 34 before Luther. It is to Luther's credit that he was courageous enough to employ it in his official rendering of the New Testament.

Luther's use of the proverb in his official Bible and Emser's clear rejection of it in his own formal Bible do not end the story of this exciting verse. As every student of Luther knows, it is mentioned prominently in the famed *Sendbrief vom Dolmetschen.* It seems that Luther was very proud of it, so proud in fact that he included it in his most elaborate defense of his New Testament. Thus we have the slightly ironic situation that an expression first used by Geiler and then, of all people, by Emser, became in Luther's mind a veritable model of his efforts to put the Bible into the "best" German. He liked it so much that he cited it as an illustration of his method of Biblical translation.

There are two aspects of Luther's *Sendbrief* discussion of this verse which interest us primarily. First, his contention not only that this is the best German imaginable for the rendering of this passage but that a literal translation is downright bad and even incomprehensible to German ears: "Auss dem uberfluss des hertzen redet der mund. Sage mir, Ist das deutsch geredt? Welcher deutscher verstehet solchs? . . . Das kan kein deutscher sagen, . . . sondern also redet die mutter ym haus und der gemeine man: Wes das hertz vol ist, des gehet der mund uber, das heist gut deutsch geredt, des ich mich geflissen, und leider nicht allwege erreicht noch troffen habe, . . ." (WA 30^2, 637)

There can be little doubt that the proverbial expression is excellent German, immediately and readily understood. Luther is on solid ground here. But there is likely to be far less unanimity that *uberfluss des hertzen* is quite as unsatisfactory as Luther made it out to be in 1530. With all due respect to Luther's standing as a literary master, it could be held that a literal translation is not so hopelessly unintelligible as Luther insisted in the *Sendbrief.* We may not accept the authority of the traditional German rendering of this passage from Old High German days to the printed pre-Lutheran Bibles, but the fact that two rather important contemporaries, Johann Lang, a friend, and Hieronymus Emser, a bitter foe but able writer in his own right, do not hesitate to employ the literal version should perhaps make us pause a little in taking Luther's words too uncritically.

If there is at least some room for doubt that *vberflus des hertzen* is not quite so reprehensible as Luther urged, even in his own 16th century, this controversial genitival phrase may be said to have staged a real comeback during the 18th century. It is found, first of all, in several Protestant Bibles of this century as well as in post-Emser Catholic Bibles.

But this phrase is by no means restricted to translations of the Bible. It is also found, without reference to Biblical material, in secular German literature of the 18th century. In Grimm's *Wörterbuch*, where several such passages are listed, the following explanatory statement is made: "die redensart erhielt in der neueren sprache durch anschluss an die metaphern 'das herz . . . fliesst . . . über' . . . neuen bildinhalt und lebte neu auf." The phrase occurs in Moritz August von Thümmel's *Reise in die mittäglichen Provinzen von Frankreich im Jahre 1785-86:* "ich wäre, glaube ich, aus überfluss des herzens im stande gewesen, ihnen mein geheimes tagebuch vorzulesen" (6, 105). It further appears in Hölderlin: "es that uns wohl, den überflusz unsers hertzens der guten mutter in den schosz zu streuen" (2, 109). The phrase is not limited to prose; it is also found in verse. In the fourth scene of the first act of Schiller's *Wallensteins Tod* we read:

"Und was der Zorn und was der frohe Mut
Mich sprechen liess im Überfluss des Herzens."

Thus there can be little doubt that this phrase, so severely attacked by Luther as being *undeutsch,* was rather thoroughly resurrected in the 18th century by some of the most famous names in German literature.

It might also be pointed out in passing that the literal translation has been fully adopted in the English tradition:

Wicliff: *for the mouth spekith of the plente of the herte.*

Tyndale: *For of the aboundance of the hert/the mouth speaketh.*

Tyndale's version remained intact all the way to the King James Bible of 1611. It has survived all revisions of the King James Bible to our own day. Outside the strictly Biblical realm, the phrase is also found in Chaucer: *After the abundaunce of the herte spekith the mouth.* In the light of these significant examples it would seem that there is full acceptance of this phrase as good English in the English tradition. We might add, for whatever it is worth, that the phrase is also fully established in French as a proverb: *De l'abondance du coeur la bouche parle.*

So far the case has gone rather against Luther. A number of German writers, not to mention the British and French tradition at all, have employed the phrase without feeling that it was awkward or unidiomatic. Was he altogether wrong then? Hardly. Though he doubtless overshot the mark when he tried to stigmatize it as unacceptable, unintelligible German, he was probably right in preferring *Wes das hertz voll ist* for the purpose he had in mind. It certainly was excellent German, superbly adapted to the needs of the common man. Addressing himself by choice to the people, Luther could not have done any better. All that is wrong with his argument is that he underestimated the significance, the power, and the future of the phrase he rejected. His positive achievement in insisting on *Wes das hertz voll ist* . . . is beyond doubt. What is subject to doubt is his too severe attack on the literal translation.

Besides the question whether *vberfluss des hertzen* is good or bad German, there is another aspect of Luther's discussion of this passage in the *Sendbrief*. It concerns his charge that other translators rendered it literally. Luther somehow implies that he was the first to depart from the literal translation and to provide the excellent, highly idiomatic rendering with which we are all acquainted: "Wenn ich den Eseln soll folgen, die werden mir die buchstaben furlegen, und also dolmetzschen: Auss dem uberflus des hertzen redet der mund" (WA 30^2, 637). This claim is wrong if we survey the known history of the German translation of Matt. 12:34. Two men at least, Geiler and Emser, had not hesitated to employ the proverb to render this Biblical verse.

However, there are two questions which should be raised again in this connection. First, was Luther aware that Geiler and Emser had anticipated his rendering? So far as Geiler is concerned, all we can say is that his translation was objectively available and that, chronologically at least, Luther could have read it. But it is highly doubtful that he actually did. As we have observed before, there is not a single reference to Geiler throughout his vast literary output. This fact would seem to preclude the likelihood that Luther saw Geiler's casual translation. Since there is no reference to Johann Pauli either, the editor of Geiler's *Evangelibuch*, it is probably fair to say that Luther was unaware of Geiler's rendering.

With reference to Emser, the case is quite different. We know that Luther did read Emser's *Quadruplica*, in which the phrase occurred. We are compelled to assume this because he outlined a reply to be made by Amsdorf to Emser and because he finally did write the entire piece himself. The question therefore boils down not so much to *whether* he read it but *how* he read it. It is my impression that Luther often read his opponents' works fast and furiously, especially those of the lesser men. But even if he should have read it fairly carefully, it does not seem too likely that he read it with attention to philological detail such as would probably be required to catch a new translation of a

Biblical verse. This impression is perhaps reinforced by the observation made earlier in this essay that in a work of his own, apparently written shortly after he received Emser's *Quadruplica*, he himself translated Matt. 12 : 34 quite literally. If Emser's proverbial rendering failed to impress itself upon him at that time, it seems unlikely that he should have recalled it several months later when he made his official translation of the Gospel According to St. Matthew, and still more unlikely that he should be aware of Emser's casual quotation almost 10 years later when he penned the *Sendbrief*. Thus although on the face of it it would seem that Luther could not help noticing Emser's translation of 1521, it is perhaps not so definite a fact as Arno Schirokauer suggests: "Emser hatte . . . Luthern selbst die prächtige Wendung in den Mund gelegt, auf die sich nun Luther so viel zu gute tut."⁷ It is possible that this was so but not as certain as all that.

Beyond Luther's knowing or not knowing Emser's casual rendering of 1521 there is another important question. Even if it could be shown conclusively that Luther took over the translation of Matt. 12 : 34 from Emser early in 1522, it may perhaps be doubted that Luther was thinking of casual quotations of this passage when he discussed the matter in the *Sendbrief* in 1530. It is probable that he was thinking of regular translations of the New Testament rather than of the vast field of occasional quotations found in profusion throughout German writings of the times. If we restrict the discussion to these formal renderings, it will have to be granted that Luther was right in asserting that the passage in question had always been translated literally. Our survey of the pre-Lutheran translations confirms Luther's claim. What we must not forget is that Emser's official translation of 1527 had reverted to a literal translation of our verse. It is my opinion that when Luther made his remarks in 1530, it was the passage in Emser's translation of 1527 that he had in mind rather than the quotation of 1521. It is my contention that Luther's charge contained in the *Sendbrief* was made on the basis of the pre-Lutheran German Bibles and of Emser's formal translation of the New Testament.

Let us sum up. Luther did not create the German proverb *Wes das hertz voll ist* nor was he the first to employ the proverb to render Matt. 12 : 34. The proverb is first found around the middle of the 15th century, and the translation of Matt. 12 : 34 by this proverb occurs in Geiler and Emser before Luther. Luther, however, was the first to incorporate the proverbial translation of this passage in a formal version

---

⁷*Modern Language Notes*, LIX (1944), 221.

of the German Bible. The decision and the achievement to render the Bible idiomatically and, if need be, freely, were Luther's and Luther's alone. While Emser was bold enough to make such a rendering as an occasional quotation, he clearly shrank from taking this step in his official translation of the New Testament. It was this that Luther scored in the *Sendbrief*: Neither the older German Bibles nor the then new Catholic New Testament of Emser was really idiomatic. This step was taken only by Luther on any systematic scale. That's why he could, with a good measure of justice, call the past and even the most recent efforts to render the Bible *Buchstabilismus*. Whatever else Luther may have been, he was not a *Buchstabilist* in rendering the Scriptures.

c. "GEGRÜSSET SEIST DU, HOLDSELIGE"

One of the best-known passages in all of Luther's writings is his spirited defense in the *Sendbrief vom Dolmetschen* of his rendering of a portion of Luke 1:28: "Gegrusset seystu holdselige." Most books on Luther discuss or at least mention this extraordinary rendering. Histories of German literature, even those devoting only a few pages to Luther and the Reformation, seldom fail to point out this splendid example of Luther's singular manner of putting the Bible into German. Whoever lays claim to any acquaintance with Luther at all seems to be familiar with the *Sendbrief vom Dolmetschen* in general and our passage in particular. However, while Luther's translation of the *Ave Maria* and his strong justification of it belong to the commonplaces of our knowledge of the Reformer, there is little awareness that Luther's animated discussion of his rendering in the *Sendbrief* is only one of several references to it in the course of his public life. Even Kawerau, Emser's biographer, believes that the only time Luther reacted to the attack on his translation was in the *Sendbrief* of 1530.[1] It is apparently not generally known that Luther commented on his bold rendering of the Salutation of the Angel long before and long after the year 1530.

It is the purpose of this essay to relate the discussion of the translation of Luke 1:28 in the *Sendbrief* of 1530 to Luther's earlier and later remarks on the same subject. The entire history of this highly controversial rendering, so far as I have been able to put it together, is to be presented here for the first time to my knowledge. But before proceeding to a discussion of Luther's various relevant utterances, let us examine somewhat closely the actual origin and consequent history of Luther's rendering as such. We must try to find out what we can about

[1] Gustav Kawerau, *Hieronymus Emser* (Halle: Schriften des Vereins für Reformationsgeschichte, No. 61, 1898), pp. 63, 64.

Luther's translation itself, prior to the controversy it called forth from friend and foe alike.

The earliest recorded translation of Luke 1 : 28 on the part of Luther is found in the *Septembertestament* of 1522: "Gegrusset seystu holdselige." It may very well have emerged in just this perfect shape in a moment of inspired translating. But we do not really know the actual story of its coming into being since we are not so fortunate as to possess the manuscript of Luther's *Septembertestament.* Whoever has worked with the manuscripts of Luther's translation of parts of the Old Testament, especially of the Psalter, is quite aware of how impossible it really is to say with full assurance whether the word *holdselige* is due to a sudden inspiration or whether Luther came upon it only after more or less protracted effort and reflection. If one remembers that many words and phrases of the German Psalter which were printed for the first time in 1524 were arrived at only after striking out often whole series of other translations in the manuscript, one may indeed wonder what the history of *holdselige* may have been before it reached the printer: was it a sudden felicitous gift of the moment or was it the product of long and arduous thought and experimentation? We shall perhaps never know unless the manuscript should yet turn up miraculously. All we can say, in the absence of definite information about the pre-publication history of the passage, is that "holdselige" is the earliest discernible Lutheran translation of the text. Although we cannot trace it all the way back to its manuscript stage, we can nevertheless date it with a certain degree of accuracy. The *Septembertestament,* as the name itself indicates, came off the press in the month of September 1522. The actual translation of the New Testament had been made rather more than half a year earlier, between the last days of December 1521 and March 1522. The first chapter of the Gospel according to St. Luke, of which our phrase is a part, was probably translated late in January or early in February, so far as one can reconstruct the various stages of Luther's work on the New Testament. Whatever the *exact* date of the translation of the first chapter of Luke, in March Luther took the manuscript back to Wittenberg, where he put the finishing touches on it with the expert help of Melanchthon, the university's distinguished Greek scholar. There remains the possibility, remote though it may seem, that Melanchthon could have suggested the famous word! This is of course not very likely, since Melanchthon's chief concern was apparently not so much with the artistic aspects of the German rendering as with questions of the meaning of the Greek text. Moreover Luther, when bitterly attacked in later years for just this particular verse, might conceivably have adduced the considerable authority of the almost universally recognized Melanchthon had the latter actually had a hand in the coining of this phrase. In fact Luther, usually ready to give credit where credit was due, speaks of this word as his own in the *Sendbrief:* "darumb hab ichs vordeutscht: Du holdselige. . . ."[2] The weight of the *ich* in *hab ichs vordeutscht* becomes evident when one contrasts it with the *wir* in another place of the same essay: "Im Hiob erbeiten wir also, M. Philips, Aurogallus und ich. . . ."[3] Thus, though absolute certainty is lacking in the nature of the case, we are pretty safe in believing that *du holdselige* is Luther's very own creation.

Although the matter well merits a separate investigation, we shall discuss the source of Luther's novel rendering of the *Ave Maria* only very briefly in this connection. The first thing to be pointed out is that it almost certainly rests on the Greek original: χαῖρε κεχαριτομένη. Luther would probably not have come upon his translation without calling upon the Greek. It seems rather unlikely that the familiar Vulgate phrase, *gratia plena,* would have resulted in *holdselige.* Even a literary genius of Luther's stature could hardly have produced this from *gratia plena.* The real issue is perhaps not so much whether *holdselige* is based on the Greek or the Latin but rather what induced Luther to understand the verb χαριτόω in just the way he did. The word has a double meaning: endued with grace in the general, secular sense or in the specific, religious sense. What we have to explain is why Luther should have so clearly preferred the secular to the religious meaning. Apart from the rather obvious fact that Luther wanted to avoid any continuance of the medieval misinterpretation which tended to ascribe the power of bestowing grace to Mary herself, there is, I believe, another reason why Luther chose the nonreligious interpretation—the philological authority of Erasmus, the man who was the first to make the Greek text of the New Testament available to Luther in 1516. Although the great humanist, in the new Latin translation he furnished alongside of the Greek original, retained the traditional words *gratia plena,* he appended a fairly elaborate discussion of this phrase in the *Adnotationes,* where he emphasized the general, secular meaning of the Greek word in question: "Nec ē gratia plena, sed ut ad verbum reddam gratificata, quo tamen participio Homerus usus est pro unice dilecto, ἐμῷ χαριτομένη θυμῷ, i.e. meo dilecto animo. Est autem vox velut amorem alicuius erga virginem nunciantis, quod sonet amatorium quiddā. Unde et turbata virgo cogitabat, qualis

[2] WA 30², 638.   [3] WA 30², 636.

esset ea salutatio."[4] After deciding in favor of the classical, pre-Christian meaning the word had in Greek literature, Luther had the task of rendering this in idiomatic German. There can be little question that the resultant adjective *holdselig* is a superb German rendering of the idea Luther wished to express.

So far as all succeeding editions of Luther's German Bible are concerned, whether of the whole Bible or of the New Testament separately, the word *holdselige* remained intact throughout without the slightest change. One may conclude that Luther was quite satisfied with it and that he saw no reason to alter it in his official German Bible.

The official German Bible is, however, not the only rendering of Biblical material into German that Martin Luther made. His writings as a whole abound with Biblical quotations of every variety. This rich source of more or less casual renderings of many a Bible verse has as yet scarcely been tapped. Checking our verse, Luke 1 : 28, against the list of all of Luther's German Biblical citations compiled at Yale University, we find that it is, understandably enough, one of the most infrequently quoted verses in Luther's writings. We need not concern ourselves here with the rather obvious theological and psychological reasons for this fact. It is quoted only twice in the whole mass of German writings which Luther himself saw through the press. Both of these quotations occur, quite significantly, rather early in his career, in 1522 and 1523 respectively. They are however of more than passing interest.

The first is found in the well-known, immensely popular *Betbüchlein* of 1522. The translation Luther used here will doubtless astonish the modern reader conversant with the Reformer's forceful discussion of the proper German translation of this phrase in the *Sendbrief vom Dolmetschen* of 1530. The quotation of 1522 actually reads: "Gegrusset seystu Maria, voll gnaden. . . ."[5] After the Protestant reader has somewhat recovered from the initial shock, he will surely wish an explanation of this definitely literal translation of the Vulgate, upon which Luther eight years later was to turn the full fury of his attack. What Luther did his best to make almost ridiculous in 1530 he himself employed in 1522!

This literal translation warrants closer inspection. Let us first try to establish the probable date of the writing of the *Betbüchlein*. While it seems next to impossible to pin it down exactly, it was apparently

---

[4]Erasmus, *Novum Instrumentum omne* (Basileae: in aedibus I. Frobenij, 1516), p. 318. Cf. Luther, WA 47, 703, ll. 32–35.   [5]WA 10^2, 408.

The Original's Intent and the Modern Idiom 155

composed in the early summer of 1522.[6] This means that it is considerably later than the actual translation of the New Testament which was finished before Luther left the Wartburg in early March. We thus reach the somewhat startling conclusion that the translation *voll gnaden*, to be spurned so brusquely a few years later, was actually used by Luther himself several months after the famous phrase *du holdselige* originated to the best of our knowledge!

Before undertaking an explanation of this strange phenomenon we might just as well face the further fact that the second casual quotation of Luke 1 : 28 in Luther's German writings is practically identical with the one just discussed. What is perhaps still more distressing is that the second quotation occurs as late as 1523. In a sermon of March 22, 1523, seen through the press by Luther himself, the *Ave Maria* is quoted in this fashion: "Bisz gegrüst, Maria voller gnaden. . . ."[7] If one could possibly, though with a high degree of discomfort, get over the first quotation of 1522 as occurring after all in the same year as the *Septembertestament* when Luther might conceivably not yet have had time to quote himself as it were, there would appear to be no excuse for another such lapse in the following year, by which time the new translation had met with the widest popular approval and applause imaginable.

Without any doubt, the twice repeated rendering of the *Ave Maria* by *voll gnaden* is difficult to explain. The first thing one should perhaps bear in mind is that almost all of Luther's works, with the exception of the translation of the Bible, were produced in great haste, many of them reaching the printer before the ink was dry. It is therefore quite conceivable that Luther just followed the path of least resistance and employed the rendering long familiar to himself and everybody else and well-nigh hallowed by centuries of public and private use. Furthermore, one can very well argue that Luther, in occasional writings of this sort, may even have consciously preferred to hew close to the line of the accepted ancient rendering and to make his bow to tradition, linguistically at least. This seems especially likely in the case of a work like the *Betbüchlein*. In a prayerbook, naturally intended for mass consumption, an author is perhaps apt to leave traditional renderings undisturbed so as to preserve the continuity of formal religious utterances. This argument gains in strength if one remembers a similar situation in Luther's Catechism even later than 1522 or 1523. Contrary to his really new translation of the Lord's Prayer in the New Testament of 1522, Luther used as late as 1529, in the very popular

[6] Ibid., p. 340.   [7] WA 12, 456.

catechism, the traditional German version which differs so markedly from the one contained in the official German Bible. It would seem that in the case of frequently used liturgical matter, which had taken on definite German form long before, Luther, wisely recognizing traditional formulations, decided not to make any changes for liturgical or semi-liturgical purposes though he did not hesitate to alter the established readings in the regular translation of the New Testament. As regards the use of the well-known *voll gnaden* in a sermon of 1523, one could perhaps bring forward similar arguments.

Whatever the actual reasons (perhaps there are no reasons at all!) for using *voll gnaden* in two isolated passages in 1522 and 1523, the fact remains that Luther did use them and that he must have somehow thought them good enough for his purpose at that time. We might also remember that even in the *Sendbrief* of 1530 he did say at one point that the customary rendering *voll gnaden,* though anything but "gut deutsch,"[8] is nonetheless a simple, straightforward translation of the Latin, the only difference being that in his formal German New Testament he could not be satisfied with a plain (*schlecht*) rendering from the Vulgate. He does seem to imply, even if somewhat reluctantly, that the "plain and simple" translation would do in less important connections as it apparently did in 1522 and 1523, relatively early years in Luther's activity.

This, then, was the state of affairs early in 1523: In the New Testament Luther had boldly and freely rendered Luke 1 : 28 by *holdselige;* in two occasional quotations he had, conservatively and informally, retained the conventional *voll gnaden*. It was in the fall of the same year, 1523, that the storm which had been gathering around *Das Newe Testament Deutzsch* broke in full force. By some strange coincidence this happened exactly one year after the publication of the first edition of Luther's New Testament in September 1522. In September 1523 Hieronymus Emser, secretary at the court of Duke George of Saxony and former teacher of Luther at the University of Erfurt, launched a strong attack on Luther's translation as a whole and on his rendering of the *Ave Maria* in particular. In this essay our only concern is with this single passage.

In his *Ausz was grund* . . . Emser takes Luther to task in this manner for the word *holdselige:*

> In diesem örsten capitel do der Ertzengel gabriel tzu Maria sagt Aue gratia plena. Gegrüszt seyest du vol genaden. Tewtschet Luther dise wort auff gut bulerisch nämlich. gegrüsset seyest du hold-

[8] WA 30², 638.

selige. wie wol nu gratia zu weylen ouch huld heyszt oder gunst die einer bey den lewten hat. vnd gratiosus holdselig. so hat doch der engel hie nit geredt von menschlicher huld. sonder von der gnad gotes. vnd Maria die ehr vnd wirdikeit, das sie werden solt ein mutter gottes. nit ausz menschlicher holdseligkeyt, sonder ausz gottes gnaden gehabt. Derhalben wir disz orts nit du holdselige, sonder du vol genaden lesen, vnd betten sollen. dann die gnaden die Eua vor schüt, hat Maria vns wider erhollet, vnd ist die maledeyung Eue jn die benedeyung Marie bekert worden.[9]

Luther is thus reproached for having translated the phrase disrespectfully, for having somehow trespassed against the dignity of the Virgin. Though Emser is ready to admit that *gratia* and *gratiosus* may occasionally mean *huld* and *holdselig*, he insists that the angel is not speaking here of human favor but of divine grace. For this reason Emser urges that we must read and pray *du vol genaden* and not *du holdselige*. It is important to note that Emser does not find fault with Luther's translation on artistic or literary grounds. While he does not go out of his way to praise it, he appears to accept it implicitly as a good rendering so far as it goes. What Emser said about Luther's New Testament as a whole, namely that it was "etwas zierlicher und süsslautender"[10] than the older German Bibles, probably also applies to Luther's rendering of Luke 1 : 28 in particular. It seems pretty clear that Emser went quite far in recognizing the literary excellence of Luther's New Testament. The man who, as Arno Schirokauer has been able to show,[11] preceded Luther in the superb translation of *Ex abundantia cordis os loquitur* by *Wes das Herz voll ist, des geht der Mund über*, was surely a person of more than ordinary literary ability and taste. The fault he finds with Luther's rendering of the *Ave Maria* is thus not so much artistic as theological and, to a certain extent, philological. It is of considerable interest to realize that he attacks not only Luther but also Erasmus, by implication at least, for it was the latter who had in all likelihood given Luther a good deal of the philological justification for his translation. From a theological point of view, Emser argues that the angel spoke to Mary as to one upon whom divine favor had been showered; he does not believe that the angel meant by his salutation that she had found favor with other people or that she was well liked and popular in earthly matters. In his fervor to give due credit to the grace of God—what irony to harp on this point with a man like Martin Luther!—Emser went so far as to place

[9]WA 17¹, 153.   [10]Kawerau, p. 65.
[11]*Modern Language Notes*, LIX (1944), 221. Cf. also L (1935), 380–82.

Mary over against Eve. Both women are held to play complementary roles in the drama of redemption. What Eve forfeited Mary is said to have recovered. Thus the gist of Emser's attack on Luther's rendering is theologically inspired. He appears to have accepted it on literary grounds.

How did Luther react to this relatively early criticism of his widely heralded translation? According to the prevailing view he did not reply to it for a number of years, not until 1530 when he unleashed his powerful counterattack in the *Sendbrief vom Dolmetschen*. Although this was to become his strongest utterance in the matter, it was, contrary to general opinion, neither his first nor his last public response. It would indeed have been strange if Luther, of ever ready tongue and pen, should have let seven years pass before defending himself. As a matter of fact, Luther made his first reply before six months had gone by.

As early as March 1524 he saw fit to discuss his rendering briefly in the course of his sermons on Genesis: "Ego 'holdselig' reddidi...."[12] He is quick to add that he has been taken to task for it: "... quod culpant...."[12] Though Emser is not mentioned by name, it seems likely that he must be counted among those who are accusing Luther for this rendering. Carefully and patiently Luther explains what is implied in his translation: "Hoc est 'holdselig,' cui omnes favent, qui inspiciunt."[12] He also suggests the word *holdreich*, both words meaning someone "dem Gott und eyn iglicher hold ist."[12] In a bold anticipation of the phrase *du liebe Maria* of the *Sendbrief*, he goes so far as to propose *fruntliche metz*,[12] but he almost immediately withdraws it as perhaps too informal, saying: "ridiculum esset"—to go to such extremes in the language of everyday life. But Luther does not rest his case there. He is not satisfied with merely defending himself against those who "culpant" him. Leaving the defensive he takes the offensive himself; strongly he accuses his opponents of a certain coarseness, theological and otherwise, which he for one detects in *voll gnaden*: "ipsi putant gratiam tale quiddam esse, quod infundatur vasi...."[12] Taking this inartistic picture for his point of counterattack Luther proceeds to point an accusing finger at the hostile camp: "ego iam culpo."[12]

Following this rather subdued initial skirmish, one of Luther's admirers, Urbanus Rhegius, the reformer of Lüneburg, rushed to the defense of the leader. On October 15, 1524, he published a little book entitled *Ob das new testament yetz recht verteutscht sey*.[13] So far as our passage is concerned, he declared emphatically that Luther's translation was not an attempt to belittle the Virgin. Rhegius praises Luther

[12] WA 14, 440.   [13] Augsburg.

for discarding the Vulgate as his authority and for basing his epoch-making rendering on the Greek original and Erasmus' new Latin translation added to his edition of the Greek New Testament: ". . . hat vorgemelter tolmetscher sich geflissen des griechischen buchs vnd des rechten lateynischen, das Erasmus Rotterdam hat Bapst Leoni dem zehenden zugeschriben."[14] Any effort to disparage Luther's new translation is an unwarranted attack on responsible scholarship and involves a like attack on Erasmus: "derhalb wellicher dise tolmetschung verwirfft, der verwürfft dem Erasmo seyn nutzliche trewe notwendige arbayt, die all gelert leüt griechischer vnnd lateynischer sprach loben müssen. . . ."[14] After thus defending Luther and, significantly enough, Erasmus in the same breath, Rhegius takes it upon himself to discuss our passage which had given so much offense. He insists that it is not only based on the Greek original but also executed in superb idiomatic German:

> Nun weis ein Jeder, der Teutsch kann, dass ein holdselig Mensch so viel ist, als der viel Huld, Gunst und Gnad bei den Leuten hat, dem man viel Gutes gönnet, den man lieb hat, der selig, der reich an Gunst und Hulden ist. Darum soll Niemand dafür halten, dass dieses Wörtlein holdselig reiche zur Verkleinerung der allerhochwürdigsten, seligsten Jungfrau Maria, als ob sie Mangel an Gnad hab', denn wie sie die holdselige, sonderlich geliebte Magd Gottes war, also war sie auch voll Gnaden nicht von ihr selbst, sondern aus Gütigkeit Gottes.[15]

The next utterance to come from Martin Luther himself occurs in March 1525. At the occasion of discussing the *Ave Maria* once again Luther feels constrained to point out that he is severely arraigned for his unconventional rendering. "Hic culpant me"[16] is his renewed complaint. It is most interesting to note that Luther finds himself in basic accord with Emser's charge that he actually rendered this passage "auf gut buhlerisch," for he writes: "angelus verba fere carnaliter loquitur, ideo timet periculum virtutis."[16] The only difference between Luther and Emser is that the former, in fundamental agreement with Erasmus, considers this to be the correct interpretation whereas the latter regards it as essentially wrong, trespassing upon the honor of the Virgin.

In 1527 Luther's Sermons on Genesis were finally published. They had been delivered in 1523 and 1524. As a matter of fact, Luther's

---
[14] WA, *Deutsche Bibel* 6, lxxiv.
[15] Gerhard Uhlhorn, *Urbanus Rhegius* (Elberfeld: R. L. Friderichs, 1861), p. 63.
[16] WA 17¹, 153.

earliest recorded statements on his disputed rendering of Luke 1 : 2 were made in the course of these sermons. What we have in th printed version of 1527 is considerably expanded beyond what is con tained in the version of 1523/24. Instead of the rather disconnected presentation of the earlier redaction we now have a well-polished con nected narrative. The relevant words *gratia plena* are now expressed by a whole group of vernacular phrases: "Sey mir günstig und hold zörne nicht mit mir odder sey mein freund, ich wil auch dein freund sein."[17] The most striking of them all is perhaps: "Sey gegrüsset, du gnadenreiche odder holdselige, Denn was heysst gnade haben ander denn holdselig sein? Als wir von einer magd sagen: du feine freund liche metze. . . ."[17] Luthers' attack on the traditional *voller gnaden* o the *lumpen prediger* is also carried out at greater length: ". . . so vo als ein blase vol winds, gerade als were gnade ein ding, das Gott yn hertz giesse, wie man wein ynn die kandel geusset, das oben ube gehet. . . ."[17] Impatient with this rendering, Luther says simply abou his own *holdselige*: "Wir künnens nicht besser nennen denn 'hold selig,' 'dem yderman hold und günstig ist,' Davon unser deudsche name Huldereich gemacht ist. . . ."[17] As if to make sure that he can not be charged with tampering with the idea of grace, Luther explain the meaning of *gratia* more fully in the Latin version of these sermons ". . . 'Ave gratia plena,' id est: quae invenisti gratiam apud Deum cui favet Deus, gratia non in te est, sed in Deo, gratiosus holtselig, cu Deus et nemo non favet. . . ."[18] This eloquent passage, more detailed than in the early version of 1523/24, is characteristic of Luther' singular concern with a religion of divine grace *par excellence*. Obviou though it is by itself, he still thought it important to restate it so as to show that he, of all men, was quite fully disposed to recognize grace wherever it had its legitimate place. He made it absolutely clear tha the grace here spoken of is of necessity divine grace, which is be stowed on Mary as the humble recipient.

This is how matters stood in 1527 before the appearance of Emser' New Testament later in the same year. The controversy, if such it can be really called up to this point, had been fairly restrained and schol arly. Neither Emser's attack on Luther nor Luther's or Rhegius' vig orous defense of *holdselige* had actually, at least in terms of the 16th century, exceeded the limits of a strong difference of opinion. If the issue had not gone beyond this point, it would have remained on the then customary level of a heated but still reasonable literary and theological feud. The chief reason for Luther's real flaring up in the *Sendbrief* of 1530 was doubtless the appearance of Emser's New Testa

---

[17] WA 24, 570.   [18] Ibid., pp. 569, 70.

ment in 1527. Duke George, not satisfied with Emser's pointing out Luther's "errors" in 1523 and 1524, had commissioned his able secretary to produce a version of the New Testament that was to take the place of the immensely popular version provided by Martin Luther. It took Emser several years to come out with his rival version. The full title of Emser's work was *Das naw testament nach lawt der Christlichen kirchen bewerten text, corrigirt, vnn widerumb zu recht gebracht*.[19] It is important to note that Emser does not claim to be the translator of this edition of the New Testament. The fatal and erroneous designation of Emser as the translator of the work did not appear on the title page till after Emser's death in November 1527. But the second edition, which was published in the following year, already contains the false information on the title page: *Das New Testament, So durch H. Emser Säligen verteuscht . . . aussgangen ist Anno. 1528.*[20] From this time on Emser was generally regarded as the translator of the New Testament the publication of which he had undertaken at the urgent request of Duke George. A letter which Cochläus, Emser's successor as secretary to Duke George, wrote on October 28, 1529, is of considerable interest in this respect. It is addressed to Princess Margaret of Anhalt and reads as follows:

> Ich sende hiermit E. F. G. das neue Testament, das von meinem lieben Vorfahren Herrn Hier. Emser, in Gott seligen, verdeutscht und diesen vergangenen Sommer zu Cöln gedruckt und gebunden worden ist, mit unterthäniger Bitte, E. F. G. wollens gnädiglich im besten verstehen und annehmen. Denn weil mir wohl wissend ist, dass E. F. G. obgemeldetem meinem Vorfahren mit sonderen Gnaden wohl geneigt gewesen, kann ich zu dieser Zeit nichts finden, welches sollte oder möchte mehr angenehm sein, denn das Wort Gottes, christlich verdeutscht und mit solchem Fleiss gedruckt. Wiewohl mir aber nicht zweifelt, E. F. G. habens längst gehabt aus dem ersten Druck, so hie zu Dresden ausgegangen ist, hab' ich doch diesen Druck auch wollen übersenden, E. F. G. dadurch erkennen zu geben, wie eine gute selige Arbeit der gute Mann kurz vor seinem Ende gethan habe, die das fünfte Mal jetzt gedruckt ist in grosser Anzahl der Exemplarien, darin viel mehr denn im 1. Druck begriffen wird und meines Bedünkens auch besser gedruckt ist. Hoffe E. F. G. werden's dem Emser seligen zu Ehren behalten. . . .[21]

---

[19]Georg Wolfgang Panzer, *Versuch einer kurzen Geschichte der römisch-catholischen deutschen Bibelübersetzung* (Nürnberg: G. P. Monath, 1781), p. 34.
[20]Ibid., p. 47
[21]Kawerau, pp. 71, 72.

Luther's strong remonstrances in the *Sendbrief* of 1530 had no visible effect on Cochläus; 19 years later, in 1549, he still possessed the effrontery to write as follows: "Hieron. Emser Novum Testamentum ex recepta et approbata per totam ecclesiam translatione latina vertit in Theutonicum quam fidelissime . . . opus maxime commendabile."[22]

If this was the spirit of Luther's opponents, it is not difficult to see that his ire was aroused when he first heard Emser praised as the actual translator of his own New Testament revised according to the Vulgate. This attitude of the hostile camp helps to explain in some measure the very sharp tone of his next and best-known utterance on the subject of the *Ave Maria*. We should, however, bear in mind that this wrong and regrettable claim did not originate with Emser himself. Let us now turn to the discussion of the proper translation of the verse in Luther's celebrated *Sendbrief vom Dolmetschen* of 1530.

Luther begins by stating that the traditional and conventional German translation is "Gegrüsset seistu, Maria vol gnaden. . . ."[23] He does not denounce it by any means but simply remarks: "Wolan, so ists biss her, schlecht den lateinischen buchstaben nach verdeutschet. . . ."[23] Though the accuracy of this claim of Luther's has never been challenged to my knowledge, the matter is of sufficient interest to be examined briefly in passing. I have been able to collect the following data on pre-Lutheran renderings of our phrase:

1. *Gegruzet sistu, Maria, vol der genaden, . . .*[24]
2. *heil und gruz si dir, Maria, vol der genaden, . . .*[25]
3. *hail wistu, völliu gnade, . . .*[26]
4. *Maria, du pist voll aller genaden.*[27]
5. *Voll der genaden.*[28]
6. *Gegrusst seistu vol der genaden:*[29]
7. *Gegrusst seistu vol genaden:*[30]
8. *. . . du voll genaden Maria. . . .*[31]

There are two fundamental faults that Luther finds with this ancient

---

[22]Richard Neubauer, *Martin Luther*, 7th and 8th ed., Part One (Halle: Waisenhaus, 1923), p. 284.
[23]WA 30², 638.
[24]Anton E. Schönbach, *Altdeutsche Predigten* (Graz: Styria), I (1886), 150.
[25]Ibid., I, 331.   [26]Ibid., III (1891), 28.
[27]H. Vollmer, *Die Neue Ee* (Berlin: Weidmann, 1929), p. 24.
[28]H. Vollmer, *Neue Texte zur Bibelverdeutschung des Mittelalters* (Potsdam: Athenaion, 1936), p. 34.
[29]W. Kurrelmeyer, *Die erste deutsche Bibel* (Tübingen: 1904), Mentel to Grüninger Bibles; Schönsperger (2d ed.) Bible.
[30]Ibid., Schönsperger (first edition) Bible; Hans Otmar and Silvanus Otmar Bibles.
[31]WA 17¹, 153.

rendering, which incidentally, as we have seen earlier in this essay, he himself had used more or less informally as late as 1522 and 1523: First, it is based on the Vulgate rather than on the Greek original; second, it is literal, all too literal. Apart from the severe scholarly criticism that it is not derived from the Greek text, there is the equally serious charge, at least from Luther's point of view, that it is simply not good German: "sage mir aber ob solchs auch gut deutsch sey?"[23] Luther obviously expects his rhetorical question to be answered in the negative, for he continues emphatically: "Wo redet der deutsch man also: du bist vol gnaden? Und welcher Deutscher verstehet, was gsagt sey, vol gnaden?"[23] Quite similarly to what he had said as early as 1524, Luther now adds a sarcastic remark: "Er mus dencken an ein vas vol bier, oder beutel vol geldes. . . ."[23] Luther then defends his own rendering as being better and more easily intelligible German: ". . . darumb hab ichs vordeutscht: Du holdselige, da mit doch ein Deutscher, deste meher hin zu kan dencken, was der engel meinet mit seinem grus."[23] In the heat of the battle Luther almost[32] forgets to mention that his translation also corrects the other fault he had found with *voll gnaden*. It is based on the Greek original as he understood it and as Erasmus had interpreted in his edition of the Greek New Testament. So far as the loud anger of his opponents is concerned, Luther brushes that aside as unimportant and proceeds to criticize his own translation as still falling short of the best German that could be used in this instance: ". . . Wie wol ich dennoch da mit nicht das beste deutsch habe troffen."[23] At this crucial point he introduces a new translation that he himself would consider superior even to *holdselige*: "Und hette ich das beste deutsch hie sollen nemen, und den grus also verdeutschen: Gott grusse dich, du liebe Maria. . . ."[23] Rising to his full height as one of the geniuses in the history of translation, he adds with a fair measure of pride in his own ability: ". . . so vil wil der Engel sagen, und so wurde er geredt haben, wan er hette wollen sie deutsch grussen. . . ."[23] Knowing that his translation is unacceptable to the Roman Church, Luther tells his foes plainly that they may translate as they wish as long as they will allow him to translate as he wishes. As a matter of fact, he is going to translate as he sees fit without paying any attention to the opposition at all: "Das hörestu wol, ich will sagen: du holdselige Maria, du liebe Maria, und las sie sagen: du volgnaden Maria."[23] It is in this connection that Luther utters the following memorable words which testify so eloquently to his extraordinary grasp of the genius of the German language:

[32]WA 30², 639.

Wer Deutsch kan, der weis wol, welch ein hertzlich fein wort das ist: die liebe Maria, der lieb Gott, der liebe Keiser, der liebe fürst, der lieb man, das liebe kind. Und ich weis nicht, ob man das wort "liebe" auch so hertzlich und gnugsam in Lateinischer oder andern sprachen reden müg, das also dringe und klinge ynns hertz, durch alle sinne, wie es thut in unser sprache.[33]

Before letting this whole matter of the proper translation of the *Ave Maria* drop, Luther at the end comes up with a few alternate renderings which he also considers readily intelligible to his ever-present criterion, *der deutsche man*: "du medliche junckfraw, du zartes weib, und der gleichen."[32]

Contrary to general opinion, this justly famous discussion of 1530 does not conclude Luther's pronouncements on the problem of the best possible translation of Luke 1 : 28. In a sermon of March 25, 1539, he again touched on this passage. Rather differently from the passionate words he had spoken nine years earlier in the *Sendbrief*, Luther now expresses himself in more subdued tones and with a tolerance usually not associated with him. He starts out by quoting the two renderings in question, his own and the traditional one: "*Holdselig. Vol genaden.*"[34] Having used both of them in this sermon, he goes on to say, somewhat to our surprise: "Qui vult, servet."[34] This probably means that Luther for one is now willing to leave it up to the individual which rendering he prefers. In other words, Luther does not object strongly, if at all, to the use of the conventional translation. It is of course a fact that he had never, not even in the trenchant *Sendbrief*, insisted on his own free and imaginative rendering to the radical exclusion of the long-established phrase.

What makes the discussion of the *Ave Maria* in this sermon of 1539 of more than ordinary interest is that Luther here advances theological and religious reasons for his finding fault with *vol genaden*: "Tantum ideo hinweg gethan, quod voluerunt gratiam per ipsam quaerere et collocabant matrem super filium. Invocata ipsa, ut a qua veniret gratia."[34] It is the attitude voiced by Emser toward the end of his criticism of Luther's new translation[9] which Luther, at this late date, makes responsible for his decision to abandon the old phrase. This naturally does not mean that Emser began the cult of the Virgin. He merely rode on the crest of it. What Luther fought in his rendering was the too high place accorded to Mary: ". . . voluerunt gratiam per ipsam quaerere et collocabant matrem super filium."[34] This is why he devised his new rendering: "Ideo vocavimus ein 'holdselige,' ger-

[33]WA 30², 638, 39.   [34]WA 47, 703.

manice: du liebe Maria."[34] Luther himself was thoroughly devoted to the mother of his Savior, but he wanted to make sure that she would no longer be "invoked as one by whom grace was bestowed."[34] He loves the Virgin Mary, in her proper sphere to be sure, for he writes "O man hat dich lieb, du bist eine liebe, werde Maria."[34]

The discussion of our verse in this late sermon of 1539 is of major importance. It really supplements the philological and literary arguments advanced in the *Sendbrief*. The whole truth is apparently that Luther objected to *voll gnaden* on both religious and artistic grounds. In the earlier period of his life he stressed the literary aspects while in his old age the fundamental religious considerations came to the fore.

Luther's last utterance on the subject of the *Ave Maria* is found in the *Hauspostille* of 1544. Again he points out that Mary is not to be thought of too highly since she is just as much without merit before God as any other sinful human being. He repeats the charge that under the papacy people were instructed to turn almost more to the Virgin than to Christ himself for the attainment of grace.[35] More interesting to us than this familiar strain is a new translation brought forward in this place: "'Gegrüsset (spricht er) seist du holdselige' oder begnadete. . . ."[36] It is this alternate translation of *begnadete* which is especially noteworthy. All things considered, this is probably the very best translation yet devised. It is both philologically correct and definitely more idiomatic than *voll gnaden*. The superiority of *begnadete* over *holdselige* is pretty clear: the Greek word κεχαριτομένη is a passive past participle, meaning that divine grace has descended upon her. Luther's final rendering, if such indeed it can be called, definitely rules out the possible misunderstanding that Mary herself can bestow grace upon others, a misunderstanding engendered by *voll gnaden*. The essential correctness of *begnadete* is vouchsafed by Carl Weizsäcker's employment of this very word in his well-known and quite authoritative translation of the New Testament.[37] However delightful and charming both *holdselige* and *liebe Maria* may be, Protestant scholarship, while recognizing its literary excellence, really disagrees with Luther's official rendering on strictly philological grounds. Both Kawerau[38] and Neubauer[39] record their actual divergence from Luther's formal translation of this phrase. These men, yielding to none in their general admiration of Luther, would have been very happy if

---

[35]WA 52, 627.   [36]Ibid., p. 626.
[37]Carl Weizsäcker, *Das Neue Testament*, 11th ed. (Tübingen: J. C. B. Mohr, 1927).
[38]P. 64.   [39]P. 236.

they had realized that their hero, in a casual quotation of Luke 1 : 28 in the year 1544, actually did use *begnadete* himself.[40]

In conclusion[41] it might be said that Luther in his own writings covered the whole distance from the inherited *voll gnaden* via his own *holdselige* and *liebe* to the final *begnadete*. Over a period of 22 years, from 1522 to 1544, Luther really wrestled with a phrase that was firmly embedded in German practice. His own superb word *holdselige* in turn has become a tradition in German Protestantism, to say the least. Both *voll gnaden* and *holdselige* represent interesting stages in the long history of German effort to find appropriate vernacular equivalents for the Vulgate and Greek terms. Neither is altogether satisfactory. It is a tribute to Luther's genius that toward the end of his career he should suggest that translation which appears thus far to be the most adequate yet found: "Gegrüsset seist du begnadete."[36]

---

[40]There remains a measure of doubt whether *begnadete* is definitely and absolutely by Luther himself. The sermon of 1532 (WA 36, 141), on which this portion of the *Hauspostille* is largely based, does not yet contain it.

[41]Cf. also John G. Kunstmann, "And Yet Again: 'Wes das Herz voll ist, des gehet der Mund über,'" *Concordia Theological Monthly*, XXXIII (July 1952), 509-527.

PART III. SHAPING THE ENGLISH BIBLE

Chapter 7

William Tyndale: Ephesians

THE SUBJECT of the literary evolution of the English Bible is so vast that no single scholar can hope to do it full justice. Certainly none has done so thus far. Though an impressively large number of books and essays both scholarly and popular have been written on the English Bible, which together with Luther's German Bible is probably the most distinguished Protestant version in the world, all of them fall short of their goal in one respect or another.

Because of the magnitude of the task, even scholars have allowed themselves rather greater dependence upon the work of their predecessors than is customary in studies of English literary history. Hence it is perhaps not surprising that the popularizers and summarizers should have been content with merely repeating the results of the labors of their more learned colleagues. While there is thus a comprehensive literature on the subject of the English Bible, a good deal of it is little more than a repetition of previous work.

One shortcoming of this literature is that there is disappointingly little discussion of the influence of Luther on the English Bible in general. True, the important matter of Luther's definite influence upon the first printed English New Testament of William Tyndale has been investigated with some care. But though considerably more has been written on Luther and Tyndale than on Luther and Coverdale, an examination of the literature on Tyndale's debt to Luther reveals an inadequate presentation of the facts even in this well-plowed field. Among the more recent publications the following are probably the most important: James L. Cheney's *The Sources of Tyndale's New Testament* (Halle, 1883, 41 pp.), L. Franklin Gruber's *The First English New Testament and Luther* (Burlington, Iowa, 1928, 128 pp.), Albert H. Gerberich's Johns Hopkins dissertation *Luther and the English Bible* (Lancaster, Pa., 1933, 59 pp.), and the relevant chapters in J. F. Mozley's brilliant *William Tyndale* (London, 1937, 364 pp.). In addition to these more or less specialized investigations there are of course the many general books on the history and nature of the English Bible, among the best of which would seem to be Charles C. Butterworth's *The Literary Lineage of the King James Bible* (Philadelphia, 1941, 394 pp.).

None of these scholars does justice to Luther. Even Gerberich's dissertation falls short of its goal of recording the chief Lutheran traces in Tyndale's New Testament. It is my aim to supplement Gerberich's basic though inadequate research, which has unfortunately been ignored by other students of the subject. Even Mozley and Butterworth have been unaware of the fundamental work done by Gerberich.

In general, I find myself in agreement with Mozley's view that Tyndale's version is basically an independent piece of work. It rests solidly on Erasmus' edition (probably the third edition of 1522) of the Greek New Testament accompanied by a new translation of that text into Latin. Yet it has been all too readily assumed that Tyndale consulted nothing but the Greek text. What has not been sufficiently examined by students of Tyndale is the degree of influence which Erasmus' new Latin rendering may have had on Tyndale's translation, and whether this suffices to account for its obvious divergences from the Vulgate. Many are not caused by Erasmus' Greek text itself. The only way to decide this troublesome issue would be to make a verse-by-verse comparison of the Greek text and Erasmus' own Latin version. Only those verses in which there is a difference between the two can be used as a basis for determining Tyndale's actual procedure. So far as I know, this time-consuming but indispensable study has not yet been undertaken by Tyndale scholars. But, whatever the outcome of this necessary examination, of one thing there can be little doubt: Tyndale's translation was made from the Erasmian texts, whether Greek or Latin or, most probably, both.

Clearly, there is inadequate evidence for the claim, sometimes made by too eager Luther enthusiasts, that Tyndale translated more or less directly from Luther's German version. The strong rejection of this claim does not mean, however, that Tyndale ignored Luther's work. On the contrary, Tyndale was very much aware of the pioneer achievement of the man who set the general pattern for Tyndale's own popular, highly idiomatic rendering. As a literary genius in his own right he more often than not provided his own relatively free translation. He was quite obviously not content with merely copying Luther. He was too independent a person to be content with such procedure. Instead, he reproduced in his own tongue the general spirit of Luther's German, thus succeeding in creating a New Testament in the vernacular second, in Mozley's opinion, only to Luther's masterful version.

In spite of the fundamental verbal independence of Tyndale's rendering, there are a number of passages where he saw fit to follow, beyond the general method of Luther's translation, actual phrases and words found in the German New Testament. It is these verbal agreements, above and beyond the general Lutheran tenor of Tyndale's New Testament, which form the subject of this essay.

By restricting the scope of the material to be examined it is hoped that some of the pitfalls of many an investigation of a similar nature may have been avoided. I shall deal only with one of the shorter Pauline Epistles, Ephesians. In this way I hope to escape the very real danger of covering too much ground with too little attention to detail. All I wish to do is to point out what appear to me clear-cut Lutheran traces in the superb text of the man who gave us the first printed New Testament in English. I shall present the evidence and discuss it as far as possible or necessary. To save space, only the relevant phrases, not the entire verses, will be quoted.

EPH. 1 : 4 Tyndale, 1526–1536: *before the foundacion of the worlde was layde*
   Erasmus' Greek, 1519 and 1522: πρὸ καταβολῆς κόσμου
   Erasmus' Latin, 1519 and 1522: *antequam iacerentur fundamenta mundi*
   Vulgate: *ante mundi constitutionem*
   Wicliff, 1380: *bifor the makynge of the world*
   Luther, 1522–1546: *ehe der welt grund gelegt war*

It is quite clear, to begin with, that Tyndale went beyond the Vulgate. Neither did he merely copy Wicliff's version so obviously based on the Vulgate. It is also clear that the Greek original by itself does not readily lead to Tyndale's English rendering. All that the Greek means is "before the foundation, or beginning, of the world." Erasmus' imaginative Latin version comes much closer to Tyndale. It is Erasmus who, several years before Luther, decided to convert the first genitive of the double genitive construction to a verbal phrase, changing in this process the preposition πρὸ to the conjunction *antequam* and the genitival noun καταβολῆς to the phrase *iacerentur fundamenta*. πρὸ καταβολῆς κόσμου thus emerges as *antequam iacerentur fundamenta mundi*.

Close as the correspondence between Tyndale's English and Erasmus' Latin version is, there is a still closer correspondence, in fact an almost complete identity, between Tyndale's English and Luther's German. *Before the foundacion of the worlde was layde* is the exact counterpart of Luther's *ehe der welt grund gelegt war*.

Although this is not the place for a detailed discussion of the genesis of Luther's rendering, we should at least say that he was doubtless indebted to Erasmus' Latin version. He appears to owe the general structure of this particular phrase to Erasmus. But he did not copy Erasmus literally, he adapted it to more idiomatic German by making a free rendering of Erasmus' *iacere* as *legen*. He also replaced the plural *fundamenta* by the singular *grund*. What emerged in this evolution was a highly idiomatic German phrase.

Tyndale, it would seem, availed himself fully of Luther's excellent German rendering. Without wishing to rule out Erasmus' Latin version as at least a secondary source, we are probably safe in maintaining that Luther's German version, indebted as it may have been to Erasmus itself, was his primary source. The very least we can say is that Tyndale agrees verbatim with Luther.

EPH. 1 : 10 Tyndale, 1526–36: *when the tyme were full come*
    Erasmus' Greek, 1519 and 1522: τοῦ πληρώματος τῶν καιρῶν
    Erasmus' Latin, 1519 and 1522: *plenitudinis temporum*
    Vulgate: *plenitudinis temporum*
    Wicliff, 1380: *into dispensacioun of plenty of tymes*
    Luther, 1522–1546: *da die zeyt erfullet war*

This is a famous and characteristically Lutheran phrase. It does not occur before him in the printed German Bibles. Unless and until it should, unexpectedly, turn up in some pre-Lutheran manuscript, it can be held to be Luther's own creation.

Though the phrase is unmistakably Lutheran, having that indefinable Lutheran ring, its origin is not necessarily shrouded in mystery. It is actually based on a favorite literary device of Luther's. He simply did not like double genitives. Wherever they occur in the Greek original and the Vulgate, he almost invariably succeeded in avoiding them in his German translation. Our verse, Eph. 1 : 10, is just one example, though a particularly familiar one, of this definite tendency of his. He decided to replace the double genitive by a dependent clause.

Tyndale, it would seem, followed Luther closely. All of his known sources have the double genitival construction. The Vulgate and Erasmus kept the Greek original's τοῦ πληρώματος τῶν καιρῶν. Tyndale's English predecessor Wicliff also retained it in his *of plenty of tymes*. Tyndale obviously broke with the Graeco-Latin and English traditions and threw in his lot with Martin Luther.

EPH. 1 : 19 Tyndale, 1526–1536: *accordynge to the workynge of that his mighty power*

Erasmus' Greek, 1519 and 1522: κατὰ τὴν ἐνέργειαν τοῦ κράτους τῆς ἰσχύος αὐτοῦ
Erasmus' Latin, 1519 and 1522: *secundum efficaciam roboris fortitudinis eius*
Vulgate: *secundum operationem potentiae virtutis eius*
Wicliff, 1380: *bi the worchynge of the mygt of his vertue*
Luther, 1522–1546: *nach der wirkung seyner mechtigen sterck*

All of the Latin and English translations available to Tyndale preserve the double genitive of the Greek original: τοῦ κράτους τῆς ἰσχύος. Tyndale departed from this tradition by converting the second genitive noun into an adjective, thereby producing a much better rendering, for a modern language at any rate. Since Luther, his principal model in his struggle for a highly idiomatic version, preceded him in this device, it is reasonable to assume that Tyndale, clearly approving of Luther's handling of this phrase, preferred to follow the German rather than the painfully literal tradition. It is interesting to note that the King James Bible, which usually shied away from Tyndale's freer renderings, kept this particular reading. It was too good to let go. This action in itself is an indirect tribute to the originator of this felicitous phrase, Martin Luther.

EPH. 1 : 22 Tyndale, 1526–36: *the heed of the congregacion*
Erasmus' Greek, 1519 and 1522: κεφαλὴν ... τῇ ἐκκλησίᾳ
Erasmus' Latin, 1519 and 1522: *caput ... ipsi ecclesiae*
Vulgate: *caput super omnem ecclesiam*
Wicliff, 1380: *heed over al the chirche*
Luther, 1522–46: *zum heubt der gemeynen*

Tyndale's use of the word *congregacion* instead of *church* (as used by Wicliff and resumed by the Authorized Version) has, practically from its inception, been looked upon as evidence of his intrinsic Lutheranism both theological and literary. Tyndale was probably the first to introduce Luther's exciting new term into English. Erasmus had seen no reason to alter the Vulgate's *ecclesia*. In the entire British tradition from Wicliff to the Authorized Version only William Tyndale and Miles Coverdale (including the Cranmer Bible of 1539), the "Lutheran" authors of the first printed English New Testament and of the first printed English Bible, respectively, were sufficiently close adherents of the German Reformation to incorporate this distinctive word of Martin Luther's.

Wherever the word *ecclesia* occurs in Ephesians, both Luther and Tyndale use *gemeyne* and *congregacion*. There is no exception. All eight occurrences (1:22; 3:10; 3:21; 5:23; 5:24; 5:25; 5:29; 5:32) in Ephesians have *congregacion* in Tyndale's version.

Eph. 2:2 Tyndale, 1526–36: *after the governer that ruleth in the ayer*
   Erasmus' Greek, 1519 and 1522: κατὰ τὸν ἄρχοντα τῆς ἐξουσίας τοῦ ἀέρος
   Erasmus' Latin, 1519 and 1522: *iuxta principem cui potestas est aeris*
   Vulgate: *secundum principem potestatis aeris huius*
   Wicliff, 1380: *aftir the prince of the power of this eire*
   Luther, 1522–1527: *nach dem fursten der vbirkeyt, die ynn der lufft regirt*
   Luther, 1530–1546: *nach dem fursten, der ynn der lufft herrschet*

For the purposes of this essay, we are primarily interested in Tyndale's relative clause, *that ruleth in the ayer*. It is obviously a free rendering. The dependent clause clearly takes the place of the double nominal genitive τῆς ἐξουσίας τοῦ ἀέρος, literally reproduced by the Vulgate's *potestatis aeris huius*. Now Luther was not the first to resolve this double genitive phrase into a relative clause. Erasmus had preceded him with his *cui potestas est aeris*. It is not inconceivable that Luther got his inspiration for his own version of this passage from Erasmus. At least the suggestion to do something about the Greek and Vulgate phrases may easily have come from Erasmus, who had labored so hard to produce a more readily intelligible and stylistically more satisfactory translation than the Vulgate provided in his opinion.

Yet, with all due respect to Erasmus' literary genius, the simple fact remains that he did not fully anticipate Luther's rendering of this phrase. It was left for Luther to supply a single verb (*regirt* and, from 1530 on, *herrschet*) for Erasmus' more complicated construction.

Probably taking his cue from Erasmus (though this assumption is by no means necessary), Luther further evolved the process initiated by the prince of the humanists. Whatever the ultimate origin of Luther's excellent phrase, Tyndale went with him all the way, including the verb in the relative clause: his *ruleth* seems to indicate strongly a Lutheran rather than an Erasmian source. We may assume that his whole phrase stems from Luther directly.

Eph. 2:14 Tyndale, 1526: *and hath broken doune the wall in the myddes that was a stoppe bitwene us.*
   Tyndale, 1534–1536: *and hath broken doune the wall that was a stoppe bitwene us*

William Tyndale: Ephesians

Erasmus' Greek, 1519 and 1522: καὶ τὸ μεσότοιχον τοῦ φραγμοῦ λύσας
Erasmus' Latin, 1519 and 1522: *et interstitium macerie diruit*
Vulgate: *et medium parietatem macerie solvens*
Wicliff, 1380: *& unbindynge the myddil wall of a wal*
Luther, 1522–27: *vnd hat abbrochen die mittelwand, die der zawn war zwischen vns*
Luther, 1530–1546: *vnd hat abgebrochen den Zaun, der da zwischen war*

Luther's influence is discernible in two ways. First, there is Luther's rendering of λύσας by *abbrochen,* taken over by Tyndale as *broken doune;* and secondly, the conversion of the nominal genitive τοῦ φραγμοῦ into an explicit relative clause: *die der zawn war zwischen vns* appearing as *that was a stoppe bitwene us* in Tyndale.

As regards the first point, Luther's method is quite clear. He decided to use a specific word to render the rather more general Greek λύσας, which the Vulgate merely took over as *solvens,* in turn reproduced literally by Wicliff's *vnbyndynge.* Tyndale appears to have been impressed by Luther's employment of the specific word for taking down a wall in German, *abbrechen,* and he transferred it to his own rendering as *break down.* Again we must acknowledge Erasmus as being the first to leave behind the Vulgate's general *solvens* and to substitute for it the more specific *diruit.* It is not at all unlikely, though again by no means necessary, that Luther was influenced by Erasmus' imaginative rendering. Since Tyndale agrees verbatim with Luther, it is more probable than not that he followed Luther directly, though it is of course impossible to say so categorically. It is interesting to observe that all English Bibles from Tyndale to the Authorized Version retained Luther's rendering, with the sole exception of the Catholic Rheims version, which, translating the Vulgate literally, has *dissolving.*

The second phrase, *that was a stoppe bitwene us,* pretty clearly goes back to Luther, without even a trace of a possible anticipation by Erasmus, for the latter is content, in this instance, with merely retaining the Vulgate's *macerie.* Luther's favorite device of turning a nominal genitive into a dependent clause—particularly when the genitive by itself does not make for clarity of meaning—was taken over by Tyndale. *Die der zawn war zwischen vns* is quite unmistakably the origin of Tyndale's *that was a stoppe bitwene vs.* All that the Greek original, the Vulgate, Erasmus' Latin version, and Wicliff have is a noun in the genitive—τοῦ φραγμοῦ, *macerie,* and *of a wal.* Tyndale, it would seem, decided to follow Luther's example. However, he did not follow Luther's superb simplification from 1530 on.

Eph. 2 : 15 Tyndale, 1526–1536: *the lawe of commaundements contayned in the lawe written*
 Erasmus' Greek, 1519 and 1522: τὸν νόμον τῶν ἐντολῶν ἐν δόγμασιν
 Erasmus' Latin, 1519 and 1522: *legem mandatorum in decretis sitam*
 Vulgate: *legem mandatorum decretis evacuans*
 Wicliff, 1380: *the lawe of maundementes, bi domes*
 Luther, 1522–1546: *das gesetz der gepot, so fern sie schrifftlich verfasset waren*

Erasmus was again the first to interpret, by way of his rendering, the meaning of this obscure passage; by inserting *sitam* he started its elucidation. How obscure the phrase was can be gathered from Wicliff's literal rendering of the Vulgate: *bi domes*. What Luther's genius added to Erasmus' very helpful *sitam* was an interpretation of the word δόγμασιν, *decretis—schrifftlich verfasset*. Tyndale decided to follow his two chief authorities in this difficult verse. If his word *contayned* can be said to originate either in Erasmus' *sitam* or in Luther's *verfasset* (or in both, Luther probably reinforcing Erasmus in Tyndale's mind), there can be little doubt as to the probable sole source of Tyndale's word *written*. Only Luther and Luther alone, without Erasmus, suggested this interpretative addition to Tyndale. Luther's *schrifftlich* would appear to be the inspiration of Tyndale's *written*.

This is obviously not a case of a literal copying of a Lutheran phrase. It is rather an illustration of Tyndale's taking over an idea of Luther's, couching it in the process in a phrase of his own suggested, however, by Martin Luther.

Eph. 3 : 5 Tyndale, 1526–1536: *in tymes passed*
 Erasmus' Greek, 1519 and 1522: ἑτέραις γενεαῖς
 Erasmus' Latin, 1519 and 1522: *in aliis aetatibus*
 Vulgate: *aliis generationibus*
 Wicliff, 1380: *to other generaciouns*
 Luther, 1522–1546: *ynn den vorigen zeytten*

Luther's free rendering was fully taken over by Tyndale. A literal translation of the Greek is found in the Authorized Version's "in other ages." One could argue that Tyndale's *tymes* could conceivably be derived from Erasmus' Latin *aetatibus*, though *ages* would seem to be a more likely rendering of this word. But Erasmus' Latin version would never do as the source of Tyndale's *passed*. Neither the Greek ἑτέραις nor the Vulgate's or Erasmus' *aliis* could easily yield *passed*. Luther's *vorigen* is the only word that corresponds exactly to Tyndale's phrase.

Eph. 3 : 15 Tyndale, 1526–1536: *father over all that is called father*
Erasmus' Greek, 1519 and 1522: ἐξ οὗ πᾶσα πατριά
Erasmus' Latin, 1519: *in quo omnis parentela*
Erasmus' Latin, 1522: *ex quo omnis a communi patre cognatio*
Vulgate: *ex quo omnis paternitas*
Wicliff, 1380: *of whom eche fadirheed*
Luther, 1522–1544: *der der recht vatter ist vber alles was vatter heyst*

This obscure passage presents a real problem to the translator. Luther, it is clear, handled it very freely. Tyndale, it seems, followed his leadership closely. This does not mean of course that Luther's rendering was particularly satisfactory. As a matter of fact, it took Luther a long time to come upon a version that was definitely superior to his earlier efforts. It was not till 1545 that he saw fit to change the second *vatter* to *kinder*. Unfortunately Tyndale was no longer alive to take advantage of Luther's late, much improved rendering.

The amazing fact remains that Tyndale took over one of Luther's less felicitous and less successful phrases, a clear indication of how strongly he felt himself to be under the influence and tutelage of his German predecessor and mentor.

Eph. 3 : 19 Tyndale, 1526–1536: *which is the love of Christ, which love passeth all knowledge*
Erasmus' Greek, 1519 and 1522: τὴν ὑπερβάλλουσαν τῆς γνώσεως ἀγάπην τοῦ χριστοῦ
Erasmus' Latin, 1519: *praeeminentem cognitioni dilectionem Christi* (In 1522, Erasmus changed *cognitioni* to *cognitionis*)
Vulgate: *supereminentem scientiae charitatem Christi*
Wicliff, 1380: *the charite of crist more excellent thanne science*
Luther, 1522–1543: *die liebe Christi, die doch alle erkentnis vbertrifft*

Tyndale, beyond following Luther in the substitution of a relative clause for the present participle of the Greek original and the non-Lutheran translations, would also seem to have inserted the word *all* in agreement with Luther's addition of *alle*. At least there is no other objective source for Tyndale's extra word.

Eph. 4 : 18 Tyndale, 1526–1536: *straungers from the lyfe which is in god*
Erasmus' Greek, 1519 and 1522: ἀπηλλοτριωμένοι τῆς ζωῆς τοῦ θεοῦ
Erasmus' Latin, 1519 and 1522: *abalienati a vita Dei*

Vulgate: *alienati a vita Dei*
Wicliff, 1380: *aliened fro the liif of god*
Luther, 1522–1546: *entfrembdet von dem leben das aus got ist*

Tyndale's conversion of the genitive τοῦ θεοῦ, *Dei*, into a relative clause is probably due to Luther's rendering. No other translator anticipated Luther's version in this phrase. It is true that Tyndale did not follow Luther all the way in that he changed the preposition. Luther's *aus* emerges as *in* in Tyndale. All that is claimed here is that Tyndale took over the general structure of the phrase. Tyndale was no slavish imitator.

Eph. 4 : 24 Tyndale, 1526–1536: *in true holynes*
  Erasmus' Greek, 1519 and 1522: ἐν ὁσιότητι τῆς ἀληθείας
  Erasmus' Latin, 1519 and 1522: *per sanctitatem veritatis*
  Vulgate: *in sanctitate veritatis*
  Wicliff, 1380: *in holynesse of truth*
  Luther, 1522–1546: *yn rechtschaffener heylickeyt*

Luther was the only translator prior to Tyndale to turn the genitive τῆς ἀληθείας into an adjective. Tyndale it would seem followed him in this procedure. The Vulgate and Erasmus kept the genitive *veritatis*. Wicliff did not depart from this literal translation. It is interesting to note that Tyndale's free version, probably based on Luther, was retained in the Authorized Version.

Eph. 5 : 2 Tyndale, 1526–1536: *of a swete saver*
  Erasmus' Greek, 1519 and 1522: εἰς ὀσμὴν εὐωδίας
  Erasmus' Latin, 1519 and 1522: *in odorem bonae fragrantiae*
  Vulgate: *in odorem suavitatis*
  Wicliff, 1380: *in to the odour of swetnesse*
  Luther, 1522–1546: *zu eynem sussen geruch*

The significance of Luther's version for Tyndale is again to be found in the conversion of the genitive noun εὐωδίας into an adjective. There is hardly room for much doubt that Tyndale's phrase *swete saver* derives from Luther's *sussen geruch*. Luther, it is clear, was the first to undertake this change, and Tyndale the first Englishman, followed by Miles Coverdale, to prefer the German version to the traditional literal translation as found in Wicliff in English.

Eph. 6 : 2, Tyndale, 1526–1536: *the fyrst commaundement that hath eny promes*
  Erasmus' Greek, 1519 and 1522: ἐντολὴ πρώτη ἐν ἐπαγγελίᾳ

Erasmus' Latin, 1519 and 1522: *praeceptum primum in promissione*
Vulgate: *mandatum primum in promissione*
Wicliff, 1380: *the first maundement in biheest*
Luther, 1522–1546: *das erst gepot, das eyn verheyssung hat*

There can hardly be any doubt as to the source of Tyndale's phrase *that hath eny promes*. It is a striking phrase, not readily arrived at on the basis of the Greek original or the various Latin and English versions prior to Tyndale. It was Luther who converted the prepositional phrase ἐν ἐπαγγελίᾳ (retained as *in promissione* by the Vulgate and Erasmus) into a full explanatory clause *das eyn verheyssung hat*. It would appear that Tyndale derived his practically identical phrase from Luther.

EPH. 6 : 11 Tyndale, 1526–1536: *agaynst the crafty assautes*
Erasmus' Greek, 1519 and 1522: πρὸς τὰς μεθοδείας
Erasmus' Latin, 1519 and 1522: *adversus assultus*
Vulgate: *adversus insidias*
Wicliff, 1380: *agens aspiynges*
Luther, 1522–1546: *gegen den listigen anlaufft*

Tyndale's method of translating μεθοδείας by means of two words, an adjective and a noun, does not have a parallel in any of the Latin and English versions before Tyndale. Since it occurs in Luther and Luther alone, it would again seem reasonable, in the light of Tyndale's relation to Luther, to assume that *crafty assautes* is due to Luther's *listigen anlaufft*. At least there does not appear to be any more satisfactory explanation.

Though Tyndale did not follow Luther very closely, there are important Lutheran traces in his English version. In support of this contention 15 passages of some significance have been discussed in detail. So far as these passages are concerned, it seems all but certain that Tyndale took them over from the man who preceded him with both the theory and practice of an idiomatic, forceful rendering of the Bible. The passages adduced in this connection were chosen with care. In order to be included in this selected list, the phrase under review had to be markedly different from the original Greek and from all of the Latin and English pre-Tyndalian versions. In other words, the passage had to be rendered in a somewhat unusual way to warrant inclusion here. If, upon close examination, this unusually Englished phrase was found to correspond closely to, or even to be completely identical with, Luther's translation, it was assumed that the German Reformer was ultimately responsible in some manner for Tyndale's rendering. Only passages for which no other source, whether primary (Greek) or secondary (Erasmus' Latin, the Vulgate, or Wicliff), would do have been brought to the attention of scholars. It is only passages of this sort that prove, or all but prove, Tyndale's consultation of his distinguished predecessor's epoch-making version. There is strong evidence—some of it incontrovertible, it would seem to me—of Lutheran traces in the first printed English New Testament.

Chapter 8

Miles Coverdale

a. THE TWENTY-THIRD PSALM

THERE IS a great deal of uncertainty and even misunderstanding abroad about the influence of Martin Luther on the first printed Bible in the English language, published by Miles Coverdale in 1535. Opinions of the most eminent students of the history of the English Bible vary considerably. They range all the way from an almost indignant denial of any influence whatsoever to the recognition that in some parts, such as the First Epistle of John, there are traces of specifically Lutheran origin.

What accounts for this bewildering diversity of scholarly views? The answer to this legitimate question is simple enough—a lack of close analysis and, consequently, of reliable information.

In the following two essays, on Psalm 23 and Galatians, I refer to the existence of serious shortcomings in the majority of the studies on the English Bible. Certainly one of these shortcomings is a failure to recognize the considerable debt which the creator of the important first complete printed English Bible owes to the literary genius of Martin Luther. If this is true of the responsible work of original scholars, it applies still more to the many popularizers in this field. So far as I know, no systematic study has yet been undertaken of the influence Luther exerted on Miles Coverdale. Yet this influence was still greater and more palpable than the influence of Luther on Tyndale.

There should never have been any doubt that Coverdale's translation of the Bible leans heavily on German sources; the translator himself established this fact by indicating on the original title-page that his English Bible was "faithfully and truly translated out of Douche and Latyn." The only real question has always been, or at least should have been, about the identity of the German versions involved. In this rather important matter Coverdale does not help us, since he merely remarked, in the Dedication to the King, that he translated "out of fyve sundry interpreters."

So far as I know, there is virtual agreement among scholars that the Zurich Bible and Luther's Bible were his "Douche" and the Vulgate and Pagninus' Latin Psalter of 1528 his "Latyn" sources. As for the fifth source mentioned by Coverdale, there is some disagreement in scholarly circles, most investigators referring to Tyndale's partial translation of the Bible,[1] and a few to Jerome's *Psalterium iuxta Hebraeos*.

With reference to the relative importance of the German and Latin sources, the translator, aside from putting "Douche" before "Latyn" on the title-page,[2] states fairly unequivocally in the Prologue to the Christian Reader that his chief debt is to his German sources: "I have had sondrye translations, not onely in Latyn but also of the Douche interpreters: whom (because of theyr synguler gyftes and speciall diligence in the Bible) I have ben the more glad to folowe for the most parte...." Thus, unless Coverdale's own words are to be ignored, there cannot be, nor should there ever have been, any doubt of a major influence of the "Douche interpreters" on the first printed English Bible of 1535.

Strange as it may seem, it is only in the last 100 years that this intellectual debt, so unmistakably set forth by none other than the translator himself, has been recognized by students of the English Bible. As late as 1861 the British scholar C. D. Ginsburg did not hesitate at all to write publicly that he was "amazed at the ignorance prevalent upon the sources of our first published English Bible."[3] It is characteristic of the then widespread lack of proper information that Ginsburg dared to state bluntly, apparently without fear of contradiction, that it was "generally asserted"[3] that Coverdale's version of the Old Testament was made from the Hebrew. A number of English publications from 1838 to 1859 are quoted to corroborate this fairly sweeping remark.[3] So far as I am aware, Ginsburg was the first modern scholar to call attention to the non-Hebrew sources of Coverdale's translation. After firing the first shot in 1861, he reiterated his "discovery" the following year in an article on Coverdale in the third edition of John Kitto's *Cyclopaedia of Biblical Literature*.[4] The general theory advanced by Ginsburg in both places was that Coverdale relied chiefly on the Zurich Bible of 1531.

---

[1] I am somewhat skeptical about Tyndale's being one of the "fyve sundry interpreters" from whom he "translated." Would Coverdale really have used the word "translate" when speaking of an earlier *English* version?

[2] Cf. H. R. Willoughby, *The Coverdale Psalter* (Chicago, 1935), p. 20: "... the order, German first and Latin second, indicating his own preference in his dependence on these earlier versions."

[3] C. D. Ginsburg, *Coheleth, Commonly Called the Book of Ecclesiastes* ... (London, 1861), Appendix II, p. 524.

[4] Available to me only in a reissue, Philadelphia, 1865–66.

It is no exaggeration to say that ever since Ginsburg's severe attack on the views generally held in his time the great majority of publications on the history of the English Bible refer specifically to the Swiss Bible[5] as a primary, if not the prime, German source of Coverdale's English version.

While there is doubtless some truth in Ginsburg's theory, the modern student cannot avoid the uncomfortable feeling that most of the writers on this subject since his initial discovery have largely lost sight of the peculiar circumstances which led him to come out with his revolutionary view. It should never have been forgotten that he arrived at his theory on the basis of studies incidental to his *Commentary on Ecclesiastes* and that he drew his original illustrations only from this brief portion of the Bible. His subsequent article on Coverdale in Kitto's *Cyclopaedia*, in addition to referring the reader to the *Commentary* just quoted, contains only one verse from Isaiah in further support of his theory. But while Ginsburg himself may surely not be absolved from generalizing too soon and too easily from what is clearly rather sketchy evidence, it is also the scholars after him who must be charged with unwarranted generalizations made on the basis of insufficient source material. The most serious flaw in the publications of almost all post-Ginsburg students of our Bible is that, with the principal exception of Westcott,[6] they do not appear to rest on independent investigations so far as the sources of Coverdale's translation are concerned. Many major works on the history of the English Bible repeat as a *general* truth what Ginsburg and, after him and under his avowed[7] influence, Westcott had found on the basis of *individual* passages, though it must be admitted that both these scholars had themselves not presented their views as *specific* but also as *general* truths. No matter how relatively small the sections of the Bible examined by Ginsburg and Westcott are, these men had at least some definite albeit disappointingly restricted ground on which they stood to rest their case.[8] The trouble with most writers since their day is that, quite apart from their uncritical generalizing on the basis of very limited data, they themselves did not produce much, if any, further proof for their views.

There is, however, one gleam of light in the otherwise dark picture of the present state of research on the "Douche" sources of Coverdale's

[5]Scholars to be sure no longer speak of the edition of 1531 but of editions between 1524 and 1530.
[6]B. F. Westcott, *A General View of the History of the English Bible* (London, 1868, 1872, 1905. First, second, and third editions, respectively).
[7]Ibid., p. 162 (third edition).
[8]Incidentally, I am not sure that the passages adduced as evidence prove the point.

English Bible. D. Daiches in 1941 went so far as to suggest that Westcott's conclusions regarding the greatly preponderant influence of the Zurich Bible were really drawn from rather insufficient evidence.[9] Yet even Daiches, one of the more recent scholarly writers on the subject, relegated his well-taken observation to a mere footnote. In the main text of his book he maintains that for the Old Testament "the Zurich Bible is certainly Coverdale's primary source, with occasional renderings of Pagninus and Luther preferred to those of the Zurich version."[10] It is only in a footnote to this passage that he points out that "a complete collation shows more important variations."[10]

So far only general investigations of Coverdale's English Bible as a whole have been touched upon. As for special detailed examinations of specific parts of the first printed English Bible, there appears to be a great dearth of relevant material. As a matter of fact, only one study has come to my attention, Ernest Clapton's *Our Prayer Book Psalter*.[11] Unfortunately this ambitious work, in which the sources of Coverdale's rendering of the Psalter are analyzed, is not without serious errors, in spite of the high praise it has received.

In view of the unsatisfactory state of our present information on the sources, particularly the German sources, of Coverdale's translation, it would appear to be advisable, if not downright necessary, to subject closely circumscribed parts of the first printed English Bible to a somewhat searching analysis and to limit the conclusions reached specifically and expressly to the section thus examined. We must by all means stay away from premature generalizations while still engaged in detailed investigations of restricted scope. It is the purpose of this essay to examine the German sources of Coverdale's translation of a single psalm, the well-known and beloved twenty-third. In order to proceed as carefully as possible we shall take up each of the six verses by itself. Although the primary emphasis in this essay is upon the German sources, the relevant Latin sources will also be given as supplementary background material.

V. 1

Coverdale (1535)[12]: *The LORDE is my shepherde, I can want nothinge.*

Zurich (1525)[13]: *Der HERR ist mein hirt / mir wirt nüts mangeln.*

---

[9] D. Daiches, *The King James version of the English Bible* . . . (Chicago, 1941).
[10] Ibid., p. 175.
[11] E. Clapton, *Our Prayer Book Psalter* (London, 1934).
[12] In W. A. Wright, *The Hexaplar Psalter* (Cambridge, 1911).
[13] In J. J. Mezger, *Geschichte der deutschen Bibelübersetzungen in der schweizerisch-reformirten Kirche* . . . (Basel, 1876).

Zurich (1530)[14]: *DEr HERR ist mein hirt / mir wirdt neüts manglenn.*
Zurich (1531)[15]: *DEr HERR hirtet mich / darumb manglet mir nichts.*
Luther (1524, 1528, 1531, 1534)[16]: *DEr HERR ist mein hirtte / mir wird nichts mangeln.*
Psalterium Gallicum[17]: *Dominus regit me et nihil mihi deerit.*
Psalterium Romanum[17]: Identical with Psalterium Gallicum.
Psalterium iuxta Hebraeos[17]: *Dominus pascit me et nihil mihi deerit.*
Pagninus[18]: *Dominus pascens me, non deficiam.* (Marginal note: *pascit*)

So far as the first half of the verse is concerned, two points should be noted. First, Coverdale agrees with Zurich 1525 and 1530, and not with Zurich 1531 as Ginsburg thought. Secondly, the two early Zurich editions agree with Luther. Inasmuch as we know that these early Swiss Bibles are practically identical with Luther's earliest versions, that they are in fact admittedly based on the Wittenberg professor's labors, we may conclude that, whether or not either of the early Zurich Bibles was the mediate source, Coverdale's phrase The LORDE is my shepherde appears to stem ultimately from Luther's translation of 1524 ff.

The second half of the verse offers a certain difficulty. Coverdale's use of the modal "can" does not seem to be based on any source either German or Latin. It is important to bear in mind, however, that the man who gave us the first printed English Bible was by no means a slavish translator. Wherever he saw fit to do so, he added or changed words "to give vividness,"[19] a fact pointed out by Clapton as one of the "special peculiarities in Coverdale's style."[20] Aside from this slight modification of his source or sources, the second half of the first verse also might come directly, or indirectly via the early Swiss Bibles, from the pen of Martin Luther. There is, however, no absolute certainty in this part of the verse. The Latin versions could also have inspired the English translation.

---

[14]Quoted from a copy available in the Library of Union Theological Seminary, in New York City.
[15]Available in the Library of the American Bible Society in New York City.
[16]The Luther items important for this paper were accessible to me as follows:
   1524: *Das 3. Teil des allten Testaments:* New York Public Library.
   1528: *New deudsch Psalter:* Library of the Hartford (Conn.) Seminary Foundation.
   1531: *Der Deudsch Psalter:* Also in Hartford, Conn.
   1534: *Biblia, das ist, die gantze Heilige Schrifft Deudsch:* New York Public Library.
[17]In Faber Stapulensis, *Quincuplex Psalterium* (Paris, 1509). Available at Yale.
[18]*Psalmi Davidis* . . . (Geneva, n.d.).
[19]Clapton, *Psalter*, XXIII.
[20]Ibid., XXII.

V. 2

Coverdale (1535): *He fedeth me in a grene pasture, ād ledeth me to a fresh water.*

Zurich (1525): *Er lasst mich weiden, da vil grass stadt, und fürt mich zum wasser, das mich erkület.*

Zurich (1530): *Er lasst mich weyden da vil grass stadt / vnd fürt mich zum wasser / das mich erkület.*

Zurich (1531): *Er macht mich in schöner weyd lüyen / vnd fürt mich zu stillen wassern.*

Luther (1524, 1528): *Er lesst mich weyden da viel gras stett / vnd furt mich zum wasser das mich erkulet.*

Luther (1531, 1534): *Er weidet mich auff einer grunen awen / und füret mich zum frisschen wasser.*

Psalterium Gallicum: *In loco pascuae ibi me collocavit. Super aquam refectionis educavit me.*

Psalterium Romanum: Identical with Psalterium Gallicum.

Psalterium iuxta Hebraeos: *In pascuis herbarum acclinavit me: super aquas refectionis enutrivit me.*

Pagninus: *In tuguriis germinis faciat accubare me: super aquas requietum ducet me.*

This is in many respects the most interesting verse of the entire psalm from our comparative point of view. It is, with a relatively high degree of certainty, based directly on Luther's revised translation of 1531. Let us examine it in more detail.

The verse as a whole shows two things pretty conclusively. First, it is another good illustration of the fact, long recognized by German scholars but still largely unrealized by American and British students of the English Bible,[21] that the early Zurich versions of 1525 and 1530 are to all intents and purposes identical with Luther's first published translation of the Twenty-third Psalm of 1524, which they merely reproduce, with orthographical changes to be sure. Secondly, the revised Zurich edition of 1531, which departs from Luther rather considerably, is quite clearly and unmistakably not the basis for Coverdale's version of 1535. All relevant editions of the Zurich Bible are thus eliminated, so far as our verse is concerned, as a source of the first printed English Bible.

It is in this important matter that a serious error in Clapton's book, the only detailed study of the sources of Coverdale's English Psalter

---

[21]Only H. E. Jacobs, *The Lutheran Movement in England and its Literary Monuments* (Philadelphia, 1891), appears to be correctly informed on this important point.

available, should be emphatically pointed out.[22] In discussing the sources of Coverdale's translation of the second verse of the Twenty-third Psalm Clapton makes the remark that the Zurich Bible, about the various editions of which he is incidentally singularly uninformed,[23] is completely identical with Luther's revision of this verse in 1531. This assertion is altogether unfounded. Luther's revision of 1531 did not find its way into any edition of the Zurich Bible so far as I know. It is therefore necessary to conclude that the Swiss Bible cannot possibly have been the source of Coverdale's rendering of the second verse. There is no room for doubt that Coverdale made direct and first-hand use of Luther's revised version of 1531.

After establishing the fact that Coverdale rests securely on Luther, and on Luther alone, we should not fail to note in the second verse as we did in the first that the Englishman's evident dependence on the German by no means rules out slight verbal deviations. Instead of Luther's "*zum* frisschen wasser" Coverdale writes "to *a* fresh water."

V. 3

Coverdale (1535): *He quickeneth my soule, & bringeth me forth in the waye of rightuousnes for his names sake.*
Zurich (1525): *Er erquicket myn seel: er fürt mich uff rechter straass umb synes namens willen.*
Zurich (1530): *Er erquickt mein sel: er fürt mich auff rechter strass vmb seines namens willen.*
Zurich (1531): *[Mit denen] erfristet er meyn seel / treybt mich auff den pfad der gerechtigkeit vmb seines namens willen.*
Luther (1524, 1528, 1531, 1534): *Er erquickt meine seele / er furet mich auf rechter strasse vmb seyns namens willen.*
Psalterium Gallicum: *Animam meam convertit. Deduxit me super semitas iustitiae: propter nomen suum.*
Psalterium Romanum: Identical with Psalterium Gallicum.
Psalterium iuxta Hebraeos: *Animam meam refecit / duxit me per semitas iusticiae: propter nomen suum.*
Pagninus: *Animam meam conuertet per semitas ducet me in orbitas iustitiae propter nomen suum.*

Since this verse presents certain difficulties, it is expedient to take it up in parts. As regards the first phrase, *He quickeneth my soule*, it is obvious that this is very probably based on Luther either directly or indirectly by way of the early Zurich editions. It is not necessary to discuss this phrase further, I believe.

[22] Loc. cit., p. 48.   [23] Ibid., p. xvi.

Our troubles begin with the second phrase, *& bringeth me forth*. It is manifestly not a literal translation of Luther and the identical early Zurich versions or of the Zurich Bible of 1531 or of any of the Latin renderings. My impression is that Coverdale struck out on his own and rendered his German and Latin sources freely. Since he is generally held to be an accomplished stylist, it is not inconceivable that he did not wish to repeat the word *lead* used in the preceding verse. Whatever the cause, it was probably stylistic.

The third phrase, *in the waye of rightuousnes*, offers another problem of some intricacy. It should first be pointed out perhaps that Clapton is quite wrong when he writes "Apparently Coverdale uses singular 'way' contrary to all Versions."[22] While it is true that all Latin versions have a plural noun in this passage, both Luther and the Zurich editions have clearly a singular noun. So far as Coverdale's employment of the singular is concerned, it would seem to me to stem from Luther or the Swiss Bibles. But the real problem this phrase poses is strangely enough not touched upon at all by Clapton—the origin of the genitive *of rightuousnes*. It is here that Clapton's lack of exact information on the various editions of the Zurich Bible proves disastrous for establishing Coverdale's sources. There can be no doubt that Coverdale's phrase *waye of rightuousnes* departs markedly from Luther's *auf rechter strasse* and from the early editions of the Zurich Bible identical with Luther's striking wording. But the Zurich Bible of 1531, definitely breaking with Luther, has *pfad der gerechtigkeit,* a rendering which, together with the Latin versions' *iustitiae*, would appear to be mainly responsible for Coverdale's phrase. Whatever may have induced the Englishman to part company with Luther in this instance, it is evident that he preferred the genitive construction of the revised Zurich version of 1531 and of the Latin translations.

Little need be said about the last phrase, *for his names sake*. It sounds like a close translation of Luther's *vmb seyns namens willen*, although that is by no means a foregone conclusion inasmuch as the same phrase had already been used in the English Psalter of 1530, which is apparently the earliest psalter ever to be printed in English[24] and which reveals no trace of Luther's influence.

V. 4

Coverdale (1535): *Though I shulde walke now in the valley of the shadowe of death, yet I feare no euell, for thou art with me: thy staffe & they shepehoke cōforte me.*

[24]C. C. Butterworth, *The Literary Lineage of the King James Bible* (Philadelphia, 1941), p. 285; 64.

Zurich (1525): *Und ob ich schon wandlete im finstern tal, vörcht ich kain unglück: denn du bist by mir: dein stecken und stab trösted mich.*

Zurich (1530): *Und ob ich schon wandlete im finsterenn thal, förcht ich kain unglück: dann du bist bey mir: dein stäcken vnd stab trösted mich.*

Zurich (1531): *Und ob ich mich schon vergienge in das göw des tödtlichen schattens / so wurde ich doch nichts übels förchten: dañ du bist bey mir / zu dem tröstend mich dein stäcken vnd stab.*

Luther (1524, 1528, 1531, 1534): *Vnd ob ich schon wandert ym finstern tal / furcht ich keyn vngluck / Denn du bist bye myr. Deyn stecken und stab trösten mich.*

Psalterium Gallicum: *Nam et si ambulavero in medio vmbrae mortis: non timebo mala quoniam tu mecum es. Virga tua & baculus tuus ipsa me consolata sunt.*

Psalterium Romanum: *Nam et si ambulem in medio vmbrae mortis: non timebo mala quoniam tu mecum es. Virga tua & baculus tuus ipsa me consolata sunt.*

Psalterium iuxta Hebraeos: *Sed et si ambulavero in valle mortis: non timebo malum quoniam tu mecum es. Virga tua & baculus tuus ipsa consolabuntur me.*

Pagninus: *Etiam cum ambulauero in vallem vmbrae mortis, non timebo quoniam tu mecum: virga tua & fulcrum tuum, ipsa consolabuntur me.*

With the exception of one important and highly interesting phrase, this verse appears to stem largely from Luther's version either directly or indirectly by way of the early Swiss Bibles, which are practically identical with Luther. In addition to this German source, it is quite possible that the revised Zurich edition of 1531 may be responsible for Coverdale's "I feare no *euell*"; at any rate the later Zurich Bible's *übels* would seem to be closer to Coverdale than Luther's and the earlier Zurich Bibles' *unglück*. Be this as it may, by and large this verse is greatly indebted to Luther.

There is, however, one significant phrase for which there does not appear to be any "Douche" source. I mean the well-known words, *in the valley of the shadowe of death*, still very familiar to most of us because of their retention in the Authorized Version. In the absence of proper German sources, it is surely in accordance with Coverdale's own directions to look for the origin of our phrase in the Latin versions. Now Clapton did just that, quoting the Vulgate's *in medio umbrae mortis* and the Psalterium Hebraicum's *in valle mortis*.[22] But the trouble with these sources is obviously that neither one corresponds, by itself, to Coverdale's phrase. If one were willing to accept this composite source, one would have to assume that Coverdale combined the two Latin phrases to give us the resultant somewhat unusual and rather striking wording. While this naturally is not impossible, there is however another Latin source, generally admitted to have been consulted by Coverdale and ordinarily made use of by Clapton in his analysis of Coverdale's sources. For some reason or other,[25] Clapton must have overlooked the following passage in Pagninus' Latin Psalter: *in vallem vmbrae mortis*. In my opinion this phrase is the exact equivalent of Coverdale's *in the valley of the shadowe of death*. So far as I can see, Pagninus' version of this passage appears to be the source of our English phrase; I for one cannot agree with Clapton's theory that a combination of the Vulgate and the Psalterium iuxta Hebraeos is its origin.

V. 5

Coverdale (1535): *Thou preparest a table before me agaynst mine enemies: thou anoyntest my heade with oyle, & fyllest my cuppe full.*
Zurich (1525): *Du bereytest vor mir einen tisch gegen mynen fyenden. Du machest myn houpt feisst mit öl, und schenkest mir voll yn.*
Zurich (1530): *Du bereytest vor mir einenn tisch gegen meinen feyndenn / du machest mein haupt feisst mit öl / vn schenckest mir voll ein.*
Zurich (1531): *Du richtest mir ein tisch zu vor minen feynden / du begeüssest mein haupt mit gesälb / und füllest mir meinen bächer.*
Luther (1524, 1528): *Du bereyttest fur myr eynen tisch gegen meyne feynde / du machst meyn heubt fett mit öle vnd schenckest myr voll eyn.*
Luther (1531, 1534): *Du bereitest fur mir einen tisch gegen meine feinde / Du salbest mein heubt mit öle / vnd schenckest mir vol ein.*
Psalterium Gallicum: *Parasti in conspectu meo mensam: adversus eos qui tribulant me. Impinguasti in oleo caput meum: et calix meus inebrians quam praeclarus est.*
Psalterium Romanum: *Parasti in conspectu meo mensam: adversus eos qui tribulant me. Impinguasti in oleo caput meum: et poculum tuum inebrians quam praeclarum est.*
Psalterium iuxta Hebraeos: *Pones coram me mensam: ex adverso hostium meorum. Impinguasti oleo caput meum: calix meus inebrians.*
Pagninus: *Dispones ad facies meas* (marginal note: *praeparabis coram me*) *mensam contra hostes meos: impinguasti in oleo caput meum. calix meus exuberans* (marginal note: *erit saturus*).

This verse together with the second contains convincing proof that

[25]Unfortunately I have access only to what appears to me to be an (undated) later edition. It is therefore not impossible that the reading given above may not occur in the first edition of 1528. In that event Clapton would of course be exonerated.

Luther's final revision of the Twenty-third Psalm in 1531 is the chief source of Coverdale's translation. I refer particularly to the phrase *thou anoyntest my heade with oyle*. The Zurich editions of 1525 and 1530 are identical with Luther's earlier versions of 1524 and 1528, except for the dialectal substitution of *feisst* for Luther's Low German *fett*. The phrase *du machst meyn heubt fett mit öle*[26] cannot in my opinion constitute as good a source for Coverdale as Luther's version of 1531, *Du salbest mein heubt mit öle;* it is not necessary to point out that the Swiss Bible of 1531 is even further from Coverdale's rendering than the earlier Swiss texts had been.

Aside from this almost incontrovertible evidence for Coverdale's indebtedness to Luther's German Psalter, another phrase of the fifth verse also strongly suggests this source. *Thou preparest a table before me agaynst mine enemies* appears to be an exact rendering of Luther's corresponding phrase even though the Vulgate (*parasti*) and Pagninus' marginal note (*praeparabis*) could also have caused the choice of the *word* "preparest" but not of the *tense* to be sure.

The final phrase of this verse, however, while possibly owing one word to Luther, is probably based on the Zurich Bible of 1531. The latter's *füllest mir meinen bächer* can surely be held to account for Coverdale's *fyllest my cuppe full*. It would seem that the Englishman recoiled from following Luther's amazingly free rendering and that he preferred the unquestionably more conservative Zurich version of 1531. Still there is one word which cannot be quite explained on the basis of this late Swiss Bible, the word *full*. While it can of course be argued that Coverdale's fondness for independent insertions of his own[19] may be sufficient to account for the added *full*, it seems to me that the use of *full* in connection with *fyllest* is a little strained and forced in English to be merely a wholly free and voluntary addition on the part of Coverdale. I rather think that it may be due to Luther's *vnd schenckest mir* vol *ein*. Coverdale must have been impressed by the ring of Luther's superb phrase and, although it was apparently too free for him as a whole, he could not altogether help yielding to its power, at least to the extent of adding the word *full*. It is obvious of course that in the nature of the case this theory is merely a guess.

V. 6

Coverdale (1535): *Oh let thy louynge kyndnes & mercy folowe me all the dayes off my life, that I maye dwell in the house off the LORDE for euer.*

[26] "du machest mein haupt feisst mit öl" (Zurich, 1525 and 1530).

Zurich (1525): *Guts vn barmherzigkeyt werdent mir nachloufen min läben lang, und wird bleyben im huss des HERRN jmmerdar.*
Zurich (1530): *Guts vn barmherzigkeyt werdend mir nachlauffen min läben lang, und wird bleyben im hauss des HERRN jmmerdar.*
Zurich (1531): *So wölle dein güte vnd gnad ob mir halten meyn läben lang / das ich in dinem hauss wonen möge ewigklich.*
Luther (1524, 1528): *Gutts vnd barmhertzikeyt werden myr nachlauffen meyn leben lang / vnd werde bleyben ym hause des HERRN ymmerdar.*
Luther (1531, 1534): *Gutts vnd barmhertzikeyt werden myr folgen meyn leben lang / vnd werde bleyben ym hause des HERRN ymmerdar.*
Psalterium Gallicum: *Et misericordia tua subsequetur me: omnibus diebus vitae meae. Et ut inhabitem in domo domini in longitudinem dierum.*
Psalterium Romanum: *Et misericordia tua subsequitur me: omnibus diebus vitae meae. Et ut inhabitem in domo domini: in longitudine dierum.*
Psalterium iuxta Hebraeos: *Sed et benignitas et misericordia subsequetur me: omnibus diebus vitae meae. Et habitabo in domo domini: in longitudine dierum.*
Pagninus: *Veruntamen bonum & misericordia sequentur me omnibus diebus vitae meae & reuertar in domum* (marginal note: *habitabo in domo*) *Domini in longitudinem dierum.*

The last verse of the Twenty-third Psalm is doubtless the most complicated so far as the sources are concerned. It apparently owes something to almost every source established by scholars to have influenced Coverdale's version. We must again examine each phrase by itself.

The general construction of the verse as a whole would seem to stem from the Zurich Bible of 1531. *Oh let* appears to have been inspired by *So wölle,* and *that I maye dwell* by *das ich . . . wonen möge* or by the Gallican and Roman Psalters' *ut inhabitem.* Structurally this verse agrees with the late Zurich version and, in part at least, with the Vulgate.

Turning now to details, we find the first phrase, *louynge kyndnes & mercy,* very difficult to trace. It could be based on either Luther's *gutts vnd barmhertzikeyt* or the 1531 Zurich version's *güte vnd gnad.* Regarding the expression *louynge kyndnes* I should be inclined to prefer a Latin source, the Psalterium iuxta Hebraeos' *benignitas,* to the German sources. The second phrase *folowe me* departs from both the early Luther and the early Zurich versions' *nachlauffen* and the later Zurich

Bible's *halten*. Its sources are either the Latin translations, especially Pagninus (*sequentur*), or, perhaps just as likely, Luther's third edition, *folgen*. The next phrase, *all the dayes off my life*, does not appear to rest on any German source at all but rather on the Latin versions' *omnibus diebus vitae meae;* Luther's very free *meyn leben lang*, found in all post-Lutheran German Bibles under review, was manifestly not followed by Coverdale. The verb *dwell* in the phrase *that I maye dwell* may have been suggested either by the Latin translations' *habitare, inhabitare* or by the 1531 Swiss Bible's *wonen;* it is probably impossible to decide which was the source, the Latin or the German, or both perhaps. The phrase *in the house off the LORDE* rests again on both German and Latin sources, except that in this case the German source is Luther and the earlier Zurich Bibles rather than the Zurich edition of 1531. The final words, *for euer*, are definitely not based on the Latin *in longitudinem dierum* but quite clearly on the German, although it is difficult to make up one's mind between Luther's *ymmerdar* and the later Zurich Bible's *ewigklich*.

If at the end of our detailed analysis we try to see the Twenty-third Psalm as a whole, the following picture presents itself. The chief source for Coverdale's translation of this psalm in 1535 is Luther's revised German Psalter of 1531; it is impossible to say whether it was this very edition or a later one of the separate Psalter or whether it may have been the 1534 or the 1535 edition of the entire German Bible. Whichever edition it was cannot be established now since they all have practically the same version of the Twenty-third Psalm. The source next in importance to Luther is the 1531 revised edition of the Zurich Bible, but it is of considerably less significance in that only two phrases and the general structure of one verse appear to stem from it. So far as the Latin sources are concerned, we noted that they play a very minor rôle indeed, with the exception of one basic phrase very important for the subsequent history of our English Bible.

It should also be recalled that Coverdale did not follow his indicated sources slavishly. His own individuality asserted itself, even if only moderately, in an occasional insertion not to be accounted for on the basis of any source now known to have been used by him.

At the outset it was stated that the conclusions to be reached in this paper would be considered valid only for the very small portion of the Bible here analyzed. In view of the unfortunate tendency of past students of the English Bible to generalize too soon on insufficient evidence, it should be insisted again at the end of this investigation that what has been found with reference to the Twenty-third Psalm may not necessarily apply to the rest of the Bible, perhaps not even to the Psalter. The results of the present examination are specific and strictly circumscribed; they are limited to the psalm here investigated: for the rendering of the Twenty-third Psalm in the first printed English Bible translated out of the German and Latin by Miles Coverdale, Martin Luther's revised version of this psalm in the German Psalter of 1531 has been found to be the primary "Douche" source.

b. GALATIANS

In the last essay I discussed Miles Coverdale's debt to Martin Luther in the Twenty-third Psalm. In the present essay I shall consider the nature and extent of Coverdale's debt to Martin Luther in Paul's Epistle to the Galatians.

The state of research in this area is such that it is necessary to begin at the beginning, i.e., by subjecting a clearly circumscribed section of the Scriptures to close scrutiny. The time for generalizations, desirable as they are, is far away. What we need first is a series of careful analyses of limited scope. The initial investigation is offered here. It should be borne in mind that whatever conclusions are arrived at in the course of this particular study are in all likelihood not applicable to the Bible as a whole, as a matter of fact not even to the New Testament as a whole. Speaking quite strictly, they apply only to the Epistle to the Galatians. It is hoped, however, that the method here employed may prove helpful to other investigators. Only after all the other books of the Bible have been analyzed in this fashion shall we be able to sketch the full picture of the relation of the first printed English Bible to the German Bible of Martin Luther.

In order to present the essential evidence it will be best to discuss each chapter by itself first. Only then, after such inductive procedure, will a strictly limited generalization be undertaken applicable only to the Epistle to the Galatians.

GALATIANS 1

The first problem we must face is that of the relation between the two editions of Tyndale's New Testament which were available to Coverdale in 1535. What are the differences if any, between Tyndale's first edition of 1525 and the second of 1534? Inasmuch as Tyndale's great translation was in all probability the basic English text with which Coverdale started his own work, it is important for us to be fully informed about the first two Tyndale editions.

Of the 24 verses of the first chapter, as many as 18 are identical in both editions. Only 6 differ: 2, 5, 10, 14, 18, 24. For the first chapter we shall discuss all changes between the two editions. In the other chapters only a selection will be presented.

1:2

Tyndale, 1525: *congregacion*
Tyndale, 1534: *congregacions*

In 1534 Tyndale corrected an obvious error of his first edition: the Greek text as published by Erasmus has the plural ταῖς ἐκκλησίαις. There were, however, editions of the Vulgate which had this noun in the singular, and it is not impossible that Tyndale in 1525 was still under the influence of the Vulgate. It is also possible that this was just an oversight or a misprint.

1:5

Tyndale, 1525: *for ever*
Tyndale, 1534: *for ever and ever*

This is doubtless primarily a stylistic change. Tyndale's second edition is the first occurrence of the well-known phrase that still survives in the King James Bible.

1:10

Tyndale, 1525: *Seke I nowethe faveoure offmen or off God?*
Tyndale, 1534: *Preache I mannes doctrine or Godes?*

The translation contained in Tyndale's first edition is rather literal, at least when compared with the second edition. It appears to be based on the Greek πείθω, for the Latin *suadeo* could hardly yield *Seke I the faveoure*. The revision of 1534 is manifestly a free rendering, the verb *preache* almost certainly suggested by Luther's *predige*.

1:14

Tyndale, 1525: *and moche more fevently (sic!) mayntayned the tradicions*
Tyndale, 1534: *and was a moche more fervent mayntener of the tradicions*

The first edition with its verbal construction is free in comparison with the second edition's substantive translation of the Greek ζηλωτής.

1:18

Tyndale, 1525: *I returned to Jerusalem unto Peter*
Tyndale, 1534: *I returned to Jerusalem to se Peter*

The first edition is free in its substitution of the dative phrase for the verb-plus-accusative construction of the Greek text ἱστορῆσαι Πέτρον, which he follows in the revision of 1534.

1 : 24

Tyndale, 1525: *they glorified God in me*
Tyndale, 1534: *they glorified God on my behalffe*
The first edition is strictly literal, the second is free.

What interests us primarily in this connection is naturally what Coverdale does in the face of these differences between the first and second editions of Tyndale's New Testament, the principal source of his own translation. Of the six passages briefly discussed above, Coverdale follows Tyndale's second edition in all but the last. In Gal. 1 : 24 he "preferred" Tyndale's original *in me* to his later *on my behalffe*. It is of course impossible to insist that the source of Coverdale's *in me* is exclusively or even primarily Tyndale's original *in me* since the Vulgate also has *in me*. All we can say safely is that Coverdale in one passage out of six, in which Tyndale's first and second editions diverge, is not in agreement with Tyndale's second version (with which the other five agree) but with the first edition or with the Vulgate, which are identical in this phrase.

So far as the question of which edition of Tyndale Coverdale followed is concerned, we can state that, for the first chapter of Galatians, it was in all probability the second revised version of 1534. The evidence points strongly in this direction. It should naturally be remembered that we are speaking only on the basis of those passages in which the two Tyndale editions under review here were found to differ one from the other.

The next problem to be considered is the question of Coverdale's relation to the Tyndale text, i.e., probably the second edition of 1534. It is quite clear that Coverdale's version of 1535 is by no means identical with the Tyndale translation of 1534 or, for that matter, of 1525. There are in fact a considerable number of divergences from Tyndale. Of the 24 verses of the first chapter, as many as 20 depart to a greater or lesser extent from the Tyndale text of 1534, the edition probably used by Coverdale. Only four verses, or as little as one-sixth of the chapter, are taken over without change. In other words, with the exception of vv. 5, 6, 7, and 15, each verse of the first chapter shows some alteration. In the light of this fact it is hardly possible to agree with a British scholar's claim that the whole of the N. T. in Coverdale's Bible contains practically Tyndale's text. This sweeping statement surely does not apply to the first chapter of Galatians, in which five-sixths of the verses differ in some way or other in the Coverdale and Tyndale versions.

If one counts phrases or words rather than verses, there are actually as many as 37 passages in which Coverdale diverges from Tyndale. Of these 37, the preponderant majority, 27 to be exact, are in full agreement with Luther's German text. However, not all of these necessarily go back to Luther alone. As a matter of fact, as many as 19 could, theoretically at least, have a double provenance—the Vulgate and/or Luther. Since, however, there is not a single case where Coverdale follows the Vulgate against Luther, and since there are on the other hand a number of cases in which Coverdale follows Luther against the Vulgate, it would seem reasonable to conclude that it is more likely that these 19 Vulgate-identical-with-Luther cases are Lutheran rather than Vulgate in origin. But there can be no final certainty in this matter because the evidence is in the nature of the case inconclusive. We can only speak of probability here.

There are, however, a number of what seem to me quite clear cases in the first chapter where Coverdale manifestly uses Luther's version alone. In these passages, in which Luther departs more or less radically from the Vulgate, Luther is almost certainly the source of Coverdale's divergence from the Tyndale text. In view of the primary relevance of these passages to the subject of this essay, the most important of them will be discussed in some detail.

1:9

Vulgate: *Sicut praediximus, et nunc iterum dico*
Greek (Erasmus, 1519): ὡς προειρήκαμεν, καὶ ἄρτι πάλιν λέγω
Erasmus' Latin, 1519: identical with the Vulgate
Tyndale, 1525: *As I sayde before/so saye I nowe agayne*
Tyndale, 1534: identical with 1525

Tyndale was apparently unhappy about Paul's "inconsistency" in shifting from the plural προειρήκαμεν to the singular λέγω. He decided to eliminate the irregularity by putting both verbs in the singular—*I sayde ... saye I*.

Coverdale also saw fit to regularize, but diverging from Tyndale he preferred to use the plural in both cases: *As we have sayde afore, so saye we now agayne*. In this decision he followed (if indeed he followed anyone) Luther rather than Tyndale, the former rendering the line: *Wie wir ... gesagt haben, so sagen wyr.* ...

1:16

Vulgate: *ut evangelizarem illum*
Erasmus' Latin: *ut praedicarem ipsum*
Greek: ἵνα εὐαγγελίζωμαι αὐτὸν
Tyndale, 1525: *that I shuld preache him*
Tyndale, 1534: identical with 1525

Coverdale departs from Tyndale's version by adding a significant phrase: *That I shulde preach him thorow the Gospell*. The origin of these additional words is clearly Lutheran. Only Luther, of all sources indicated above, made the bold insertion: *durchs Euangelion*. This apparently appealed to Coverdale so much that he decided to use the Lutheran expansion in his own translation.

1:22

Vulgate: *ecclesiis iudaeae quae erant in Christo*
Erasmus: identical with Vulgate
Greek: ταῖς ἐκκλησίαις τῆς Ἰουδαίας ταῖς ἐν Χριστῷ.
Tyndale, 1525: *vnto the congregacions of Jewrye which were in Christ*
Tyndale, 1534: identical with 1525

Coverdale's version is a startling departure from Tyndale: "*To ye Christen congregacions in Jewrye.*"

While differing radically from Tyndale, Coverdale is in full agreement with Luther who has this phrase: *den Christlichen gemeynen ynn Judea*.

What did Luther do to produce this amazing version? He converted the Greek phrase ταῖς ἐν Χριστῷ, which the Vulgate and Tyndale rendered quite traditionally by a relative clause (*quae erant in Christo; which were in Christ*), with audacious simplicity into an adjective, *Christlichen*, preceding the noun *gemeynen*. Coverdale, a superior stylist in his own right, was apparently taken with this Lutheran phrase and reproduced it faithfully in his own Bible: *Christen congregacions*.

1:24

Vulgate: *et ... clarificabant deum*
Erasmus: *et glorificabant ... deum*
Greek: καὶ ἐδόξαζον ... τὸν θεόν
Tyndale, 1525: *and they glorified God ...*
Tyndale, 1534: identical with 1525

Coverdale replaced *glorified* by *praysed: and they praysed God*. Inasmuch as Luther has *vnd preyssetten Got*, it would seem reasonable to assume that his *preysseten* is primarily responsible for Coverdale's *praysed*.

GALATIANS 2

Of the 21 verses in the second chapter, 13 are identical in the two Tyndale editions of 1525 and 1534, with eight verses showing divergences between these principal Tyndale texts. Differences occur in vv. 1, 2, 4, 9, 11, 14, 16, 21. Of these eight changes, six are of a relatively minor stylistic nature and need not be discussed in this connection. Only two, vv. 9 and 14, are sufficiently important to be presented here.

2:9

Tyndale, 1525: *and as sone as James, Cephas, and Jhon which seemed to be pilares perceaved the grace that was geven vnto me they gave to me and Barnabas their hondes*
Tyndale, 1534: *and therefore when they perceaved the grace that was geven vnto me, then James, Cephas and John, which seemed to be pilers, gave to me and Barnabas the ryght hondes*
Tyndale's second edition contains a major stylistic revision of the first. The sentence structure is completely changed, and the adjective *ryght* is inserted before the noun *hondes*. The edition of 1534 is closer to the Greek original than the first edition; it is definitely more literal than the first.

2:14

Tyndale, 1525: *why causest thou the gentyls to folowe the Jewes?*
Tyndale, 1534: *why causest thou the gentyls to live as do the Jewes?*

Both renderings, *to folowe the Jewes* and *to live as do the Jewes*, are honest efforts to express in idiomatic English a single Greek verb, ἰουδαΐζειν. The Vulgate offered no help here at all by simply retaining the verb *iudaizare*. Tyndale's two successive attempts are creditable, with the second perhaps preferable to the first. It is quite likely that Tyndale, in evaluating his first rendering, decided to cast his lot with Luther, who has the verb *leben*. At any rate, he replaced *folowe* by *live*.

So far as these eight passages are concerned, Coverdale follows the second edition of Tyndale rather than the first, with the exception of verses 9 and 11, in which he is independent of Tyndale altogether. There is no evidence, in the second chapter, that Coverdale made use of Tyndale's first edition.

It should be clearly understood, however, that agreement in these passages does not mean agreement in these verses as a whole. There is not a single verse in the entire second chapter in which Coverdale does not depart to some degree from Tyndale. Contrary to the situation in the first chapter, in which four verses were left unchanged by Coverdale, every single verse of the second chapter underwent some change. There is, to be exact, a total of 50 changes in individual passages in this chapter. Of these, 10 cannot be attributed to any source known to me and should probably be credited to Coverdale himself. But the preponderant majority of the changes, 40 in number, are in full agreement with Luther's text. Fourteen of these 40 also agree with the Vulgate. For 26 of the 40 Luther's Bible alone appears to be the source of Coverdale's translation. It is these 26 changes in which we are primarily interested. We shall select some of them for detailed discussion.

2:2

Vulgate: *seorsum autem his qui videbantur aliquid esse*
Erasmus: *sed privatim cum iis qui erant in precio*
Greek: κατ' ἰδίαν δὲ τοῖς δοκοῦσιν
Tyndale, 1525: *but apart with them which are counted chefe*
Tyndale, 1534: *but apart with them which were counted chefe*
Coverdale: *but specially with them which were in reputacion*

Coverdale's phrase is markedly different from Tyndale's. It would seem that Luther's text provided the basis for this version: *besonders aber mit denen, die das ansehen hätten*. We are not discussing, in this connection, the origin of Luther's excellent rendering. If we were, one would probably refer to Erasmus' Latin version as at least a partial inspiration for Luther's delightfully free translation. It is not inconceivable that Erasmus was not without direct influence upon Coverdale himself in this instance. Of Coverdale's indirect debt to Erasmus, via Luther's German, there can hardly be any doubt. However, so far as any direct influence is concerned, it would appear to be Lutheran rather than Erasmian: Coverdale's *specially* is closer to Luther's *besonders* than to Erasmus' *privatim*.

2:6a

Vulgate: *Deus enim personam hominis non accipit*
Erasmus: *Personam hominis deus non accipit*
Greek: πρόσωπον ἀνθρώπου θεὸς οὐ λαμβάνει
Tyndale, 1525: *God loketh on no mans person*
Tyndale, 1534: identical with 1525
Coverdale: *For God loketh not on the outwarde appearaunce of men.*

Coverdale made a major change in this passage. The chief source for this astonishing departure from Tyndale would seem to be Luther's phrase *das ansehen der menschen*. It is true that Coverdale has an additional word, *outwarde*, before *appearaunce*. This is not a very troublesome matter, however, because Coverdale never was a slavish follower. He had a mind of his own and was quite prepared to proceed with some independence as he so obviously did in this particular case. Luther gave him the idea, and Coverdale developed it further on his own.

2:6b

Vulgate: *mihi . . . nihil contulerunt*
Erasmus: identical with Vulgate
Greek: ἐμοὶ . . . οὐδὲν προσανέθεντο
Tyndale, 1525: *added nothynge to me*
Tyndale, 1534: identical with 1525
Coverdale: *taught me nothinge*

Coverdale has an altogether different rendering of this concluding phrase of the sixth verse. The verb *taught* is surely surprising! A glance at Luther's Bible supplies the answer, for here we find: *nichts . . . geleret*. We need look no further.

2:15

Vulgate: *Nos natura iudai*
Erasmus: identical with Vulgate
Greek: Ἡμεῖς φύσει Ἰουδαῖοι
Tyndale, 1525: *We which are Jewes by nature*
Tyndale, 1534: identical with 1525
Coverdale: *Though we be Jewes by nature*

Coverdale turns this passage into a concessive clause. In this noteworthy change he clearly follows Luther's example: *Wie wol wyr von natur Juden . . . sind*. Coverdale is quite willing, on occasion, to take over a whole Lutheran sentence structure, though that may represent a radical departure from Tyndale and the other translators.

2:16a

Vulgate: *Scientes . . .*
Erasmus: *quoniam scimus . . .*
Greek: εἰδότες
Tyndale, 1525: *We . . . knowe . . .*
Tyndale, 1534: Identical with 1525
Coverdale: *yet in so moch as we knowe*

Coverdale begins his sentence differently. The introductory *yet* was almost necessary after Coverdale had changed, following Luther, the preceding sentence to a concessive clause, *Though we be*. He now merely relates the main clause to it by starting out with *yet*. In this he again kept close to Luther, who has *doch weyl wyr wissen*. Thus Luther's entire sentence structure, ranging over two verses, was incorporated by Coverdale into his rendering. He obviously preferred it to all other versions accessible to him.

2:16b

Vulgate: *per fidem Jesu Christi*
Erasmus: identical with Vulgate
Greek: διὰ πίστεως 'Ιησοῦ Χριστοῦ
Tyndale, 1525: *by the fayth of Jesus Christ*
Tyndale, 1534: identical with 1525
Coverdale: *by the faith on Jesus Christ*

Coverdale made a minor though very interesting change. This substitution of *on* for *of* may not appear to be a very important change on the face of it. But it really is. The changing of a genitive to a prepositional phrase is one of Luther's favorite devices. It is so characteristically Lutheran that, even when taken by itself, it almost invariably indicates dependence on the German Bible. Luther's phrase here is *durch den glawben an Jhesu Christ*.

The ten changes made by Coverdale for which there are no Lutheran examples are strictly stylistic. In other words, in the second chapter Coverdale made no important independent changes over against the Tyndale text. Whenever there is a significant departure from Tyndale in this chapter, it is always due either to Luther alone or to both Luther and the Vulgate agreeing with each other against Tyndale.

GALATIANS 3

There are 29 verses in the third chapter, 17 of which are identical in the two Tyndale versions of 1525 and 1534. That is to say, as many as 12 show some divergence or other in these two editions: 2, 4, 7, 8, 12, 13, 16, 17, 19, 21, 27, 28.

Of these 12, all but two are quite minor and need not concern us here. Only verses 19 and 28 are important enough to be discussed in this connection.

3:19

Tyndale, 1525: *tyll the seed came vnto which seede the promes was made*

Tyndale, 1534: *tyll the seed came to which the promes was made*

The revised edition dropped the second occurrence of the word *seede*, which is not found in either the Greek or the Vulgate. The revision was thus in the direction of greater accuracy. Coverdale is in agreement with Tyndale's second edition, in accordance with his general practice.

3 : 28

Tyndale, 1525: *Now is ther no Jewe nether Greke*
Tyndale, 1534: *Now is ther no Jewe nether gentyle*

In this phrase, the first edition is more literal than the second. The Greek original has Ἕλλην and the Vulgate *graecus*. Coverdale uses the word *Greke,* perhaps not so much because he found it in Tyndale's first edition but because it occurred in Luther's German version, *Krieche.* But this point cannot be established with anything even approaching certainty. It could also be argued that Coverdale here preferred the Vulgate or Erasmus' Latin version to Tyndale's second edition. In other words, in this particular case, as many as four possible sources could be adduced. The only thing of which we are sure is that Coverdale did not follow Tyndale's revision of 1534.

So far as Coverdale's whole relation to Tyndale in the third chapter is concerned, there are only two verses in which he merely reproduces Tyndale's text of 1534: only vv. 9 and 16 are in full agreement. That is to say, as many as 29 verses of the chapter contain departures of some kind or other from the second edition of Tyndale.

If we count phrases or words rather than verses different from Tyndale, the surprising total of 69 emerges. Of these, 21 appear to be due to Coverdale himself. At least none of the familiar sources accounts for any of these 21. That leaves the large number of 48 for which we are in a position to run down one or more sources.

All 48 can be accounted for by referring to Luther's German text. This is tantamount to saying that not a single one of these 48 requires that we go beyond the German Bible. It should be pointed out, however, that for 16 of them the Vulgate can also be considered a possible source; these are found in vv. 2, 4, 7, 8 (two passages), 10, 12, 14, 15, 19, 21, 22, 24, 28 (two passages), 29. For two phrases, occurring in vv. 7 and 28, Tyndale's first version of 1525 could be the source besides Luther's German text. That is to say, while Luther suffices as the source for all 48 passages under review here, 16 could also be explained on the basis of the Vulgate and two on the basis of Tyndale's first edition. As in the first two chapters we shall restrict ourselves in the third chapter to those passages for which Luther alone appears to be the source. That is the imposing total of 30 individual phrases or words occurring in the following verses: 1, 2, 3 (two passages), 4, 5 (two passages), 6, 7, 8, 10 (three passages), 11, 13, 14 (two passages), 17, 18 (three passages), 19, 20, 22, 25, 26 (two passages), 27, 28 (two passages). Only a selection from these will be discussed in detail.

3:3

Vulgate: *Sic stulti estis, ut cum spiritu coeperitis, nunc carne consummemini?*
Erasmus: *Adeo stulti estis, ut spiritu coeperitis, nunc carne consummamini?*
Greek: οὕτως ἀνόητοί ἐστε; ἐναρξάμενοι πνεύματι νῦν σαρκὶ ἐπιτελεῖσθε;
Tyndale, 1525: *Are ye so vnwyse that after ye have begonne in the sprete ye wolde nowe*
Tyndale, 1534: identical with 1525
Coverdale: *Are ye so vnwyse? Ye beganne in the sprete, wolde ye....*

Coverdale departs from Tyndale's sentence structure and models his after Luther's. This structure corresponds closely to Luther's *seyt yhr so vnverstendig? ym geyst habt yhr angefangen, wolt yhr denn ym fleysch*

3:4

Vulgate: *Tanta passi estis sine causa? si tamen sine causa*
Erasmus: *Tam multa passi estis frustra, si tamen & frustra*
Greek: τοσαῦτα ἐπάθετε εἰκῇ; εἴ γε καὶ εἰκῇ
Tyndale, 1525: *So many thinges there ye have suffred in vayne, iff it be so that ye have suffred in vayne*
Tyndale, 1534: *So many thinges there ye have suffred in vayne, if that be vayne*
Coverdale: *Have ye suffred so moche in vayne? Yf it be els in vayne*

Coverdale's version is completely different from both the first and second Tyndale editions, which differ somewhat from each other. His text bears hardly any relation to Tyndale's at all. The first part of the verse can be explained on the basis of the Vulgate and Erasmus' Latin version as well as of Luther's *habt yhr denn so viel vmb sunst erlitten?* The second part, however, appears to be due very largely if not entirely to Luther alone. *Yf it be els in vayne* corresponds very closely to *ists anders vmbsonst*. The word *els* in particular stems directly from the German Bible, it would seem.

3 : 5

Vulgate: *et operatur virtutes in vobis*
Erasmus' Latin: identical with Vulgate
Greek: καὶ ἐνεργῶν δυνάμεις ἐν ὑμῖν
Tyndale, 1525: *and worketh myracles amonge you*
Tyndale, 1534: identical with 1525
Coverdale: *and doth soch greate actes amonge you*

Again Coverdale departs radically from Tyndale in this passage. There can be little doubt of his indebtedness to Martin Luther's "vnd thutt solche thatten vnter euch." It is interesting to observe again that Coverdale does not imitate mechanically or slavishly. He inserts, on his own, the adjective *greate* between *soch* and *actes*. It will never do to underestimate Coverdale as an imaginative translator. He is a master of the well-turned phrase without violating the inner meaning of the text. It can only enhance Luther's standing as a great translator that as able and aesthetically sensitive a man as Coverdale should have chosen to follow in Luther's footsteps as frequently as he did. Luther himself, had he known of this fact, would have been proud of so distinguished a disciple.

3 : 6

Vulgate: *et reputatum est illi*
Erasmus' Latin: *& imputatum*
Greek: καὶ ἐλογίσθη αὐτῷ
Tyndale, 1525: *and it was ascribed to him*
Tyndale, 1534: identical with 1525
Coverdale: *and it was counted to him*

Coverdale saw fit to change the verb. It is probable that *counted* was inspired primarily by Luther's phrase, *vnd es ist yhm gerechnet*, although one should not rule out the Vulgate as a possible supplementary or even independent source.

3 : 10

Vulgate: *Quicumque enim ex operibus legis sunt*
Erasmus' Latin: *Nam quotquot ex operibus legis sunt*
Greek: Ὅσοι γὰρ ἐξ ἔργων νόμου εἰσίν
Tyndale, 1525: *For as many as are vnder the dedes of the lawe*
Tyndale, 1534: identical with 1525
Coverdale: *For as many as go aboute with the workes of the lawe*

Here is another radical departure from Tyndale on the part of Coverdale. His rendering bears no resemblance to Tyndale at all. This phrase, so markedly different from Tyndale's, in all likelihood goes back to Luther and to Luther alone: *Denn alle die mit des gesetzs wercken vmbgehen.* This case is so clear that it is superfluous to discuss it further. This is Luther speaking through the mouth of Myles Coverdale.

3:13

Vulgate: *factus ... maledictum*
Erasmus' Latin: *dum ... factus est maledictum*
Greek: γενόμενος ... κατάρα
Tyndale, 1525: *and was made a cursed*
Tyndale, 1534: identical with 1525
Coverdale: *whan he became a curse*

Coverdale's sentence structure differs from Tyndale's. Instead of resolving the participle *factus* into a main clause as Tyndale had done ("and was made ..."), he turned it into a dependent clause. This procedure is in agreement with Luther's *da er wart eyn vermaledeyung*. It is possible of course that Coverdale could also be indebted to Erasmus' Latin version, *dum ... factus est*.

3:14

Vulgate: *ut pollicitationem spiritus accipiamus*
Erasmus' Latin: *ut promissionem spiritus acciperemus*
Greek: ἵνα τὴν ἐπαγγελίαν τοῦ πνεύματος λάβωμεν
Tyndale, 1525: *that we might receave the promes of the sprete*
Tyndale, 1534: identical with 1525
Coverdale: *that we might so receave ye promysed sprete*

Coverdale departs significantly from Tyndale's translation, and he does so in a characteristically Lutheran manner. He turned a noun into a past participle serving as an adjective. This would seem to be a practically indisputable case of Luther's influence on the Englishman. Only Martin Luther was bold enough to recast the original construction of a noun followed by a genitive into a noun (i.e. the original genitive) preceded by an "adjective" (the original noun as an accusative object): *wyr also den verheyssen geyst empfiengen.* Unless we wish to credit Coverdale himself with this audacious rendering, we must hold that this is the voice of Martin Luther speaking through the tongue of Myles Coverdale.

3:18a

Vulgate: *Nam si ex lege hereditas, iam non ex promissione*

Erasmus' Latin: *Nam si ex lege est hereditas, non iam est ex promissione*
Greek: εἰ γὰρ ἐκ νόμου ἡ κληρονομία, οὐκέτι ἐξ ἐπαγγελίας
Tyndale, 1525: *For yff the inheritaunce come of the lawe, it cometh not of promes*
Tyndale, 1534: identical with 1525
Coverdale: *For yf the inheritaunce be gotten by the lawe, then it is not geven by promes*

It is clear that the main problem in this part of the verse for the translator is what to do about the verbs which remain unexpressed in both the Greek and the Vulgate. Erasmus apparently felt the lack of a verb and supplied, in both clauses, the auxiliary *est*. Tyndale, ingeniously, introduced a more colorful verb: *come* and *cometh*. Coverdale, again departing from Tyndale, did not use one and the same verb but two different verbs. Remembering that there is no explicit verb in either the original or the Vulgate, any verb or verbs supplied by Coverdale must either be of his own making or stem from some source. It seems quite definite that Coverdale again turned to Luther. In view of the excellence of Tyndale's solution of the problem, there really did not seem to be any necessity for Coverdale to dissociate himself from his distinguished predecessor, yet he apparently preferred Luther's handling of the matter. This is what Luther had done with this passage: *Dann so das erbe durch das gesetz erworben wurde, so wurde es nicht durch verheyssung geben*. It would seem that Coverdale's *be gotten* is largely if not entirely due to Luther's *erworben wurde; geven* is of course in complete agreement with Luther's *geben*.

3 : 18b

Vulgate: *Abrahae autem per repromissionem donavit Deus*
Erasmus' Latin: *atque Abrahae per promissionem donavit deus*
Greek: Ἀβραὰμ δι' ἐπαγγελίας κεχάρισται ὁ θεός
Tyndale, 1525: *But God gave it vnto Abraham by promes*
Tyndale, 1534: identical with 1525
Coverdale: *But God gave it freely vnto Abraham by promes*

Coverdale kept Tyndale's version as his basic text, but he added an important word not actually occurring in the Greek or Latin. It was unmistakably Luther who was responsible for this "liberty," for his rendering reads, *Got aber hats Abraham durch verheyssunge frey geschenckt*. The addition of the adverb *frey* is manifestly a Lutheran feature. Luther's strong emphasis on God's free gift to man is fully brought out in his German Bible. Coverdale cheerfully retained Luther's heavy underscoring of this vital point of Lutheran theology.

3 : 20

Vulgate: *Mediator autem unius non est*
Erasmus' Latin: *Intercessor autem unius non est*
Greek: ὁ δὲ μεσίτης ἑνὸς οὐκ ἔστιν
Tyndale, 1525: *A mediator is not a mediator of one*
Tyndale, 1534: identical with 1525
Coverdale: *A mediator is not a mediator of one onely*

Coverdale again makes a significant addition to the text. This wa probably suggested to him by Luther's rendering: "Ein mitteler abe ist nicht eyns eynigen mitteler." Additions of this sort indicate quit plainly and convincingly the influence of Martin Luther on Myle Coverdale.

3 : 22

Vulgate: *ut promissio ex fide Jesu Christi daretur credentibus*
Erasmus' Latin: identical with Vulgate
Greek: ἵνα ἡ ἐπαγγελία ἐκ πίστεως Ἰησοῦ Χριστοῦ δοθῇ τοῖς πιστεύουσιν
Tyndale, 1525: *that the promes by the fayth of Jesus Christ shuld b geven vnto them that beleve*
Tyndale, 1534: identical with 1525
Coverdale: *that the promes shulde come by the fayth on Jesus Christ geven vnto them that beleve*

Coverdale's version represents a considerable departure from Tyn dale's. This reconstructed passage comes almost certainly from Luther': rendering of the verse: "auff das die verheyssung keme, durch der glawben an Jhesum Christum, gegeben denen die da glewben." Luthe inserted the verb *keme*, replaced the mere genitive *Jesu Christi* by ¿ full prepositional construction, *an Jhesum Christum*, and completec the sentence by turning *daretur* into a past participle, *gegeben*. It wa: obviously Luther's endeavor to make Paul's tight sentence more ex plicit. Coverdale apparently was so impressed with this performance that he incorporated it in his own translation.

3 : 26

Vulgate: *filii Dei*
Erasmus' Latin: identical with Vulgate
Greek: υἱοὶ θεοῦ
Tyndale, 1525: *the sonnes of God*
Tyndale, 1534: identical with 1525

Coverdale replaced *sonnes* by *children*. Since Luther alone of all hi:

sources has *kinder,* it is more than probable that Coverdale's departure from Tyndale is due to Luther.

3 : 27

Vulgate: *Quicumque enim . . . estis*
Erasmus' Latin: *Nam quicunque . . . estis*
Greek: ὅσοι γὰρ
Tyndale, 1525: *For all ye that are . . .*
Tyndale, 1534: identical with 1525

Coverdale changed this phrase to *For as many of you as are. . . .* In view of the fact that Luther has *Denn wie viel ewr . . . sind,* it is reasonable to assume that this is the source of Coverdale's rendering.

In the third chapter of Galatians there are, as already stated, a large number of departures from Tyndale's text, 29 in number, for which there does not seem to be any outside source, Lutheran or other. They appear to be due to Coverdale himself. With the exception of two, they are all of a more or less minor stylistic nature and do not require any comment. The two passages of more than ordinary interest occur in verses five and eight.

3 : 5

Coverdale: *and doth soche greate actes*

As discussed earlier in connection with Coverdale's indebtedness to Luther for this phrase in general, the adjective *greate* is as it were the personal property of Coverdale himself. He added it independently because he felt, it would seem, that it brought out the implications of the text still more forcefully than Luther's rendering had done. It seems to me that Luther, had he ever known of Coverdale's version, would have approved of it. Coverdale was merely carrying out Luther's own principles of translation. The master would have recognized one of his true sons.

3 : 8

Coverdale: *and sayde*

Coverdale added this phrase on his own. He probably thought it would make the long sentence in which it occurs easier to understand. It is hard to disagree with him, though the addition is not really necessary.

Aside from these two passages, it can safely be stated that whenever there is any significant departure from Tyndale's text, this is invariably due either to Luther alone or to both Luther and the Vulgate agreeing with each other against Tyndale. This is definitely the pattern of the third as well as of the first two chapters.

GALATIANS 4

Of the 31 verses of the fourth chapter, 20 are identical in the Tyndale editions of 1525 and 1534. The following 11 verses differ to some degree in these two principal editions of the English N. T.: 3, 5, 7, 8, 10, 11, 12, 13, 15, 16, 30. These differences are all relatively minor and really need no discussion in this connection. Suffice it to say that Coverdale never followed Tyndale's first edition where that differs from the second, so far as the fourth chapter is concerned.

As regards Coverdale's relation to Tyndale's second edition, then, it is a little closer than it was in the third chapter. In the fourth chapter, as many as seven verses contain the unaltered text of Tyndale's second version of 1534: 10, 12, 14, 19, 20, 22, 27. In 24 of the 31 verses making up the fourth chapter, Coverdale chose to depart to a greater or lesser extent from Tyndale.

If, instead of counting verses, we count phrases or words differing in Coverdale and Tyndale, we come up with as many as 46 passages. Of these 46, 13 appear to have no other source than Coverdale himself. That leaves the fairly large number of 33 for which we can establish one or more outside sources. Every single one of these 33 passages can be explained on the basis of Luther's German text. All we need to account for these 33 departures from Tyndale is the German Bible. We should, however, again point out that for the following 10 of the 33 passages the Vulgate can also be regarded as a possible source in addition to Luther's text: 1, 2, 4, 8, 14, 21, 29 (three phrases), 30.

We shall again limit our discussion to those passages for which Luther alone seems to have been the source. The following is the list of the 23 individual passages in question: 1 (three phrases), 3, 4, 5, 6 (two phrases), 9, 13, 14, 17, 18, 23, 24 (two phrases), 25, 26, 29, 30 (two phrases), 31 (two phrases). We do not have the space to analyze all of them. It is necessary to present a small selection.

4 : 1a

Vulgate: *nihil differt a servo*
Erasmus' Latin: identical with Vulgate
Greek: οὐδὲν διαφέρει δούλου
Tyndale, 1525: *differeth not from a servaunt*
Tyndale, 1534: identical with 1525
Coverdale: *there is no difference betwene him and a servaunt*

Coverdale has a somewhat longer phrase, obviously not rendered very literally. This freedom, however, is not original with Coverdale. The decisive step was taken by Martin Luther, whose free rendering Coverdale apparently preferred to Tyndale's more literal translation: *so ist vnter yhm vnd eynem knecht keyn vnterscheyd.*

4:1b

Vulgate: *cum sit dominus omnium*
Erasmus' Latin: identical with Vulgate
Greek: κύριος πάντων ὤν
Tyndale, 1525: *though he be Lorde of all*
Tyndale, 1534: identical with 1525
Coverdale: *though he be lorde of all ye goodes*

Coverdale, interestingly enough, adds a noun at the end of the phrase. There is no other source for this unusual addition than Luther's German Bible, which has this reading: "ob er wol eyn herr ist aller guter." It can hardly be doubted that this is the origin of Coverdale's expansion of the text.

4:3

Vulgate: *sub elementis mundi*
Erasmus' Latin: identical with Vulgate
Greek: ὑπὸ τὰ στοιχεῖα τοῦ κόσμου
Tyndale, 1525: *vnder the ordinacions of the worlde*
Tyndale, 1534: *vnder the ordinaunces of the worlde*
Coverdale: *vnder the outwarde tradicions*

Coverdale's rendering of this phrase is radically different, so different in fact that one scarcely recognizes it as the same passage. The noun has been changed and, perhaps more important than that, the nominal genitive *of the worlde*, which is a literal translation of τοῦ κόσμου, emerges as an adjective modifying the noun στοιχεῖα, *elementis: outwarde*. Again, there can be little doubt that this major alteration is due to Luther's Bible, which reads as follows: "vnter den euserlichen satzungen." Whether *tradicions* was directly suggested by *satzungen* is difficult to say. However, it can be stated with assurance that *outwarde*—both the word itself and the construction within which it occurs—were definitely inspired by Luther.

4:4

Vulgate: *At ubi venit plenitudo temporis*
Erasmus' Latin: identical with Vulgate

Greek: ὅτε δὲ ἦλθεν τὸ πλήρωμα τοῦ χρόνου
Tyndale, 1525: *But when the tyme was full come*
Tyndale, 1534: identical with 1525
Coverdale: *But whan the tyme was fulfylled*

Coverdale's phrase would seem to stem directly from Luther's famous and familiar words, *Da aber die zeyt erfullet wart.*

4:5

Vulgate: *ut adoptionem filiorum reciperemus*
Erasmus' Latin: *ut adoptione ius filiorum acciperemus*
Greek: ἵνα τὴν υἱοθεσίαν ἀπολάβωμεν
Tyndale, 1525: *that we thorow eleccion shulde receave the inheritaunce that belongeth vnto the naturall sonnes*
Tyndale, 1534: *myght* for *shulde*
Coverdale: *that we mighte receave ye childshippe*

Coverdale departs radically from Tyndale's astonishing rendering which is really a lengthy interpretation of the passage. However one may look at it, Tyndale's version is an extension and elaboration of the original. Coverdale did not follow him at all. There is no problem in recognizing the source of this translation. Martin Luther's version has this reading: "das wyr die kindschafft empfiengen." We need look no further.

4:6

Vulgate: ... *clamantem: Abba, Pater*
Erasmus' Latin: identical with Vulgate
Greek: κρᾶζον· Ἀββᾶ ὁ πατήρ
Tyndale, 1525: ... *which cryeth Abba father*
Tyndale, 1534: identical with 1525
Coverdale: ... *which cryeth: Abba, deare father*

Coverdale makes an interesting insertion between *Abba* and *father*. This is of course a favorite phrase of Luther's. Throughout the New Testament he employs it with a good deal of regularity. Wherever the King James Bible has *brethren*, Luther is apt to have *lieben bruder*. Here he has *Abba, lieber vater*. It is quite certain that this is the source of Coverdale's *deare father*.

4:17

Vulgate: *sed excludere vos volunt*
Erasmus' Latin: identical with Vulgate
Greek: ἀλλὰ ἐκκλεῖσαι ὑμᾶς θέλουσιν
Tyndale, 1525: *they intende to exclude you*

Tyndale, 1534: identical with 1525
Coverdale: *they wolde make you to fall back*
Coverdale's version is altogether different. This seems like a new translation, difficult to account for on the basis of all non-German versions till we look at Luther's text: *sie wollen euch . . . abfellig machen*. It can hardly be doubted that this is the origin of Coverdale's unusual rendering.

4:18

Vulgate: *Bonum autem aemulamini in bono semper*
Erasmus' Latin: *Bonum autem est, aemulari in re bona semper*
Greek: καλὸν δὲ ζηλοῦσθαι ἐν καλῷ πάντοτε
Tyndale, 1525: *It is good alwayes to be fervent, so it be in a good thinge*
Tyndale, 1534: identical with 1525
Coverdale: *It is good to be fervent, so yt it be allwaye in a good thinge*
Coverdale puts the adverb "alwayes" in the second half of the phrase, whereas it occurs in the first part in Tyndale. Coverdale evidently prefers Luther's *Eyffern ist gut, wens ymerdar geschicht vmb das gutte*. It is not impossible that the Latin versions helped him in this decision.

4:23

Vulgate: *Sed qui de ancilla . . .*
Erasmus' Latin: *Verum is qui ex ancilla . . .*
Greek: ἀλλ' ὁ μὲν ἐκ τῆς παιδίσκης
Tyndale, 1525: *Yee and he which was of the bonde woman*
Tyndale, 1534: identical with 1525
Coverdale changes *woman* to *mayde,* probably following Luther, who has *magd*. The same change occurs in verses 30 and 31.

4:24

Vulgate: *quae sunt per allegoriam dicta*
Erasmus' Latin: *quae per allegoriam dicuntur*
Greek: ἅτινά ἐστιν ἀλληγορούμενα
Tyndale, 1525: *Which thinges betoken mystery*
Tyndale, 1534: identical with 1525
Coverdale: *These words betoken somewhat*
In Coverdale we find an astonishingly different rendering. There is little room for doubt that this passage is fully based on Luther's very free translation reading: "Die wort bedeuten etwas." When Luther renders a phrase as freely as he does here, and when Coverdale is in such fundamental agreement with him, it is practically a foregone conclusion that Luther is his source.

4:25

Vulgate: *Sina nunc mons est in Arabia, qui coniunctus est ei, quae nunc est Jerusalem*

Erasmus' Latin: *Sina mons est in Arabia, confinis est autem ei, quae nunc vocatur Hierusalem*

Greek: τὸ γὰρ ῎Αγαρ σινᾶ ὄρος ἐστὶν ἐν τῇ ᾿Αραβίᾳ· συστοιχεῖ δὲ τῇ νῦν ῾Ιερουσαλήμ

Tyndale, 1525: *For mounte Sina is called Agar in Arabia, and bordreth upon the citie which is now Jerusalem*

Tyndale, 1534: identical with 1525

Coverdale: *For Agar is called in Arabia ye mount Sina, and reacheth vnto Jerusalem which now is*

Coverdale diverges considerably from Tyndale. His rearranged passage appears to be based on Luther's version, *Denn Agar heyst ynn Arabia der berg Sina, vnd langet biss gen Jerusalem, das zu diser zeyt ist.*

4:29

Vulgate: *Sed quomodo tunc*
Erasmus' Latin: *sed quemadmodum tunc*
Greek: ἀλλ᾿ ὥσπερ τότε
Tyndale, 1525: *But as then*
Tyndale, 1534: identical with 1525
Coverdale: *But like as at that tyme*

While of course not necessarily so, Coverdale's phrase seems to stem from Luther's *Aber gleych wie zu der zeyt.*

As indicated before, there are 13 passages in the fourth chapter of Galatians which, while different from Tyndale's rendering, are not based on Luther or the Vulgate or any other known source. They appear to be changes which Coverdale made on his own. They occur in vv. 2, 7, 9 (two passages), 11, 14, 15, 17, 23, 24, 26 (two passages), 28. Almost all of them are minor stylistic alterations. Only two are important enough to merit special attention.

4:26

Tyndale, 1525: *But Jerusalem, which is above, is fre*
Tyndale, 1534: identical with 1525
Coverdale: *But Jerusalem, that is above, is the fre woman*

Coverdale changed *which* to *that* and turned Tyndale's single word *fre* into a longer phrase, *the fre woman.*

4 : 28

Tyndale, 1525: *Brethren we are after the maner of Isaac, chyldren of promes*
Tyndale, 1534: identical with 1525
Coverdale: *As for vs (brethren) we are the children of Isaac accordinge to the promes*

Coverdale departed radically from Tyndale, who together with Luther based his rendering on the Greek original. Coverdale struck out on his own as never before in this Epistle. Since this is hardly a responsible translation of the original or of the Vulgate for that matter, one should perhaps be grateful that Coverdale saw fit for the most part to adhere to either Tyndale or Luther, rather more reliable translators from the original text itself.

GALATIANS 5

Of the 26 verses of the fifth chapter, 21 remained unchanged from the first to the second edition of Tyndale's N. T. Only five reveal some difference: 5, 10, 12, 20, 21. Three of these are relatively minor and call for no discussion here. Two are sufficiently interesting to merit brief presentation.

5 : 5

Tyndale, 1525: *We ... hope to be justified by the sprete which cometh of fayth*
Tyndale, 1534: *We ... hope in the sprete to be iustified thorow fayth*

Both versions are comparatively free renderings, with the first edition the freer of the two. The second half of the second version shows some debt to Luther, it would seem.

5 : 20

Tyndale, 1525: *... lawynge ... parte takynges*
Tyndale, 1534: *... variaunce ... sectes*

This is a confusing verse consisting of a long enumeration of vices to be guarded against. Suffice it to say that Tyndale's first and second editions diverge considerably in the two phrases selected.

So far as Coverdale's relation to Tyndale is concerned, there are only three verses in the 26 of the fifth chapter where Coverdale is satisfied with reproducing Tyndale's text (the second edition only; there is no evidence that he used the first). That is to say, in as many as 23 verses Coverdale departs from Tyndale to some degree. If we count phrases or words, we find a total of 36 departures from Tyndale. Of these 36, 11 appear to have no outside source but to be due to Coverdale himself. At least no other influence can be established. Excluding these 11, we still have at least 25 passages for which one or more outside sources can be given.

It is again important to bear in mind that Luther's German Bible suffices to explain each and every one of these 25 passages. For nine passages both the Vulgate and Luther qualify as possible sources: 6, 8, 10, 11 (two passages), 13, 24 (two passages), 25. For 16 passages only Luther's text will do because Luther, in these, departs from the Vulgate. Coverdale preferred Luther to the Vulgate in all instances where they differed: 4, 5, 8 (two passages), 9, 12 (two passages), 13 (two passages), 14 (two passages), 15, 16, 21, 23, 24.

We shall omit from the discussion the passages with a possible double origin, and we shall restrict ourselves to those for which Luther appears to be the sole source. For lack of space, it will be necessary to select just a few from the 16 passages available for proof of Coverdale's dependence on Luther.

5:4

Vulgate: *qui in lege iustificamini*
Erasmus' Latin: *quicumque per legem iustificamini*
Greek: οἵτινες ἐν νόμῳ δικαιοῦσθε
Tyndale, 1525: *as many as are iustified by the lawe*
Tyndale, 1534: identical with 1525
Coverdale: *as many off you as wilby made righteous by the lawe*

Coverdale's text differs markedly from Tyndale's. It would seem that this change is due to Luther's *yhr durchs gesetz rechtfertig werden wolt.*

5:5

Vulgate: *Nos enim spiritu ex fide, spem iustitiae expectamus*
Erasmus' Latin: identical with Vulgate
Greek: ἡμεῖς γὰρ πνεύματι ἐκ πίστεως ἐλπίδα δικαιοσύνης ἀπεκδεχόμεθα
Tyndale, 1525: *We loke for and hope to be iustified by the sprete which commeth of fayth*
Tyndale, 1534: *We loke for and hope in the sprite to be iustified thorow fayth*
Coverdale: *But we wayte in the sprete off hope, to be made righteous by faith*

Coverdale's rendering of this very difficult verse is totally different from Tyndale's two versions. It bears no resemblance to either. His free version is, however, in complete agreement with Luther's rendering: *Wyr aber wartten ym geyst der hoffnung, das wyr durch den glawben rechtfertig seyen.* This verse is interesting also from another point of view. It allows us to determine for the first time in the Epistle to the Galatians whether Coverdale used an early or a late edition of Luther's New Testament. The Lutheran version just quoted remained intact only through 1527. It was thoroughly revised in 1530 in the following manner: *Wir aber warten im Geist, durch den glauben, der Gerechtigkeit der man hoffen mus.* From this it is quite clear that Coverdale used an edition prior to the great revision of 1530. Unfortunately we cannot run it down more specifically than that in the nature of the case.

5:9

Vulgate: *Modicum fermentum totam massam corrumpit*
Erasmus' Latin: *Paulum fermentum totam massam fermentat*
Greek: μικρὰ ζύμη ὅλον τὸ φύραμα ζυμοῖ
Tyndale, 1525: *A lytell leven doth leven the whole lompe of dowe*
Tyndale, 1534: identical with 1525
Coverdale: *A lytell leven sowreth the whole lompe of dowe*

Coverdale changed only one word in this verse, but a very important word indeed. It would seem that this change was made in conformity with Martin Luther's *versawret*.

5:12

Vulgate: *Utinam abscindantur*
Erasmus' Latin: *Utinam & abscindantur*
Greek: Ὄφελον καὶ ἀποκόψονται
Tyndale, 1525: *I wolde to God they were sondred*
Tyndale, 1534: *I wolde to God they were seperated*
Coverdale: *Wold God they were roted out*

Coverdale changes the first phrase somewhat and the final verb altogether. Since the entire passage including the crucial verb is in complete agreement with Luther's rendering, *Wolt Got, das sie auch aussgerottet wurden*, it would seem that the German Bible is the clear source of Coverdale's version.

5:24

Vulgate: *cum vitiis, et concupiscentiis*
Erasmus' Latin: *cum affectibus & concupiscentiis*

Greek: σὺν τοῖς παθήμασιν καὶ ταῖς ἐπιθυμίαις
Tyndale, 1525: *with the appetites and lustes*
Tyndale, 1534: identical with 1525

Coverdale changes Tyndale's phrase to read *with the lustes and desyres*. This corresponds exactly to Luther's version, *sampt den lusten vnd begirden*, which may quite safely be taken to be the source of Coverdale's altered rendering.

As indicated above, there are 11 passages in the fifth chapter which are different from Tyndale and from Luther and the Vulgate as well. These appear definitely to be changes which Coverdale made on his own authority. They are found in the following verses: 1, 2, 3, 4, 5, 7, 12, 14, 17, 19, 26. Practically all of them involve only minor stylistic changes. None is important enough to be singled out here for special presentation.

Galatians 6

Of the 18 verses of the sixth chapter, as many as 16 remained unaltered in the second edition of Tyndale's New Testament. Only two show some difference: 2 and 9. Only the change in v. 9 is important enough to record here.

6:9

Tyndale, 1525: *Let vs do good, and let vs not faynte*
Tyndale, 1534: *Let vs not be wery of well doynge*

Tyndale's first version appears to be based on the Greek original, translated literally by the Vulgate:
Greek: τὸ δὲ καλὸν ποιοῦντες μὴ ἐνκακῶμεν
Vulgate: *Bonum autem facientes, non deficiamus*

Tyndale's second version would seem to have been revised by the 1519 edition of Erasmus' Latin translation.
Erasmus' Latin: *Bonum autem faciendo ne defatigemur*

So far as Coverdale's relation to Tyndale is concerned, only three out of the 18 verses of the sixth chapter reproduce the Tyndale text (i.e., the second edition) unchanged. In other words, in as many as 15 verses Coverdale saw fit to depart from Tyndale. Counting phrases or words rather than whole verses we find a total of 29 departures from Tyndale. Of these 29, seven appear to be changes initiated by Coverdale himself. At least no outside influence can be discovered. If we exclude these seven passages, there are still 22 left for which we can locate external sources.

It should again be pointed out that Luther's German Bible is sufficient to account for all of these 22 changes. For 10 of them, both the Vulgate and Luther qualify as possible sources: 5, 6, 10, 12, 13, 14 (three passages), 15, 16. For 12 of them only Luther's text will do inasmuch as the Vulgate has readings different from Luther's. The following passages reveal the simple fact that wherever Luther and the Vulgate differ from each other Coverdale preferred to follow Luther: 1 (two passages), 2, 6 (two passages), 8 (three passages), 9, 11, 12, 14.

In order to conserve space we shall again ignore the passages having, theoretically at least, a possible double origin. We shall limit the discussion to those which appear to go back to Luther as their only source. Again for reasons of space, we shall select only a few of these primarily relevant passages.

6 : 1a

Vulgate: *et si praeoccupatus homo fuerit in aliquo delicto*
Erasmus' Latin: *etiam si occupatus fuerit homo in aliquo delicto*
Greek: ἐὰν καὶ προλημφθῇ ἄνθρωπος ἔν τινι παραπτώματι
Tyndale, 1525: *yf eny man be fallen by chaunce into eny faute*
Tyndale, 1534: identical with 1525
Coverdale: *yf eny man be overtaken of a faute*

Coverdale departs from Tyndale to a considerable extent. The origin of this astonishing version is probably to be found in Luther's *so ein mensch etwa von eynem feyl vbereylet wurd.*

6 : 1b

Vulgate: *in spiritu lenitatis*
Erasmus' Latin: *in spiritu mansuetudinis*
Greek: ἐν πνεύματι πραΰτητος
Tyndale, 1525: *in the sprete of meknes*
Tyndale, 1534: identical with 1525
Coverdale: *with a meke spirit*

Coverdale made a very important stylistic change. This phrase, in which an adjectival form is substituted for a nominal genitive, embodies a characteristic Lutheran method of translation. Luther did exactly this in rendering the passage *mit sanfftmutigem geyst*. There cannot be any doubt that this is the source of Coverdale's English phrase.

6 : 9

Vulgate: *metemus non deficientes*
Erasmus' Latin: *metemus non defatigati*

Greek: θερίσομεν μὴ ἐκλυόμενοι
Tyndale, 1525: *we shall repe without weriness*
Tyndale, 1534: identical with 1525

Coverdale replaced Tyndale's last word *weriness* by *ceassinge*. Inasmuch as Luther, and Luther alone, has *on auffhoren*, which is incidentally a free rather than a close rendering, it is reasonable to assume that Coverdale's translation is directly indebted to Martin Luther.

6:11

Vulgate: *Videte qualibus litteris scripsi vobis*
Erasmus' Latin: *Videtis quanta vobis epistola scripserim*
Greek: Ἴδετε πηλίκοις ὑμῖν γράμμασιν ἔγραψα
Tyndale, 1525: *Beholde how large a letter I have written vnto you*
Tyndale, 1534: identical with 1525
Coverdale: *Beholde, with how many words I have written vnto you*

Coverdale's version is altogether different from Tyndale's. This fairly free rendering was in all probability, if not with certainty, inspired by Luther's: "Sehet, mit wie vielen wortten hab ich euch geschrieben."

6:12

Vulgate: *ut crucis Christi persecutionem non patiantur*
Erasmus' Latin: *ne ob crucem Christi persecutionem patiantur*
Greek: ἵνα μὴ τῷ σταυρῷ τοῦ Χριστοῦ διώκωνται
Tyndale, 1525: *because they wolde not suffre persecucion with the crosse of Christ*
Tyndale, 1534: identical with 1525
Coverdale: *lest they shulde be persecuted with the crosse of Christ*

Coverdale's version differs markedly from Tyndale's. While the change from Tyndale's *because* to *lest* could be due to the Vulgate or Erasmus as well as to Luther, the replacing of Tyndale's phrase *suffre persecucion* by the single verb *persecuted* would seem to be due exclusively to Luther's translation *das sie nicht mit dem creutz Christi verfolget werden*. Luther's rendering rests on the Greek original having one word rather than two as found in the Vulgate and in Erasmus. It is theoretically possible that Coverdale's translation could stem from the Greek text itself. But since Coverdale knew no Greek, it is Luther whom he followed.

6:14

Vulgate: *nisi in cruce domini nostri*
Erasmus' Latin: identical with Vulgate

Greek: εἰ μὴ ἐν τῷ σταυρῷ τοῦ κυρίου ἡμῶν
Tyndale, 1525: *but in the crosse of oure Lorde*
Tyndale, 1534: identical with 1525
Coverdale: *save onely in the crosse of our Lorde*

Coverdale underscores and intensifies the idea of rejoicing in the cross of Christ and only in the cross of Christ by inserting an extra word.

This extraordinary emphasis is already found in Luther, who rendered the phrase: *denn nur von dem creutz vnsers herrn*. It would seem that this is the source of Coverdale's unusual rendering.

As stated earlier, there are seven passages in the last chapter of Galatians which differ from Tyndale but which do not stem from either Luther or the Vulgate. They appear to be changes made by Coverdale himself, independently of any of his known sources. They occur in the following verses: 1 (two passages), 3, 7, 10, 12, 13. Not one of them goes beyond minor stylistic adjustments. It is not necessary to dwell on them in detail. All they prove is that Coverdale was a stylist in his own right, with his own mind and literary taste. As should be abundantly clear by this time, he was no mere copyist.

The results of this investigation may be summarized briefly as follows:

1. There are 29 passages in Tyndale's translation of Galatians which are clearly traceable to Luther's German Bible. All of these 29 Lutheran formulations were retained by Coverdale in 1535, without a single exception. While thus not constituting a direct influence of Luther upon Coverdale, they are nevertheless indirectly due to the German master. These 29 passages were not analyzed in this essay because they belong properly in a study of Tyndale's debt to Luther. Still, the fact as such should at least be pointed to in passing in an investigation dealing with Luther's influence on Coverdale. The 29 cases of Lutheran impact upon Coverdale via Tyndale should be added to the number of direct borrowings above and beyond Tyndale.

2. In addition to the 29 Lutheran passages taken over from Tyndale, there are 113 new passages in which Coverdale followed Luther independently of Tyndale, on his own initiative.

3. Besides these 113, there are 78 passages which may have been inspired by either Luther or the Vulgate, in the sense that Luther and the Vulgate furnish identical readings. While it is theoretically impossible to decide whether Coverdale followed Luther or the Vulgate, we may, practically speaking, incline to the view that Luther should perhaps be considered the primary source here too. There are 100

passages in which Coverdale agrees with Luther against the Vulgate. There is not a single passage in which Coverdale sides with the Vulgate against Luther.

4. As regards what edition of Luther's N. T. Coverdale may have used, it is very difficult to come to a definite decision. In the nature of the case, it must have been an edition that appeared no later than 1535, probably no later than 1534, for Coverdale's own Bible came out in 1535.

So far as the evidence contained in Galatians is concerned, Coverdale appears to have used an early edition, one before Luther's major revision of the text incorporated in the edition of 1530. It is impossible to state more specifically which of the several pre-1530 editions Coverdale may have had in his hands when he prepared his own version. It does appear, however, that it was definitely an edition prior to 1530.

5. It should be clearly understood that any of the conclusions reached in the course of this investigation apply only to the Epistle to the Galatians. It seems clear that the situation changes from Biblical book to Biblical book. Until they have all been investigated separately, we are simply not in a position to make sweeping statements about Coverdale's general debt to the Lutheran Bible. Far from drawing any general conclusions we can, at the present stage of research, draw only specific conclusions strictly applicable to the book examined, in this case Paul's Epistle to the Galatians.

6. There remains a measure of doubt whether Coverdale or, for that matter, Tyndale followed Luther directly or perhaps only indirectly by way of the Zurich Bible. Since it seems that not all students of the English Bible are aware that the 1524–1529 New Testament of the Zurich Bible was practically a reprint of Luther's German Bible, it is perhaps important to lay some stress on this point so widely overlooked. Until 1574 the N. T. portion of the Swiss Bible was merely a reproduction of the Luther text, with a very few minor alterations. These alterations are not sufficient either quantitatively or qualitatively to permit us to state with assurance whether it was a Luther text or a Swiss text which actually lay before Coverdale (or Tyndale) as he was at work on the New Testament. One or two slight indications in favor of one are canceled out by similar indications in favor of the other. Whichever German text Coverdale had in front of him does not ultimately matter very much. The Swiss was practically as Lutheran as Luther himself.

Chapter 9

The Authorized Version

a. PSALM 26:8

IT IS no secret that the King James Bible is a considerably more literal rendering than Luther's German Bible. The Coverdale Bible, on the other hand, the first printed Bible in English (1535), stands somewhere between the freedom of Luther and the relative literalism of the Authorized Version. By the time the latter came out, in 1611, many of the free renderings of the Coverdale Bible had been eliminated by intervening versions.

One of the passages in which the nonliteral translation of the Coverdale Bible was retained in the King James Bible is Ps. 26:8. The question of the origin of this verse in the Authorized Version resolves itself into the question of the origin of the verse in the Coverdale Bible. Miles Coverdale himself clearly indicated both on the title page and in the preface of his Bible that he was indebted to both the Latin and the German Bibles, especially the latter.

It is worthwhile to examine Ps. 26:8 somewhat closely. In order to be sure of our ground, we should begin at the beginning and discuss the available Hebrew text, the Septuagint, and the various Latin renderings as well as the relevant German and English translations prior to the Authorized Version. For our purposes we may dispense with the first half of our verse, since it does not present a problem. We shall therefore limit the discussion to the second half of the verse.

Hebrew: וּמְקוֹם מִשְׁכַּן כְּבוֹדֶךָ

A literal translation of the Hebrew: *and the place of the dwelling* (or: *tabernacle*) *of thy honor*
Septuagint: καὶ τόπον σκηνώματος δόξης σου.
Psalterium Romanum: *et locum tabernaculi gloriae tuae*
Psalterium Gallicanum: *et locum habitationis gloriae tuae*
Psalterium iuxta Hebraeos: *et locum tabernaculi gloriae tuae*

It is obvious that the Greek and Latin versions are literal translations of the Hebrew. They faithfully reproduce the three nouns of the original. So do, incidentally, the pre-Lutheran High German Bibles from the Mentel edition of ca. 1466 to the Silvanus Otmar edition of 1518.

Mentel and Eggesteyn: *vnd die stat der entwelung deiner wunniglich*
Pflanzmann: *vnd die stat der einwonung deiner glori*
Zainer to S. Otmar: *vnd die stat der wonung deiner glori*

With Luther's appearance on the scene, the syntactical structure of this half-verse undergoes a major change. We are fortunate enough to possess the manuscript of a large section of the translation of the Psalter (1523–24), including our psalm. Verse 8 reads as follows in the second half: *vnd den ort, da deine ehre wonet*.

Unlike many a verse in Luther's manuscript, this half-verse was written down without the slightest change or correction. In other words, our phrase is one of those excellently rendered passages which received their permanent literary form at the first stroke of the pen, as it were. Luther never altered this earliest rendering of the verse —surely an indication that it met with his full critical approval throughout his life. A verse that survived the searching revision of 1531 can be said to have passed the strictest test of which Luther and his learned collaborators were capable. The chief characteristic of Luther's rendering of this passage is the resolution of the awkward noun construction into a dependent clause, which reads very easily and smoothly and is doubtless a superior translation.

The Zurich Psalters of 1524 and 1525 reproduce, aside from slight orthographical alterations, Luther's text first published in 1524. It is only the Zurich Bible of 1531 which makes changes as against the Lutheran Psalter. But, significantly enough, our verse undergoes no more than a minor revision. The fundamental structure of Luther's verse remains intact; only a single word, the verb, is replaced: *vnd das ort da dein eer ruwet*.

Thus all of the editions of Luther's Psalter and Bible as well as of the Zurich Bible of the 16th century really present but one basic text: Martin Luther's original manuscript version. This text, with its ingenious substitution of a clause for the noun construction of the original Hebrew, is a definite departure from all other relevant pre-Lutheran translations and bears the unmistakable stamp of Luther's style. We are now ready for a look at the English scene.

Coverdale (1535): *and ye place where thy honoure dwelleth*

Since the Zurich versions agree either wholly or practically with Luther's translation, and since the Latin versions (the only sources Coverdale acknowledges for the Psalter other than the German Bibles) are altogether different, it is more likely than not that Coverdale's phrase *and the place where thy honor dwelleth* stems from Martin Luther himself. Unless we are to credit Coverdale himself with this remarkable rendering, it is practically certain that the phrase under review is Luther's very own.

What is the history of this verse from Coverdale's Bible to the Authorized Version? All the Bibles published between 1535 and 1611 keep Coverdale's rendering.

The Great Bible (1539): *& the place where thy honoure dwelleth*
The Geneva Bible (1560): *and the place where thine honour dwelleth*
The Bishops' Bible (1568): *and the place where thine honour dwelleth*

The fact that these major English Bibles retain the Coverdale version surely shows that they approved of this translation of Ps. 26 : 8.

The most remarkable fact, however, is that the King James Bible also saw fit to keep the phrase. This is all the more noteworthy in that the Authorized Version, in its manifest endeavor to be as literal as feasible, usually adhered pretty closely to the noun constructions of the Hebrew original and of the Greek and Latin translations. But in the second half of Ps. 26 : 8 the scholars of the King James Bible chose to make an exception and preserved the excellent free rendering of the Coverdale Bible, which in turn rests solidly on the literary genius of Martin Luther.

It adds to the interest of this fact that our passage is not an undistinguished or even relatively unimportant verse of the Bible but quite definitely one of the best-known and surely one of the most widely used passages. It figures prominently in the services of both the liturgical and the nonliturgical Protestant churches. In fact, it is perhaps one of the most frequently quoted single verses of the Psalter, itself one of the favorite books of the Bible. If we bear this in mind, it is certainly worth pointing out that its arresting literary form is in all likelihood due to none other than Martin Luther.

b. PSALM 45 : 13

Psalm 45 : 13 is one of the most excellently rendered passages in the great King James Bible.

AV: *The king's daughter is all glorious within: her clothing is of wrought gold.*

This verse, couched in superb English, is not original with the makers of the Authorized Version. It rather belongs to those verses inherited from the past, i.e., from the earlier printed English Bibles preceding the Authorized Version by up to three quarters of a century.

We can, as a matter of fact, trace it back, step by step, in the evolution of the King James Bible.

The Bible closest in time to the Authorized Version is the Bishops' Bible, of which there were two editions, in 1568 and 1569 respectively. Psalm 45 : 13 is translated identically in these editions. This version is also identical, except in spelling, with the Authorized Version.

Bishops' Bible: *The kynges daughter is all glorious within; her clothyng is of wrought golde.*

The Bible immediately preceding the Bishops' Bible is the Geneva Bible of 1560, of which only a single edition seems to have appeared.

Geneva Bible: *The King's daughter is all glorious within: her clothing is of broydered golde.*

This Bible differs in one word from the Bishops' and King James Bibles: Instead of *wrought* it has *broydered*. The Authorized Version clearly did not follow the Geneva Bible in this instance.

The Geneva Bible was in turn preceded by the Great Bible, which first came out in 1539 and thereafter went through six editions in 1540 and 1541. In this apparently very popular Bible our verse appears as follows, consistently throughout all editions.

Great Bible: *The kynges daughter is all glorious within, her clothing is of wrought golde.*

This translation is manifestly the same as that contained in the Authorized Version, published a full 70 years later.

We now come to the first printed English Bible, produced by Miles Coverdale in 1535 and brought out again in 1537 and 1550. There are no differences in the rendering of Ps. 45 : 13 in the three editions of the Coverdale Bible.

Coverdale Bible: *The kynges doughter is all glorious within, hir clothing is of wrought golde.*

This is the earliest English source to which we can trace the translation of our verse as contained in the Authorized Version. In other words, Ps. 45 : 13 in the King James Bible of 1611 goes back in its entirety to the Coverdale Bible of 1535. All English Bibles between the Coverdale and King James Bibles have the identical rendering, with the single exception of the Geneva Bible, which departs from the other post-Coverdale and pre-King-James Bibles in one word: *broydered* for *wrought*. To put it in another way, Miles Coverdale is the (British) father of Ps. 45 : 13 in the Authorized Version. We must now examine the origin of Coverdale's translation of this verse.

The paramount fact about Coverdale's sources is that they do not include the Hebrew text. This must always be borne in mind. As a matter of record, Coverdale himself stated on the very title page of the first edition of 1535 that his Bible was "faithfully and truly translated out of Douche and Latyn." He did not for a moment maintain that his English Bible was based on the Hebrew and Greek originals. With engaging frankness he put his cards on the table: His sources were German and Latin. It has even been suggested that "the order, German first and Latin second, indicated his own preference in his dependence on these earlier versions."[1]

So far as his German sources are concerned, Coverdale was evidently referring to the Luther and Swiss Bibles in the various editions that were available before 1535. The identity of the Latin sources is somewhat less clear. Inasmuch as he mentioned a total of "fyve sundry interpreters," of whom two are doubtless German, three Latin interpreters remain to be identified. These are, probably for all the editions, and certainly for the first edition of 1535, two of Jerome's three versions (if indeed not all three of them) and, it is usually assumed, the Latin translation of Pagninus of 1528.

Let us look closely at these five versions, beginning with the Latin renderings. For good measure we shall quote all three Jeromian versions in addition to the Pagninus translation of the early 16th century.

Psalterium Romanum: *omnis gloria eius filie regum ab intus. In fimbriis aureis.*

Psalterium Gallicanum (i.e., Vulgate): *omnis gloria eius filie regis ab intus: in fimbrijs aureis.*

These two versions, based on the Septuagint, are almost identical. The only difference between them is the use of the genitive plural *regum* in one as against the genitive singular *regis* in the other. This difference is probably accounted for by variant readings in the Septuagint: βασιλέως and βασιλέων. No matter how hard we may look, it is scarcely conceivable that these versions can be the basis of Coverdale's rendering. The second half of the verse in particular cannot easily be explained by reference to the Roman and Gallican Psalters. Let us turn next to Jerome's third version.

Psalterium iuxta Hebraeos: *Omnis gloria filie regis intrinsecus: fascijs aureis vestita est.*

This final version of Jerome's is not based on the Greek Septuagint as the first two had been but, as the name implies, on the Hebrew original. While it is rather more intelligible than the two earlier versions, it cannot very well be held to yield, or lead to, the translation

[1] H. R. Willoughby, *The Coverdale Psalter* (Chicago, 1935), p. 20.

found in Coverdale's Bible. Except for the addition of the verb *vestita est*, it does not materially differ from the first two Jeromian versions.

The only editions of the Pagninus version accessible to me are an early Geneva edition of uncertain date and a London edition of 1726. They differ from each other.

Pagninus–Geneva: *Tota inclyta est filia Regis intrinsecus: ex vestibus auro ocellatis indumentum eius.*

Pagninus–London: *Tota inclyta filia regis intrinsecus: ex ocellaturis auri vestimentum eius.*

Both are closer to the Masoretic text than is Jerome's third version. They are clearly based on the Hebrew text.

כָּל־כְּבוּדָּה בַת־מֶלֶךְ פְּנִימָה

daughter of king all glorious inside

The first half of Coverdale's translation could possibly be explained from Pagninus' rendering. The latter's use of the adjective *inclyta* rather than the noun *gloria* could have inspired Coverdale's *glorious*. The second half of the verse, on the other hand, could not have been arrived at solely on the strength of Pagninus. While a close correspondence exists between *hir clothing* and either *indumentum eius* or *vestimentum eius,* it is somewhat difficult to see how Coverdale's characteristic phrase *of wrought golde* could have descended either from *ex vestibus auro ocellatis* or from *ex ocellaturis auri.* This final phrase remains something of a mystery within the framework of the Latin renderings examined here.

We may safely ignore the pre-Lutheran printed German translations. They are literal, sometimes painfully literal, renderings of the Vulgate. It is doubtful whether a non-German ever took notice of them in the 15th and 16th centuries. They appear to have been strictly for domestic consumption, and they achieved no international significance beyond the interesting fact that they were the first printed Bibles in any modern European language. Merely for curiosity's sake, and for the record, we shall quote Ps. 45 : 13 as it occurs in the earliest printed High German Bible.

Mentel Bible (1466): *All sein wunniglich seint die töchter des kunigs von inwendig: in den guldin saumen.*

The third printed German Bible changed *wunniglich* to *glory* about 1473. This single alteration is retained throughout the remaining redactions of the pre-Lutheran Bibles all the way down to 1518. No other change is made. It is a foregone conclusion that this rendering was of no use to Coverdale even if he should have had access to it.

The first German Bible to attain international stature was Martin

Luther's historic translation. It achieved this distinction almost instantaneously, while it was still in the process of evolution. Long before Luther's complete Bible appeared in 1534 the various parts had become famous as they came out in installments. It is therefore important to consider the individual editions of the Psalter. The first time Luther brought out the Psalter was as early as 1524.

Luther, 1524: *Des koniges tochter ist gantz herlich drynnen / yhr kleyd ist gewirckt gold.*

It is obvious that we need look no further than this earliest rendering of Luther's to discover the source of Coverdale's translation of 1535. The correspondence is so close that a discussion is almost superfluous. The first half of the verse, for which we had established a possible source in Pagninus' Latin translation, is practically identical in Luther's and Coverdale's versions, down to the details of word order. *The kynges doughter is all glorious within* appears to be an exact rendering of *Des koniges tochter ist gantz herlich drynnen.* If the first half of the verse could conceivably be accounted for by Pagninus' version, the second half clearly cannot. Here Luther's version comes fully into its own. None of the Latin translations we examined could in any way be considered as the chief source for Coverdale's striking translation. This source is German, Luther's rendering of 1524. *Yhr kleyd ist gewirckt gold* is as close a source as can be established for *Hir clothing is of wrought golde.* It is especially the superb phrase *wrought golde* for which we now have the exact model in Luther's *gewirckt gold.*

Our story is not yet at an end, though it might stop here. We have found what would seem to be the closest possible source for the well-known English verse under discussion. What should perhaps be pointed out is that the most distinguished British student of the Coverdale Prayer Book Psalter, Ernest Clapton,[2] was not able to establish the Lutheran source which we have suggested in this paper. In his careful analysis of the individual verses of Psalm 45 he has nothing substantial to say on verse 13. The reason for this is obvious to the student of Luther's German Bible. Clapton, who is very good on the Latin sources, has unfortunately a very inadequate picture of Luther's translation or, better, of the successive stages of his translation. He is totally, and most unfortunately, unaware of the existence of Luther's several renderings of the Psalter. All he appears to have had in mind, and on hand, when he undertook to establish the sources of the English Psalter was the first edition of Luther's complete German Bible of 1534. He obviously worked with this edition or a modern reprint of it. Small

---

[2] Ernest Clapton, *Our Prayer Book Psalter* (London, 1934), 375 pp.

wonder that it proved of no help in running down the source of the important second half of Ps. 45 : 13. It sufficed for the first half of the verse, and Clapton rightly indicated Luther's Bible as the most likely source for Coverdale. This was a perfectly correct observation, since the first half of the verse in the edition of 1534 corresponds to that in the edition of 1524 in almost every respect, only one word differing from the later version.

Luther, 1534: *Des Königes tochter ist gantz herlich jnn wendig*

It will be noted that Luther has replaced *drynnen* of the earlier edition by *jnn wendig*. This is a minor change indeed, one that does not alter the meaning. Both words can easily be translated by "within." It is obvious that the word *jnn wendig* of 1534 leads as readily and naturally to "within" as the word *drynnen* of 1524.

But while the edition of 1534 (anticipated in the Psalter of 1531) suffices to explain the first half of the verse, it is of no avail for the second half for the simple reason that Luther completely changed the second half in the later edition.

Luther, 1534: *sie ist mit gülden stücken gekleidet*

This translation, apparently the only one of Luther's which Clapton knew, is clearly of no help whatsoever in connection with Coverdale's text. There cannot be any question that Luther's later rendering, *sie ist mit gülden stücken gekleidet*, does not in any way yield, or even remotely suggest, Coverdale's phrase *hir clothing is of wrought golde*. No bridge spans the chasm between these two renderings. Since the Latin versions are similarly of no help in the matter of the source of the second half, Clapton has absolutely nothing to say and no comment to make on this important point.

Thus it would seem that by calling attention to Luther's earliest published translation we have solved a problem which Clapton could not solve with the information at his command. What authorizes our contention that it was one of the editions of 1524 that Coverdale used? Students of the German Bible know that there was another revised edition in 1528, which could have been in Coverdale's hands so far as the time element is concerned. The answer is as simple as the question is legitimate: Luther's edition of the Psalter of 1528 has a rather different text both from the edition of 1524 and from the complete Bible of 1534.

Luther, 1528: *Des koniges tochter ist vberal herlich drynnen / sie ist mit gülden spangen gekleidet.*

With this text in front of us, there can be little doubt which Lutheran version Coverdale made use of: the first edition of 1524. Perhaps we had better put it more cautiously: one of the first editions that preserve Luther's earliest translation. This could be either of the editions of 1524 and 1525, the only ones prior to the revised edition of 1528.

What about the Zurich Bible, which has long been recognized as one of Coverdale's important sources? The answer is comparatively easy. The 1525 Swiss edition of the Psalter is an exact replica of Luther's text of 1524. Thus even if Coverdale should have consulted the Zurich Bible of 1525, he was still using Luther's translation, though indirectly rather than directly. The next Swiss Bible came out in 1530. It has the same text. Only the edition of 1531 introduces changes in our verse:

Alle zierd der künigen ist biss auff das inner /
all ire kleidung von gewürcktem gold vnnd gestickter arbeit.

Even though the single phrase *von gewürcktem gold* is retained, this is a thoroughly altered reading. It does not seem likely that Coverdale used this version. If he did look at it, all he could have gained from it for his own rendering is the phrase *von gewürcktem gold,* and that, as we have established, unquestionably goes back to Luther.

Thus there would appear to remain little doubt as to the ultimate source of Coverdale's translation of Ps. 45:13: Martin Luther's version of 1524. Whether the debt is direct or only indirect, by way of the pre-1531 Zurich Bibles, we can of course not tell in the nature of the case. But whichever it was—Luther's Psalter of 1524 or an early edition of the Zurich Bible—copies of these early renderings must have found their way into English hands. This is I believe a new discovery. Scholarship in this field has so far been aware that Coverdale used the complete German Bible of 1534 or the Swiss Bible of 1531 containing the new translation of the Hagiographa. But we have not known heretofore that a partial edition of ten years earlier or early Swiss editions were also influential in England and helped shape the great English Bible. In fairness to Luther it should be insisted that the Swiss editions prior to 1531 were identical with Luther's version of 1524; they were no more than reprints of the early Luther text.

We have traced back our verse from the Authorized Version of 1611 to the Coverdale Bible of 1535 and, beyond that, to Martin Luther's translation of 1524. With this succession established, we now have every right to ask why the learned and artistically sensitive makers of the Authorized Version adopted our particular verse, among others to be sure, from the first printed English Bible. In my opinion they did so for two sound reasons. First, the verse in the Coverdale

Bible must have passed their high standards of philological accuracy, i.e., it was a correct translation of the Hebrew original, in terms of early 17th-century knowledge of Hebrew, of course. Secondly, it was couched in superb English, upon which the men who gave us the King James Bible felt they could not possibly improve. Thus they gave their philological and literary approval to the verse in the form in which it had been handed down from the days of Miles Coverdale.

It is a fairly safe assumption that they had no inkling that the verse they accepted so fully as to leave it untouched was in the last analysis Martin Luther's very own. This is, of course, not to say they did not have a Luther Bible among the various "former translations" they so "diligently compared and revised," as the title page of the Authorized Version mentions with delightful candor. As a matter of fact, it is universally accepted that they had a German Bible accessible. But this was almost certainly one of Luther's later versions. It seems rather unlikely that they could have had available the Psalter of 1524 or the partial Bible of the same year. They looked at Coverdale and saw that it was good. It is hard to imagine that they should have been interested in the source of Coverdale's superb rendering.

Assuming that they had the Bible of 1534, or one of its successors, they would not, as we have shown above, have found our verse in the form in which they took it over. In other words, the Luther Bible of 1534, or of a later date, would not have supplied them with the text they chose and adopted. Instead, if indeed they took the trouble to consult the Luther Bible in this instance at all, they simply abided by what English tradition, from 1535 on, had handed down to them. Little did they realize that by following their own English tradition (as it must have seemed to them) they actually walked in the footsteps of Martin Luther. But the entire Psalter, much more, of course, in the Prayer Book version than in the King James Bible, abounds in beautifully rendered verses, long familiar to all English-speaking peoples, that received their artistic shape from the literary genius of none other than Martin Luther himself.

Index

Aleander 52, 64, 67, 69, 70, 75
Althaus vii
Ambrose 131
Amsdorf 142, 149
Augsburg German Bible of 1487; See Schönsperger Bible
Augustine vii, 131, 132, 137
Aurogallus 153

Bach xiv
Barth 137
Beethoven vii
Behaghel 42
Betbüchlein 154, 155
Bishops' Bible 225, 226
Brodführer 80, 86
Bruchmann xi
Büchmann 138, 141
Butterworth 169f, 170, 188

Catechism 155f
Chaucer 148
Cheney 169
Christmas Postil 50ff
Chrysostom 8
Clapton 184, 185ff, 229, 230
Cochläus 161, 162
Cologne Bibles 97ff
Copinger Collection of Vulgates at General Theological Seminary in New York 40, 89
Coverdale Bible xiii, xiv, 173ff, 181ff
Cranmer Bible 173

Daiches 184

Dezembertestament 134
Diet of Worms xi, 12, 36
Duke Barnim 37
Duke George xii, 145, 156, 161

Eck x
Eggesteyn Bible 84ff, 89f, 92ff, 92, 103, 224
Emser xii, 117, 120, 142f, 145, 147, 149ff, 156ff, 160ff, 164
Enders 142
Erasmus xi, 7, 14, 37ff, 44, 46, 52ff, 62ff, 72ff, 126f, 144, 153f, 157, 159, 171ff, 197ff

Faber Stapulensis 185
Frederick the Wise 36
Freiberg ms. of the German Bible 42
Freitag xi, 50, 77

Geiler von Kaisersberg 141, 143, 147, 149f
Geneva Bible 225f
Gerbel 7, 52
Gerberich xiii, 169f
Ginsburg 182f
Goethe 3
Great Bible 225
Grimm 148
Grimmelshausen 138
Gruber xiii, 169

Halberstadt Bible 97ff
Harnack, Th. vii
Hartford Seminary Foundation 113
Haupt 139
Hauspostille 165

Hirsch ix
Hölderlin 148
Holl vii
Hugo cardinalis 39

Index of Luther's Biblical quotations at Yale x
Ising 97

Jacobs 186
Jerome viif, 8, 87, 89, 107, 123, 137, 182, 227f

Kawerau 151, 157, 161, 165
Keller, A. 139
King James Bible xii, xiv, 25, 56, 148, 173, 178, 189, 195, 212, 223, 232
King James Bible, Revised 126
Kitto 182f
Koberger Bible 11, 17, 78, 82ff, 90, 96f
Köhler xi, 77
Koenig 105
Kunstmann 166
Kurrelmeyer 10, 83, 87f, 90ff, 107, 141, 162

Lang 64, 139, 147
Lectures on Romans, Luther's 37
Leipzig Disputation 37
Lenschau 138f
Lord's Prayer 155
Lortz 131
Lübeck Bible 97ff

Margaret of Anhalt 161

Melanchthon 4, 142, 152f
Mentel Bible 5, 11, 17, 24, 34f, 78ff, 84ff, 89f, 92ff, 103, 140, 224, 228
Mezger 184
Monsee Fragments 140
Mozley 169f

Neubauer 162, 165
New York Public Library 87
Nietzsche vii
Ninety-five Theses 8

Hans Otmar Bible 34, 162
Silvanus Otmar Bible 5, 10f, 34f, 96f, 97, 99, 103, 162, 224

Pagninus 182, 184, 190, 229
Panzer 161
St. Paul 127, 131, 133f, 137
Pauli, J. 141
Pflanzmann Bible 10, 17, 34, 78, 80, 83ff, 94, 96ff, 102ff, 107, 140, 224
Pierpont Morgan Library in New York 87
Pietsch 140
Plenaria 5, 15, 51, 140
Prayerbook Psalter xiv, 232

Pre-Lutheran German Bibles xi, 5, 15, 17, 33ff, 42, 49, 51, 65, 78, 82, 92, 107, 109, 140, 150, 172, 223, 228
Psalterium Gallicum 87f, 185ff, 223ff
Psalterium iuxta Hebraeos 87f, 107, 123, 182, 185ff, 223ff
Psalterium Romanum 82, 87ff, 185ff, 223ff

Reu ix
Rhegius 158ff
Rheims Bible 175
Rosenplüt 139

Schiller 148
Schirokauer 141, 150, 157
Schmidt 104
Schönbach 162
Schönsperger Bible (1487) 96, 162
Schönsperger Bible (1490) 34
Sendbrief vom Dolmetschen xii, 117, 120, 127ff, 147
Septembertestament 4, 9, 10ff, 16ff, 43, 49ff, 61ff, 64ff, 65ff, 73ff, 97, 134f, 140, 145, 152, 155
Septuagint 223, 227
Shakespeare vii
Singer 138

Sorg Bible 11
Summarien über die Psalmen 119

Tatian 140
Taylor 138f
Teplitz ms. of the German Bible 42
Theologia deutsch 15
Thomas Aquinas 131, 137
Thümmel 148
Tyndale viii, xiii, 148, 169ff

Uhlhorn 159
Ursachen des Dolmetschens 118ff

Vollmer 162
Von der Freyheyt eynisz Christen menschen 134

Wagner vii
Walther ix, 80, 83, 92f
Wander 138
Wartburg 155
Weizsäcker 165
Westcott 183
Wicliff 148, 171ff
Willoughby 182, 227
Wordsworth and White 126
Wright 184

Zainer Bible 10, 17, 34, 78, 83ff, 90, 92ff, 97, 103f, 140, 224
Zurich Bibles 182ff, 222

Scripture Index

NEW TESTAMENT

Matthew
  General — 4, 6
  2:1-12 — xi, 51, 63, 77
  2:1 — 52, 53
  2:2 — 56
  2:3 — 58
  2:4 — 59, 62
  2:5 — 62
  2:6 — 63
  2:7 — 66
  2:8 — 69
  2:9 — 70
  2:10 — 72
  2:11 — 72
  2:12 — 74, 76, 77
  4:17 — 7
  5:4 — 34
  5:13 — 25
  5:15 — 12
  5:24 — 20
  5:25 — 17
  5:26 — 33
  5:29 — 30, 33
  5:39 — 20
  5:42 — 31
  5:45 — 26
  6:7 — 9
  6:11 — 9
  6:13 — 17
  6:19 — 35
  6:24 — 32
  6:31 — 11
  6:33 — 23
  6:34 — 23, 26
  7:3 — 31
  7:6 — 6, 20
  7:12 — 26, 28
  7:15 — 19, 35
  7:18 — 9, 11
  7:23 — 34
  7:27 — 27, 31, 35
  8:4 — 25
  8:8 — 33
  8:11 — 20
  8:26 — 10
  9:2 — 10
  9:12 — 13
  9:13 — 7, 8
  9:22 — 10
  9:38 — 18
  10:8 — 24
  10:9 — 12
  10:10 — 25
  10:22 — 31
  10:24 — 20
  10:25 — 21
  10:34f — 31
  11:7 — 21
  11:17 — 13, 27
  11:28 — 16, 18, 21, 28, 32
  11:29 — 34
  11:30 — 21
  12:34 — 35, 139-147, 149f
  12:34b — xiii, 138
  12:36 — 34
  13:29 — 21
  13:33 — 30
  13:58 — 35
  15:3 — 32
  15:7 — 35
  15:8 — 14, 21, 35
  15:9 — 14, 21
  15:14 — 34
  15:28 — 23, 31
  16:11 — 35
  16:13-19 — x, 37, 47
  16:13 — 38, 40
  16:14 — 39, 43
  16:15 — 24, 40, 47
  16:16 — 41
  16:17 — 43
  16:18 — 19, 22, 31, 44
  16:19 — 45, 46
  16:23 — 7, 17, 30
  16:24 — 35
  17:25 — 30
  17:27 — 24
  18:4 — 31
  18:6 — 19
  18:9 — 27
  18:15 — 18, 23, 35 (2)
  18:16 — 12
  18:17 — 22, 29, 33
  18:18 — 19, 35
  18:19 — 22
  18:20 — 16
  18:24 — 34
  21:3 — 22, 30
  21:5 — 22, 27
  21:9 — 33
  21:12 — 35
  21:13 — 35
  21:22 — 29
  21:31 — 28
  21:43 — 35
  22:21 — 35
  23:3 — 35
  23:10 — 35
  23:13 — 24
  23:14 — 25
  23:24 — 27
  23:32 — 35
  23:33 — 35
  24:5 — 35
  24:9 — 34
  24:13 — 26
  24:15 — 26, 29, 35
  24:23 — 35
  24:24 — 13, 19, 26, 32, 36

24:26 — 20
25:43 — 20
26:26 — 35
26:27 — 35
26:28 — 35
26:29 — 29
26:43 — 18
26:50 — 22
27:42 — 35
28:19 — 35
28:20 — 35

Luke
1:28 — xiii, 151f, 154 to 157, 160, 164, 166
6:45 — 138-141, 144 to 146

John
1:1-14 — 143

Romans
1:17 — 134f
3:28 — xiii, 117, 125f, 128f, 131-137
5:1 — 134

Galatians
General — xiv, 181, 194
1:2 — 195
1:5 — 195
1:9 — 197
1:10 — 195
1:14 — 195
1:16 — 198
1:18 — 195
1:22 — 198
1:24 — 196, 198
2:2 — 200
2:6a — 200
2:6b — 201
2:9 — 199
2:14 — 199
2:15 — 201
2:16 — 135-137
2:16a — 201
2:16b — 202
3:3 — 204
3:4 — 204
3:5 — 205, 209
3:6 — 205
3:8 — 209
3:9 — 202
3:10 — 205
3:13 — 206
3:14 — 206
3:16 — 203
3:18a — 206
3:18b — 207
3:19 — 202
3:20 — 208
3:22 — 208
3:26 — 208
3:27 — 209
3:28 — 203
4:1a — 210
4:1b — 211
4:3 — 211
4:4 — 24
4:5 — 212
4:6 — 212
4:17 — 212
4:18 — 213
4:23 — 213
4:24 — 213
4:25 — 214
4:26 — 214
4:28 — 215
4:29 — 214
5:4 — 216
5:5 — 215, 216
5:9 — 217
5:12 — 217
5:20 — 215
5:24 — 217
6:1a — 219
6:1b — 219
6:2 — 218
6:9 — 218, 219
6:11 — 220
6:12 — 220
6:14 — 220
Brief mention of 3:1-4, 6-8, 10, 11, 13, 14, 17-20, 22, 25-28 — 204; 3:2, 4, 7, 8, 10, 12, 14, 15, 19, 21, 22, 24, 28, 29 — 203; 4:1-29, 29-31 — 210; 5:1-5, 7, 12, 14, 15, 19, 26 — 218; 5:5, 10, 12, 20, 21 — 215; 6:1, 3, 7, 10, 12, 13 — 221

Ephesians
General — xiii
1:4 — 171
1:10 — 172
1:19 — 172
1:22 — 173
2:2 — 174
2:14 — 174
2:15 — 176
3:5 — 176
3:15 — 177
3:19 — 177
4:18 — 177
4:24 — 178
5:2 — 178
6:2 — 178
6:11 — 179

1 John — 18

OLD TESTAMENT

Genesis — 158
Psalms
23:1-6 — xi, xii, xiv, 64, 78, 93, 98, 103 to 105, 107, 110, 113, 184, 186
23:1 — 63, 79, 84, 94, 98, 184
23:2 — 80, 85, 92, 94, 99, 186
23:3 — 81, 85, 95, 100, 187
23:4 — 81, 85, 92, 95, 96 (2), 100, 188
23:5 — 81, 85, 89, 92, 95, 96, 101, 190
23:6 — 82, 90-92, 95, 96, 103, 191
26:8 — 223, 225
45:13 — 225-232
46 — 104

Isaiah — 183

www.ingramcontent.com/pod-product-compliance
Lightning Source LLC
Chambersburg PA
CBHW020835160426
43192CB00007B/655